WHY GOVERNMENT DOESN'T WORK

WHY GOVERNMENT DOESN'T WORK

Harry Browne

ST. MARTIN'S PRESS
New York

Library of Congress Cataloging-in-Publication Data

Browne, Harry.
  Why Government Doesn't Work / Harry Browne.
    p.   cm.
  ISBN 0–312–13623–4
  1. Federal government—United States. 2. Decentralization in government—United States. 3. Libertarianism—United States. 4. United States—Politics and Government—1993–   I. Title.
JK325. B76 1995
320.5'12—dc20   95–20251
                                                                          CIP

First Edition: December 1995

10   9   8   7   6   5   4   3   2   1

*To
Pamela*

CONTENTS

PROLOGUE

Chapter 1

The Breakdown of Government

Imagine living in a city where you felt safe walking home at ten in the evening—or even at two in the morning.

Imagine your children going to schools that respect *your* values; where teachers concentrate on reading, writing, adding, subtracting, and other academic basics; and where no one would dare teach your child a philosophy that's alien to you.

Imagine paying only half the taxes you're paying now. You could move into a better home, finance a more comfortable retirement, send your children to the private school of your choice, support your favorite cause or charity in a way that would make a significant difference, or save up to go into business for yourself.

With much lower taxes, your family could live well on the income of just one spouse—so the other parent could choose to stay home and raise your children in the values you believe, rather than leaving their moral training to strangers.

Is This a Dream?

I'm not describing Utopia. Such a society wouldn't be perfect. But as recently as 1950, it was real. The crime rate was only one fifth of what it is today. Most American school children learned to read, write, and do math competently—and they left school able to make their way in the world. Government was only *one fifth* the size it is today.

1

Government Running Wild

But today's America is quite different. It is a land where crime is a national scandal, schools turn out illiterates, and taxes drive both parents into the job market. The "American dream" has become a mirage for too many of us.

And to make matters worse, government has grown too large and too bold. It routinely tramples on our property and our liberties:

- The federal government was founded by men who warned "Don't tread on me." But that government now pries into your bank account, threatens to destroy you to collect its taxes, and tries to herd you into a health-care collective—as though you were a Soviet citizen.
- Federal, state, and local governments together take 47% of your earnings through direct and hidden taxes—cutting your standard of living to a fraction of what it could be.
- The government created to enable us to pursue happiness in peace now runs up the price of everything you buy through the regulations and mandates it lays on companies.
- The government set up to protect private property now confiscates it in the name of fighting drugs or preserving the environment.
- The courts that once defended your privacy and liberties now ratify any intrusion that can be shown to be in the government's interest.

This is a far cry from what the founding fathers had in mind—a government instituted among men to secure the blessings of life, liberty, and property.

What Changed?

No plague descended upon America to halt progress and plunge us into a world of violent crime, poor education, and big government.

So how did it happen? What transformed America from the land of the free into the land of high taxes—from the land of prosperity into the land of debt and bankruptcy—from the land of opportunity to the land of quotas and lawsuits—from the land of free enterprise to the land of regulations, mandates, and government inspectors?

The decline of America has been caused by politicians and reformers who believe that you aren't competent to run your own life, that they know better how to spend the money you've earned, that they understand which products you should be allowed to buy and what wages and job benefits are suitable for you.

To run your life for you, they have created a government that fails at everything it undertakes, but wants to undertake everything:

- The government can't deliver the mail on time, but wants to take your life in its hands by controlling your health care.
- The government can't keep the peace in Washington, D.C., but it sends troops on "peacekeeping missions" to Somalia and Haiti—to save those countries from being run by the wrong thugs.
- Government schools don't have the money and time to teach your children how to read well—yet they always find the resources to teach their favorite social theories, no matter how distressing they are to parents.

Wherever we look, government fails at what we want, and succeeds only in finding new ways to interfere with our lives.

What Went Wrong?

Once upon a time government budgets were balanced, our money was sound, the cities were safe, and the taxes of federal, state, and local governments combined took less than 10% of our income.

The graph below shows how the cost of government has grown. But no graph can show how government has intruded deeper and deeper into our lives, making decisions we used to make for ourselves. Government decides which products we're allowed to buy,

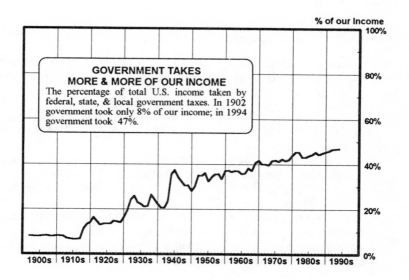

GOVERNMENT TAKES MORE & MORE OF OUR INCOME
The percentage of total U.S. income taken by federal, state, & local government taxes. In 1902 government took only 8% of our income; in 1994 government took 47%.

sets wage floors that force unemployment on teenagers, prevents most small businesses from raising capital, and stops the critically ill from using life-saving medicines while bureaucrats pretend to protect us.

Where did it all go wrong? Wasn't government supposed to be our servant, rather than our master? Wasn't government supposed to help only those who can't help themselves—rather than benefiting politicians, lobbyists, and social reformers?

What happened to the idea that government should do for the people only what they cannot do for themselves?

WHAT WE WILL COVER

We need to answer those questions before we can revive the American dream of liberty and prosperity for all.

Understand the Problem

But to understand how government went so wrong, we must first identify exactly what government is and how it operates. Because Part I does this, it may be the most important section of the book.

It shows why government programs never seem to produce the results that were promised—why laws to make America "color blind" lead to racial quotas, why programs to improve the economy end in recession and inflation, and why plans to help the poor enlarge their numbers.

Identify the Solutions

Part II examines specific issues—showing how government created the problems the politicians now pretend they can solve, and showing how we can solve these problems. We will see:

- How crime, education, and welfare went from minor problems in the 1950s to major scandals in the 1990s—and how we can end the scandals.
- How to fix Social Security once and for all—to end its periodic crises, and to guarantee that you get everything you pay for.
- How to balance the federal budget *immediately* and permanently—without raising taxes.
- How to keep government from running up the prices of the things you buy and reducing the wages you earn.
- How America can be much safer from foreign attack with a much smaller military budget.

- How to cut taxes to a fraction of where they are now.

. . . and much more.

Today's social and political problems aren't mysterious punishments inflicted by angry gods. They are man-made, and they can be fixed. If we understand what caused them, we can cure them. And we can make sure they don't recur.

Get from Here to There

Part II shows how we can get from where we are now to where we want to be—to a society where crime rates are low, education is first-class, taxes are trivial, products and services are plentiful and inexpensive, jobs are more rewarding, and each of us is free to make of his life what he will.

It has come to seem impossible that we could ever cut government and reduce taxes enough to make a real difference in our lives. We're told that everyone wants a smaller government but that no one wants to give up his own favorite program. Part II will show how we can escape that trap.

IT'S UP TO US

A revolution is sweeping through America today—as Americans have grown impatient with big government, high taxes, meddling politicians and bureaucrats, soaring crime rates, and mediocre education.

If the revolution brings the right changes, America can be free, peaceful, and prosperous again.

But to restore that free country, we first need to understand how we arrived where we are today.

So let's get started.[1]

---

[1]To keep the text from being littered with footnotes, I have put the sources for many of my assertions in Appendix B, "Notes & Background Information."

PART ONE

WHY GOVERNMENT DOESN'T WORK

Chapter 2

What Is Government?

To understand how government went wrong, we must understand what it is.

Government dominates our lives; it is at the center of most news and most public discussion. And yet not one person in a hundred can explain what we mean by "government," and no school or textbook bothers to provide a precise definition.

What is government? What makes it different from IBM or the Boy Scouts or a local security company? What is there about government that enables it to do what other organizations can't?

When a reformer decides that everyone should have health insurance or that every worker should have "family leave," why doesn't he take his project to the Red Cross or the Chamber of Commerce? Why does he turn to government?

What makes government different from every other institution in society?

Is it that only government is large enough to handle some tasks?

No. General Motors alone had revenues of $132 billion in 1992. And in 1995 Pacific Bell announced that it would raise $16 billion to rewire the entire state of California to accommodate the information "superhighway." Even larger companies than these could be organized if they were needed.

Is it that only government operates without profit?

No—so do the Salvation Army, the Rotary Club, and thousands of other organizations.

Is it that government cares more about the future than private companies do?

Hardly. A corporation may last for centuries. Its management enhances today's stock price by building tomorrow's earnings, because almost any investor will prefer a stock that's likely to pay dividends for 50 years over a stock whose dividends may end in 10 years. But politicians have little interest in anything beyond the next election.

Is it that government is the only institution that considers the well-being of all citizens?

No institution can do that—and certainly not government. Anything government gives to one group must be taken from others. So government necessarily plays favorites, which divides people into opposing camps.

Government's Unique Asset

What separates government from the rest of society isn't its size, its disregard for profit, its foresight, or its scope.

The distinctive feature of government is *coercion*—the use of force and the threat of force to win obedience. This is how government differs from every other agency in society. The others persuade; government compels.

When someone demands that government help flood victims, he is saying he wants to *force* people to pay for flood relief. Otherwise, he'd be happy to have the Red Cross and its supporters handle everything.

When someone wants government to limit the price of a product, he is asking to use force to prevent people from paying more for something they want. Otherwise, he would simply urge people not to patronize those he thinks are charging too much.

When Congress passes a bill mandating "family leave," it *forces* every employer to provide time off for family problems—even if its employees want the employer to use payroll money for some other benefit. Otherwise, employers and employees would be free to decide what works best in each situation.

Nothing involving government is voluntary—as it would be when a private company does something. One way or another, there is compulsion in every government activity:

- The government forces someone to pay for something;
- The government forces someone to do something; or
- The government forcibly prevents someone from doing something.

There is no other reason to involve government.

And by "force" I mean the real thing—the kind that hurts people.

As Long as You Comply . . .

In some government agencies, such as the police and prisons, the role of coercion is obvious. But it is at work in *every* government program—although a program's supporters rarely acknowledge it.

If this seems like too sweeping a statement, it may be that you've never tried to resist a government program. If you did, you'd have learned very quickly that the program is enforced by a gun. The easiest way to spot the gun is to imagine what would happen if you decided to ignore the government's "request."

Suppose, for example, that you're a barber. One day the state Board of Tonsorial Cutters of Hair (BOTCH) issues a regulation to stop "cut-throat competition"—decreeing that no barber can charge less than $8 for a haircut. (Many states do have laws prohibiting barbers from charging less than a stated minimum price.)

So long as you charge at least $8, you won't even notice the regulation. But suppose your price is only $6. Perhaps you're in a low-income neighborhood where people can't afford $8 haircuts, or maybe your shop is new and you want to attract customers, or perhaps business is slow and you need to stimulate sales. For whatever reason, suppose you offer haircuts for $6.

You may be able to get away with this for a month or two. But eventually the folks at BOTCH will send you a letter, ordering you to desist.

If you comply by boosting your price to $8, you'll hear nothing more. But if you keep cutting hair for $6, eventually some men in suits will come to your shop and warn you to stop undercharging.

If you continue to ignore the law, you'll receive a subpoena— telling you to appear in court. If you don't show up, or if you ignore the court's order to raise your price, your barber's license will be revoked.

If you defy the court by continuing to cut hair, another group of men will come to your shop. These fellows may not be in suits, and they probably will have guns. They will be there to close your business.

If you resist, their job will be to "take you into custody"—which is a euphemism for seizing you, handcuffing you, and taking you to jail.

At this point, it will be obvious that the regulation's purpose is to *force* barbers to charge at least $8—not by persuasion, but with a gun.

Every government program, no matter how benign it may appear, is the same. Coercion is the reason—and the *only* reason—it is a government program.

Voluntary vs. Compulsory

The IRS likes to say that our tax system is based on voluntary compliance. And that's true: so long as you comply, the system is voluntary. But the moment you choose *not* to comply, you'll find yourself in a different system—one where you'll be forced to pay.

People seek the help of business groups, charity organizations, and service clubs to *urge* others to support some cause. People turn to government to *force* others to support their cause.

Now, you may believe that government *should* set prices for haircuts and other things—or that it should force people to do what's good for them or what's good for society. But those are other issues. Before we can address them, we first need to recognize the simple truth that every government program and regulation is backed by the same kind of force that is so useful for robbing money from 7-Eleven stores. Only then will we understand why government programs turn out as they do and how government has come to where it is today.

Think through any government activity. Eventually, you'll find the coercion that keeps it from being anything but a government program.

Government Defined

So what is government? Very simply, it is an agency of coercion.

Of course, there are other agencies of coercion—such as the Mafia. So to be more precise, government is the agency of coercion that has flags in front of its offices.

Or, to put it another way, government is society's dominant producer of coercion. The Mafia and independent bandits are merely fringe competitors—seeking to take advantage of the niches and nooks neglected by the government.

Chapter 3

Oops!
Why Government Programs Always Go Astray

Being able to force people to do what you want can be an attractive prospect—especially if you don't have to admit, even to yourself, how you're getting what you want.

- If you want to feed the homeless, you don't have to persuade hundreds of people to donate money. The government can force millions of people to contribute.
- If your business is losing customers, you don't have to try harder to match your competition. The government can establish licensing laws or impose tariffs that get the competition out of your hair.
- If you don't want people reading pornography or other "bad" literature, you don't have to persuade them to find something better. Just get the government to put the smut-peddlers out of business.

Government, with its power to coerce, seems to be a magic wand that can make your dreams come true. It can seem able to summon up anything you want, do away with anything you don't like, and make everyone happy—especially you.

Because of government's power, controlling it is the grand prize—the brass ring, the pot of gold, the genie of the lamp. It beckons as the shortcut to riches, to the perfect world you imagine, to imposing your personal tastes on everyone. With government at your disposal, it appears that you can bypass the tedious process of earning a living, spreading the gospel, or persuading others that you're right.

No wonder that most TV news revolves around government. No wonder nearly everyone wants to influence government. Whoever controls it controls us all.

THE CONSEQUENCES OF COERCION

Government is a powerful tool. But it's far easier to put it in motion than to control it. When government is involved, nothing ever seems to work out as intended.

Discussions about a new government program always focus on those who "need help"—the people who will benefit immediately. They may be the intended recipients of government checks, or employees whose pay will be boosted, or companies whose markets will be enhanced. This is the stuff of great dreams.

But the dreams—of instant riches or social reform—lead inevitably to disappointment, and sometimes to nightmares.

The plans almost always ignore the inevitable complications:

- The people you want to help get past a difficult predicament will decide it's easier to continue receiving the help than to move onward.
- The people you believe need help will be joined by people who would rather receive help than give it.
- The people whose lives must be turned upside down for the program to succeed—those who must be coerced to make the program work—will do what they can to avoid complying.
- The people who are kept from doing what the reformers don't like will find something worse to do instead.

For example, a program to serve meals to 1 million children who aren't getting nutritious lunches will need 6 million meals per day—because the children's families will decide they need breakfast and supper as well, and because the parents of 1 million other children will see no reason to continue paying for something others are getting for free.

And that's just to start with. Over time, the program will need 10 million meals a day, and then 20 million, as more people learn how to qualify.

A government program goes astray as well because little forethought is given to the people who must be coerced. These are thinking, feeling human beings—just like you and me—and they have no more desire to have their lives turned inside out than we do.

If they must pay for the service, they will seek ways to avoid making full payment—meaning there will be less revenue available for the service than expected. Or if they are forced to do something, they will look for every possible way to avoid doing it without getting into trouble. Or if they're prohibited from doing something they want to do, they'll use their creative energy to find ways to continue doing it without running afoul of the law.

Trashing Medical Care

Medicare provides a good example. It was created in 1965 to make it easier for the elderly to get health care. But by reducing the patient's out-of-pocket costs, it increased the demand for doctors and hospitals. And it reduced the supply of those services by requiring doctors and other medical personnel to use their time and attention handling paperwork and complying with regulations—and looking for ways to circumvent these things. So the price of medical care rose sharply as the demand soared and the supply diminished.

As a result, the elderly now pay from their own pockets over twice as much for health care (after adjusting for inflation) than they did before Medicare began. And most older people now find it harder to get adequate medical service. Naturally, the government points to the higher costs and shortages as proof that the elderly would be lost without Medicare—and that government should be even more deeply involved.

When Medicare was set up in 1965, the politicians projected its cost in 1990 to be $3 billion—which is equivalent to $12 billion when adjusted for inflation to 1990 dollars. The actual cost in 1990 was $98 billion—eight times as much.

Upside-Down Results

When people set up a program for themselves, most of them act as they agreed to. But when a program is based on coercion, everyone involved changes his behavior—and the outcome is far different from what was intended. Government programs promoted by well-intentioned citizens are almost always derailed by unforeseen consequences:

- Poverty programs don't reduce the number of poor people. On the contrary, they encourage more people to qualify as poor and get on the gravy train.
- Rules and regulations don't reform society as expected. People respond by looking for ways around the rules they don't like.
- The War on Drugs makes drugs more profitable—increasing the incentive for drug-pushers to recruit new customers.
- The underground economy thrives as a means of earning

money without losing it to government—reducing the revenues that had been expected to pay for government programs.

Human action is always unpredictable. But you can count on government programs to produce results quite different from those promised by their sponsors.

You would think this would cause people to shun government as a way of solving problems. But just the opposite happens—as we'll see.

Chapter 4

Why Government Grows
& Grows & Grows

The bad consequences of a government program usually don't show up immediately. And the delay may be long enough to hide the connection between the program and its results.

So government never has to say it's sorry—never has to take responsibility for the misery it causes. Instead, it can blame everything on personal greed, profit-hungry corporations, and the "private sector." And the government's cure for the problems is to impose bigger programs, more regulation, and higher taxes.

Thus politicians tell us the high cost of Medicare is due to doctors, hospitals, and drug companies charging too much—not that Medicare inflated costs by running up the demand for health care and hindering the supply of it. And, even though government controls over 50% of the money spent on medical care, politicians freely refer to the high cost of a hospital stay as a "failure of the free market."

Each government program carries within it the seeds of future programs that will be "needed" to clean up the mess the first program creates. No matter how much mischief it causes, government always shows up in a cavalry uniform—riding in to rescue us from the problems it created.

- Government runs a deposit insurance program that begs savings & loans to speculate freely—and then spends billions of our dollars to clean up the mess.
- Government regulates drug companies into near paralysis—and then spends billions of our dollars to subsidize drug research.

- Government cripples American companies with punitive taxes and mountains of regulation—and then spends billions of our dollars trying to find foreign markets for those crippled companies.

By preventing people and companies from taking care of themselves, government feeds its own growth.

Equal Benefits

Government grows, too, because the subsidy given to one group inspires others to demand the same benefits. And when government protects one company or industry from competition, others wonder why they shouldn't demand the same protection.

That's why no government program ever stands still. No matter what the stated purpose or limit when implemented, it inevitably expands to cover more and more people—and wider and wider areas.

Everyone who comes to the government asking for favors has a plausible request.

Once it's considered proper to use government force to solve one person's problem, force can be justified to solve anyone's problem.

Over time, fewer and fewer requests seem out of bounds. And the grounds for saying "no" become more and more eroded. The pressure on politicians to use coercion to grant favors becomes overwhelming.

The Motives of Public Servants

But, in truth, very little pressure is needed.

Lawmakers, bureaucrats, and judges all rejoice in a government that grows and grows and grows. Big government gives lawmakers the power to make or break companies and individuals. People must bow and scrape to obtain favors—or just to keep government from destroying them.

Like Topsy . . .

So government gets bigger and bigger:

1. Because the failure of each program leads to demands for new programs;

2. Because everyone wants the special privileges he sees others getting; and

3. Because "public servants" seize on every problem as an excuse to expand their powers.

There's a fourth reason that government grows so effort-lessly—a reason we'll look at next.

Chapter 5

If You Were King (The Dictator Syndrome)

Government grows also because well-meaning people like you and me believe it should do certain things that seem beyond controversy—find a cure for cancer, stop air pollution, keep violence off television, hold back an aggressor in the Middle East—something that everyone seems to agree should be done. Whatever the goal, it's easy to imagine that a single-minded government could achieve it.

I call this *The Dictator Syndrome*. You see suffering or danger, and in your imagination you see a government program eliminating it. But in the real world the program would operate as you expect only if you were an absolute dictator—having at your disposal all of government's power to compel everyone to do things your way.

Running the Gauntlet of Political Action

Just for a moment, think about something you wish the government would do and that nearly everyone would like to see happen— provide swifter and surer punishment for criminals, teach children right and wrong, furnish health care to those who don't have it, bring peace to Bosnia, or whatever. Imagine a goal so important that it seems to justify using government's power to coerce.

And now, consider what will actually happen to your program.

To get it enacted you'll need political allies, since alone you have only limited influence. But other people will support your plan and work for it only if you modify it in dozens of ways that further *their* goals and satisfy their opinions.

Suppose you make the necessary compromises and amass enough support to pressure the politicians to vote for your revised program. Who will write the actual law? You? Of course not. It will be written by the same legislators and aides who created all the laws, programs, and problems you object to now. Each of them will compromise your program still further to satisfy his political supporters.

And if the law passes, who will administer it? You? Of course not. It will be implemented by bureaucrats—many of whom will use it to pursue goals quite different from what you had in mind. They won't care what your purpose was. It's *their* law now, and they'll use it to suit their objectives.

And, lastly, the new law probably will generate many disputes— cases that must be settled in a courtroom. Who will decide those cases? You? Of course not. It will be the same judges who today rule according to their own beliefs, rather than by reference to the written law. A judge may even rule that your law means exactly the opposite of what you had intended.

By the time your program has run this gauntlet, it will be far bigger and far more expensive (in money and disrupted lives) than you had imagined. And it will have been twisted to satisfy many factions. In fact, your program may end up being the opposite of what you had intended.

In any case, you will have provided a new tool by which others can use government for their own ends.

COLOR CONSCIOUSNESS

To see how the political process turns idealistic dreams inside out, look no further than the civil rights laws passed in the last 30 years.

For almost a century before 1964, governments in many southern states forced segregation on the people. Government prohibited companies from providing racially integrated facilities for their employees or customers. Whites and blacks were forbidden by government to sit together in restaurants or to use the same restrooms and drinking fountains—and in many cases were forbidden to shop together or work together.

Civil rights advocates fought to repeal these state Jim Crow laws, but they failed. So they appealed to the federal government, which responded with the Civil Rights Act of 1964.

But this didn't simply repeal state laws *compelling* segregation. It *prohibited* racial segregation—voluntary or otherwise. Overnight, what had been mandatory became forbidden. Neither before nor after the Civil Rights Act were people free to make their own decisions about whom they would associate with.

The civil rights movement wasn't opposed to coercion by government. It merely wanted the government to aim its force in a new direction.

Although the activists believed coercion served the noble objective of bringing the races closer together, it was coercion nonetheless.

The Giant Begins to Grow

And coercive laws never stand still. No matter what a law's backers say at the time of passage, the law always stretches in surprising directions. The expansion occurs on at least two fronts:

1. The law almost always is enforced more broadly than intended;
2. When government benefits one group, other groups are encouraged to seek similar benefits.

And this is what happened to the civil rights laws.

In the first regard, the bureaucrats and courts set out to enforce the law zealously, seeking to root out any kind of discrimination—even though ending segregation, not discrimination, was the motive behind the original law. Companies were ordered not to consider race in any way when making hiring decisions.

But usually the reasons for a business decision are hard to prove. Unless a businessman was a noisy bigot, who could say whether racial discrimination had affected his decision to hire someone?

To avoid having to read minds, the enforcers treated results as proof of discrimination. If you didn't have a suitable racial mix in your workforce (or even among your customers), you were assumed to be discriminating—and the burden of proof was on you to prove otherwise.

So an employer could avoid charges of discrimination only by, in fact, discriminating—by using quotas to assure that he hired the right number of people of the right races. The law against segregation had been transformed into a law requiring discrimination.

The law also encouraged other groups to demand similar coverage. Once it was established that government should punish racial discrimination, the door was open to using government to punish anything similar. If it's wrong for an employer, landlord, or organization to discriminate according to race, it must be just as wrong to discriminate according to gender.

So the coercion expanded to prohibit discrimination against women—and then religious believers, and then the elderly, and then people with children, and then the handicapped.

The New Ruling Classes

Civil rights laws feed lucrative lawsuits. So every imaginable group wants to be covered by the laws—to be eligible for generous settlements. There's pressure to outlaw discrimination on the basis of sexual preference, weight, looks, drug use, illness, criminal record, citizenship, and many other categories. Everyone wants to become part of the aristocracy.

And it *is* an aristocracy these groups are trying to join.

Once they're on the "A-List," they have special powers. They can sue anyone who refuses to hire them, to rent an apartment to them, or to sell his services to them—and maybe force him to pay thousands or millions of dollars in punitive damages. No company can risk such a disaster by offending someone in the aristocracy—since almost any mistake might be considered evidence of discrimination.

For example, in 1993 six U.S. Secret Service agents sued the Denny's restaurant chain—complaining they received poor service because they're black. And how do they know their color was the reason for the poor service? Because a group of white people entered the restaurant at the same time they did, and the white people finished their meals before the blacks received their first course. To many people this was proof of discrimination.

Now, if you happen to be a white male, you've probably never felt such an insult. It's true you may have endured dreadful service in a coffee shop—perhaps many times. A waiter may have refused to give you the time of day, lost your order and forgotten you were even in the restaurant, spent all his time flirting with a waitress, or refused to take care of you until he had phoned his bookie.

The family at the next table may have eaten an entire meal before anyone even asked for your order. And so you passed the time counting the designs on the wallpaper.

But it isn't called discrimination if you aren't part of a group that's been certified as oppressed. So *you* have to blame it on a bad-tempered waiter, an overcrowded restaurant, or poor management. Since you aren't part of the aristocracy, there's no chance you were insulted because of your race (or your religion, handicap, or any other recognized status). You were insulted just because you're you. And your only recourse is to find a coffee shop that will treat you better.

The Denny's customers, however, could file a law suit—and they did. To avoid a long, expensive trial and months of unfavorable news coverage, Denny's settled out of court and paid them $54 million dollars.

Neither you nor I was in the Denny's restaurant that night. And we aren't mind readers. So we don't know whether the waiter mistreated the Secret Service agents because of their race. But we do know that if it's possible to get an enormous payoff for claiming discrimination, many people will do it—whether or not they actually suffer discrimination.

So we shouldn't be surprised that so many accusations are made. And with such rewards available for minor insults, it's not surprising that more and more groups demand to be covered by the law.

How Government Expands

The civil rights laws are supposed to end discrimination and segregation, and to promote harmony.

But coercion never produces harmony. How harmonious are people who are being forced to act against their will? Most likely, those who are coerced will resent those who benefit from the coercion. This sets group against group; it doesn't bring them together.

And if we accept coercion for one purpose, we'll be asked to use it for others. Even if *you* can say "No" to the other uses, some people will say "Yes," and others will say "Yes, please, and make mine a double." The noble cause will be stretched further and further until it eventually becomes farce.

For example, a Chicago company was hauled before the Equal Employment Opportunity Commission to explain why it failed to promote a woman who claims she was discriminated against because of the microchip in her tooth that allows her to communicate with others.

Then there's the man who sued his employer who fired him for bringing a gun to work. He said he was covered by the Americans for Disabilities Act (an outgrowth of the Civil Rights Act of 1964) because he's under psychiatric care. The case will be tried before a jury.

A 220-pound woman has sued the Minnesota National Guard, claiming that its 155-pound limit discriminates against her eating disorder.

In 1993 a married couple was ejected from an airliner (before takeoff) because they had screamed a string of obscenities at other passengers. So they sued the airline, claiming it had discriminated against them as sufferers of a disease that makes them utter profanities.

Has the law really been stretched so far?

No, it has been stretched even further.

In fact, it has been stretched all the way inside out. The civil rights laws originated to end segregation of the races in the South. But in 1992 a Florida court used these laws to award a white woman permanent disability benefits—ruling that her employer should have provided a *segregated* workplace to accommodate her fear of blacks.

Although the decision seems absurd, something of the kind was inevitable. If coercion is used to protect the feelings of black people, eventually it will be used to protect the feelings of white people as well. Once government coerces on behalf of one group of "victims," it will eventually swing the club on behalf of almost every imaginable group. You can't limit coercion to the uses *you* think are right.

So don't think of any of these cases as an example of a government program gone wrong. Each is an example of a government program—period.

YOU'RE NOT A DICTATOR

I've used the Civil Rights Act as an example of the way a well-intentioned government program grows and causes far more problems than it solves. But it is just one example. *All* government programs expand to encompass the political demands of people who want to take advantage of its benefits. And almost all government programs eventually do the opposite of what their original backers had asked for.

Whatever social reform you may envision, the version the government implements will be something completely different. However lofty your purpose, it will be debased by compromises in the legislature, in the administration of the program by thousands of government employees, and in the settling of the inevitable disputes.

Not only that, the program is likely to grow far bigger and more complicated than what you wanted. And someday it will evolve into a force opposite to your intentions.

You aren't a dictator. You can't control the actions of politicians, bureaucrats, and judges.

Universal Blindness

The Dictator Syndrome affects people in all political camps—left, right, and center.

On the left, some reformers imagine how the government could spend money in intelligent and clearly defined ways to eliminate poverty. They've forgotten that the trillions of "War on Poverty" dollars already wasted sprang from plans that once seemed just as intelligent and clear-cut to their well-meaning proponents. Today's reformers can't control the outcome of their programs any more than yesterday's could.

On the right, other people say the government should spend more on police and prisons to fight drugs or crime. They don't stop to notice that trillions of "tough on crime" dollars have already been spent without making a noticeable difference in the level of crime or drug use.

In the middle, some "moderates" think the government can make health care easily affordable for everyone by forcing a few simple reforms on insurance companies. They fail to see that today's problems stem from previous reforms that seemed just as simple and helpful—but forced doctors to handle enormous paperwork, forced hospitals to treat anyone who shows up, and forced insurance companies to ignore important differences among people when setting their rates.

It's easy to ignore the failures all about us as we imagine that the next scheme will operate efficiently and fairly—whether that scheme be a hard-headed welfare reform, an effective tough-on-crime campaign, a practical health-care reform, or whatever inspires our enthusiasm.

The New World Order

The same blindness afflicts people still hoping to make the world safe for democracy.

World War I didn't convince them otherwise. Nor did World War II.

They seem to think the government that can't stop violence in American cities can somehow bring peace to the rest of the world.

But one can support the newest foreign military adventure only by ignoring the wreckage left by all the previous military adventures.

After the 1991 war against Iraq ended, many people continued to feel the U.S. had been right to become involved. Some of them said, in effect, "Going to war was the right thing to do, but it didn't settle anything because the U.S. didn't go all the way and remove Saddam Hussein from power."

So, despite killing thousands of people and spending billions of dollars, the war failed to settle matters. Why? Because the government mishandled the project. But when has government handled *anything* correctly? As Joseph Sobran has pointed out, war is just one more government program.

Before the fighting, the Dictator Syndrome had led each of the war's supporters to think the government would wage it *his* way. Perhaps he thought he would answer the phone one day and hear a voice say, "Hey, buddy, this is George. Colin Powell's here in the Oval Office and we've got Norm Schwarzkopf on the other line, waiting for instructions. On this war thing, should we go on to Baghdad or wrap it up here?"

No one was going to ask your advice on waging the war. Your ideas about how it should be handled were just idle daydreams. This is government, not Burger King; nothing is done your way.

Not Under Your Control

You don't control the government. And your dreams of what government can achieve are just that—dreams. They bear no resemblance to what government will really do if your program is enacted.

No one can control the government. Most people who tug at it end up disappointed—even if, for a while, they seem to be succeeding.

If government, the agency of coercion, is a tool that can achieve your worthy ends, why shouldn't other people see it as the tool to achieve *their* purposes—including people who are thieves, bigots, politicians, mass murderers, bureaucrats, and judges?

If government is going to do someone's bidding, is it likely to be *your* bidding—or that of people far more determined, far wealthier, and far more influential than you are?

The government that's strong enough to give you what you want by taking it from someone else is strong enough to take everything you have and give it to someone else.

The government you want to suppress your enemies can be used as easily by your enemies to attack you.

Chapter 6

How Did We Get in This Mess?

We have seen that all government activities require coercion—violence or the threat of it.

You can always locate the coercion if you look for it.

First, the activity probably costs money—which was taken by force from people, whether or not they wanted the program. Almost no one volunteers to pay taxes.

Second, people are coerced to participate in the program. Business people are forced to fill out piles of forms to show they have complied with the law. Companies must submit to endless inspections of their products and procedures. Home owners may have their property taken away—or rendered useless—by provisions of the law.

One way or another, many people will be forced to do what they don't want to do—or will be forbidden to do what they do want.

If you fail to comply, you may be forced to pay a fine or may even be sent to prison. This can happen even if you are a peaceful, productive citizen—someone who has committed no violence against anyone, has stolen from no one, and hasn't defrauded anyone.

And after all the lesser penalties have been exhausted—the demands, the fines, the seizure of your house, the jail sentence—if you continue to resist, the government will use a gun.

The gun is always there. *The gun is the essence of a law.*

When someone asks for a government program, he is saying in effect, "Tell the police to use their guns to get me what I want."

See No Evil

The beneficiaries of a program (the people receiving subsidies, companies protected from competition, or people whose values are imposed upon the community) usually don't notice the coercion that's applied for their benefit. So it's easy for them to believe the government's efforts are wholly benevolent.

If the beneficiaries had to do the dirty work themselves—use a gun to steal the money or force people out of their homes or their jobs—they might have mixed emotions about the benefits they're receiving.

If they just had to stand and watch as companies are shut down, businessmen lose their life savings, employees lose their jobs, homeowners are evicted, and other people are hurt by the government's coercion, the beneficiaries might not be so eager to claim a "right" to their subsidies.

But they aren't required to see the dark side of the program at all. That is what has made government such a success in the coercion business:

Government lets people take from others without having to face the people being hurt.

And this assures that government will grow and grow and grow:

- Because the beneficiaries are never told who has been hurt and how, there is no limit to what they will ask from the government.
- Because so many of those not yet benefiting from a government program are oblivious to the damage government does, there is no limit to the number of people who will clamor to join those getting the benefits.
- Because the politicians aren't legally liable for the human lives they wreck, there is no limit to the coercion they will vote for.
- And because the people hurt by government aren't masochists, they will try to avoid the coercion—assuring that the government will have to keep strengthening the program to make it work.

This means government programs inevitably grow—no matter what their initial "limits." It means that those being coerced will participate grudgingly—producing much less revenue, information, and cooperation than was assumed when the program was enacted. It means the programs won't work as promised.

Programs based on coercion don't work.

This is why government programs don't work.

And this is why "fixing them" doesn't work.

The program will work only if you take the coercion out of it:

- So that the beneficiaries must pay full value for what they receive;
- So that everyone involved has an incentive to produce what's wanted;
- So that no one can distribute money that doesn't belong to him.

But if you take the coercion out of a program, you no longer need the government to run it.

And that's the point: government programs don't work. There has to be a better way.

HOW IT ALL BEGAN

As we can see, there is no such thing as a little coercion—any more than a woman can be a little bit pregnant.

Coercive programs almost always fail—and on the way to failure they get bigger, more expensive, and more intrusive.

So maybe now we can see why and when the government became the unworkable monster it is today.

The seeds of today's runaway government were planted when it was decided that government should help those who can't help themselves.

From that modest, compassionate beginning to today's out-of-control mega-state, there's a straight, unbroken line.

Once the door was open, once it was settled that the government should help some people at the expense of others, there was no stopping it. If the coercion of government can endow one person with property he hasn't earned, then everyone will want to use government to get something he wants. So it's not surprising that, over the past two centuries, more and more people have concluded that *they* deserve government's help.

"Helping those who can't help themselves" is a paraphrase of Karl Marx's famous dictum: "From each according to his ability, to each according to his need."

And once that principle is adopted, more and more people will want to be part of the needy, rather than part of the able—because nearly everyone prefers to be on the "to" side of transfers, rather than the "from" side.

You can't help a few people without everyone else wanting to be helped as well.

You can't limit government's coercion to just those transfers you believe are fair, because you can't give government the power to force good on the country without also giving it the power to force enormous evil on the country—in fact, to do anything it wants. It becomes a tool for obtaining whatever anyone can't get on his own—an instrument for every frustrated ambition.

So it was inevitable not only that the government would grow and become more powerful, but that the growth would accelerate—perhaps imperceptibly at first, but then faster and faster. The potential beneficiaries (as well as Congress, the executive, and the bureaucrats) have an interest in pushing government to get bigger.

And since politicians aren't legally liable for the harm they do, there's no point at which they have a reason to stop expanding their own power and wealth by expanding the government. Thus it's no surprise that after stripping *us* bare, they continue on and mortgage our children's future to pay for further expansion.

Nor is it a surprise that people elected to change the system usually join it instead. After all, once elected, these people have the power of big government at their disposal—and power is a heady commodity. Few can resist the temptation to use it to "do good"—to receive the applause of reformers and the gratitude of those on the receiving end of government favors.

And it should be no surprise that every attempt to reform government simply makes it worse. "Reform" won't transform a gorilla into a lamb, and politicians and administrators who have spent their lives seeking power aren't suddenly going to decide not to use it.

It Was Inevitable

It's understandable that people believe government *can* protect us and educate our children, but that something has gone wrong and needs fixing.

But the system *must* go wrong eventually. A government that can tax us—confiscate our wealth—to feed the poor and punish foreign villains will soon tax us to feed political cronies and punish political enemies.

If government has the power to keep criminals off the streets, it has the power to keep you off them, too.

And it has the power to subsidize companies that put campaign contributions in the right pockets. It has the power to breed a mass of welfare clients who will be completely dependent on government, and who will vote to make it grow.

Any system that lets one person force his will on another—by confiscating resources or by compelling obedience—will inevitably break down, because everyone will want to use the coercion for his own ends. And so, sooner or later, government becomes a free-for-all to be won by those best able to deceive and manipulate.

To maintain their tenure and power, politicians have to make deals with more and more interest groups until, eventually, most of the government's resources are consumed just buying votes and satisfying political backers. This leaves almost nothing for true crime control, education, or other functions you may think are government's proper business.

So it's perfectly natural to reach the point we have now, where government fails utterly in its traditional functions while meddling in things once considered no business of government—taking over the health care system, trying to police the planet, laying down millions of rules for companies to follow, subsidizing everything from art to zoology.

- A government that tries to help those who can't help themselves will turn into a government that helps those with the most political power.
- A government we try to use as our servant inevitably will become our master.
- And a government formed to do for the people what they can't do so well for themselves will instead do to the people what they don't want done.

Chapter 7

Government Doesn't Work

If government doesn't help those who can't help themselves, who *will*?

If we don't ask the government to protect us from fraud, from avarice, from incompetence, who *will* do it? If government can't assure medical coverage for all who need it, who *will*?

Most people tolerate the worst of government—high taxes and intrusive regulations—because they feel there are some things government must do.

One purpose of this book is to show how the things you value can be done more effectively and fairly outside of government. In Part II, we'll look at non-governmental, non-coercive ways we can improve health care, education, public safety, and national defense.

But we don't want to get ahead of ourselves. Before we look for solutions that do work, we must recognize that government solutions don't—that government is the source of most of society's problems. We don't need to fix government; we need to shrink it.

Government doesn't work. It can't deliver the mail on time. It can't issue a currency that holds its value. It can't maintain the roads efficiently, or run them so that they aren't constantly congested, or reduce a highway death rate that is so scandalous that highway officials probably would go to prison if the roads were privately owned.

Government doesn't work. Its schools don't operate properly because the people who work there are government employees—and so reading and writing take a back seat to indoctrination in becoming a model citizen.

Government doesn't work. And so there's never enough money to keep the cities safe, because crime-fighting becomes a political program, just like any pork-barrel project. Politicians will always spend first on programs that gratify their political allies—on subsidies, social-reform programs, and construction projects that enrich their supporters. And then, for some reason, there's never enough money left to deal with violent criminals.

Government doesn't work. The government that pledged to defend us from foreign invaders has drafted our youth and sent them to die fighting other people's enemies—in the trenches of France, the sands of the Persian Gulf, and the jungles of Asia. Our shores have seldom been threatened—and yet a million Americans have died in wars, another million have been wounded, and *trillions* of dollars have been spent intervening in other countries' conflicts.

Government doesn't work. You work, I work, Federal Express works, Microsoft works, the Salvation Army works, Alcoholics Anonymous works, but government doesn't.

Changing Our Perspective

Once we realize that government doesn't work, we will stop asking what government *should* do, and notice instead that government *can't* do the things we want:

- We may want government regulation to protect us from fraud, but the truth is that government *doesn't* protect us from fraud. The savings and loan crisis, every class-action law suit, and every financial scandal are testaments to the government's inability to shield us from fraud or incompetence.
- We may think crime control is a proper function of government, but the truth is that government *doesn't* control crime. Our cities are war zones. At most, the government promises only to look for the person who robs, rapes, or murders you.
- We may like to think that government sets the rules of the marketplace and acts as the referee, but in reality the government's rules are arbitrary, ambiguous, and constantly changing. And the "referee" always seems to side with the team with the greatest political influence.

Once we realize that government doesn't work, we will stop dreaming that this or that social problem can be solved by passing a law—or by creating a new government program—or by electing someone who will make Washington more efficient or cost-conscious.

Once we realize that government doesn't work, we'll know that the only way to improve government is by reducing its size—by *doing away* with laws, by *getting rid* of programs, by making government spend and tax less, by *reducing* government as far as we can.

And once we realize that government doesn't work, we will know which side of any political issue to cheer for: If the proposal would *increase* the size, the reach, or the importance of government, it would be a mistake to support it—no matter how honorable its stated purpose. If the proposal would *reduce* the size, the reach, or the importance of government, it would be an improvement—no matter what its flaws—because it can't be worse than what it will replace.

Reducing government and getting it out of our way means unleashing the elements of society that do work:

- The companies that increase our standard of living with their jobs, products, and services;
- The private charities that actually improve the lives of the needy, rather than turning them into permanent wards; and
- The most innovative and creative people in society—who make their living identifying what we want and helping us get it.

How far we can reduce government is a question no one can answer today. But we know that the more we reduce it, the better.

And we delay that improvement by trying to make government more efficient, more humane, more "user-friendly." Coercion isn't efficient, it isn't humane, and it certainly isn't friendly.

Government doesn't work. That's the first lesson we must learn if we want to improve society.

Chapter 8

Once the Land of the Free

America once was unique in all the history of the world.

It wasn't its natural resources, the character of its people, or its beauty that made it special. Other countries could boast of similar things.

The essence of America was an abundance of something rarely found in other countries: *freedom from government*.

For centuries the peoples of the world had been ruled by kings, queens, tsars, shahs, ministers, satraps, chiefs, rajahs, emirs, warlords, parliaments, senates, legislatures, assemblies, gangs, and freebooters. The rulers made extravagant demands upon their subjects.

An individual couldn't refuse their demands. The rulers could take from him whatever they wanted; command him to work, fight, or kneel; and forbid him to do anything that displeased them. The government was all-powerful.

America's Founding Fathers established something unprecedented—the first government strictly limited by a written constitution to a short list of activities. The federal government was authorized to do only what was specified in the Constitution. Anything else was to be done by state or local governments, by the people themselves acting outside government, or not at all.

The Constitution didn't limit what *citizens* could do. Its only purpose was to spell out—enumerate—what was permissible for the federal government to do. And anything not authorized was forbidden to the federal government.

This ideal of limited government was sometimes violated—but

violations were the exception rather than the rule. And many of the violations that did occur were reversed later, because it was understood that the Constitution limited the role of the federal government.

For example, in January 1794 when Congress considered a bill appropriating $15,000 for French refugees, James Madison (then a Congressman) voted against it, saying he

> . . . could not undertake to lay [my] finger on that article in the Constitution which granted a right to Congress of expending, on objects of benevolence, the money of their constituents. And if they once broke the line laid down before them, for the direction of their conduct, it was impossible to say to what lengths they might go, or to what extremities this practice might be carried.

To what extremities indeed!

The Bill of Rights

Some state governments had hesitated to ratify the Constitution— fearing that it didn't make entirely clear how limited the federal government's role was to be. Many people were afraid Congress might meddle in the areas that belonged exclusively to the states or private citizens.

And so the Bill of Rights was added to forestall any misunderstanding. It listed specific prohibitions against the federal government—such as forbidding it to pass laws suppressing the freedom to voice opinions in public or in print.

The Ninth and Tenth Amendments defined the essence of limited government:

> IX. The enumeration in the Constitution, of certain rights shall not be construed to deny or disparage others retained by the people.
>
> X. The powers not delegated to the United States by the Constitution, nor prohibited by it to the States, are reserved to the States respectively, or to the people.

In other words, the United States government could do only what was specified in the Constitution. All the rest of life's activities—charity, education, regulation of business, crime control, and so on—were to be handled by state governments or by the people on their own.

Thus began a momentous experiment to tame the monster that had enslaved so many people all over the world over all the centuries. And it was very clear to the fathers of the Constitution that government *is* a monster. As George Washington said:

> Government is not reason; it is not eloquence. It is force. Like fire it is a dangerous servant and a fearful master.

The founders felt that some government was necessary, since no one knew a better way to provide for the common defense and to insure domestic tranquillity. But they knew how dangerous it was to give such an agency the power to tax, to forbid, and to compel obedience.

The Constitution was the most successful attempt ever made to keep the dangerous servant from becoming the fearful master. And it made possible the freest, most prosperous country in all history.

People everywhere envied Americans for the liberty they enjoyed. And they flocked to this country from the four corners of the earth.

America rightly became known as the Land of the Free.

Chapter 9

How Freedom Was Lost

The Constitution authorized the federal government to use coercion for certain purposes—chiefly to deal with foreign governments, to prosecute wars, to assure a "republican government" in each state, to settle disputes among states, and to collect the taxes needed for those functions. But because coercion tends to breed coercion, government tends to grow—both in size and in reach.

Most of the time, the growth has been gradual, almost imperceptible. Year by year, the federal government has taken a little more of our resources and a little more of our freedom—but too little at a time to provoke much resistance, or even much notice. Over the years, though, all the petty thefts have added up to grand larceny.

Even this, however, has been dwarfed by the wholesale looting of freedom that occurred during four fateful periods in American history, when the politicians simply pushed aside the limitations the Founders had devised for the federal government.

1. THE CIVIL WAR, 1861–1865

The first was the Civil War.

Until then, the federal government had made brief, self-conscious excursions outside its Constitutional limits. But upon the secession of the Confederate states, the federal government began to disregard the limits without pause or shame. The concept of individual rights was thrown out, and U.S. citizens became "resources" for the prosecution of the Civil War.

The government drafted soldiers for the first time, jailed people who spoke out against the war, imprisoned citizens without trial, flooded the country with paper money, and levied an income tax—each of which violated the Constitution.

By 1865 the federal government's budget was 20 times that of 1860. After the war, the budget shrank year by year until 1878. But in 1878 the government was still spending 2½ times as much per person as it had in 1860.

Although some of the war's impositions were repealed afterward, the precedent had been set: the federal government may do whatever it finds necessary. Its needs overrule the Constitution.

The federal government may have freed the slaves, but it had become everyone's master.

2. THE PROGRESSIVE ERA, 1900–1918

During the first two decades of the 20th century, politicians established the principle that the federal government should actively intervene to solve apparent social problems and to direct the economy.

Regulation

The federal government had begun regulating railroads in the late 1800s. In the first decade of the new century it expanded its reach to oil companies, steel companies, and any enterprise it considered critical to the economy. The government decided which companies were too big or too successful, and split up some firms whose share of the market it considered too large.

This "trust-busting" hit companies that provided the best service and lowest prices for their customers. It also let established companies use the government to keep more efficient competitors out of their markets.

And it brought us the Federal Trade Commission and the Interstate Commerce Commission—empowering the federal government to decide what products and services you're allowed to buy.

The Income Tax

In 1913 the income tax was brought back and became a permanent imposition in our lives. It provided a seemingly unlimited source of funds to finance ever-growing government, and it gave the government an excuse to pry into every aspect of your life.

Perhaps no other instrument so starkly demonstrates the unrestrained power of today's government.

The Federal Reserve System

Also in 1913, Congress set up the Federal Reserve System. This agency is supposed to keep the economy growing smoothly by regulating the quantity of money in circulation. Thus it became the government's job to create prosperity—something coercion can never achieve.

The Federal Reserve was sold to the American people as a way to eliminate inflation, recession, and banking panics. Instead, it presided over America's worst depression (1929–1941), its biggest banking crisis (1933), and its longest sustained inflation (starting in 1955 and still going).[1]

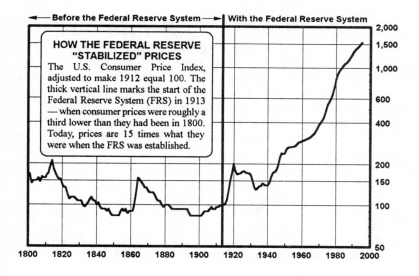

◄── Before the Federal Reserve System ──►│ With the Federal Reserve System

HOW THE FEDERAL RESERVE "STABILIZED" PRICES
The U.S. Consumer Price Index, adjusted to make 1912 equal 100. The thick vertical line marks the start of the Federal Reserve System (FRS) in 1913 — when consumer prices were roughly a third lower than they had been in 1800. Today, prices are 15 times what they were when the FRS was established.

Direct Election of Senators

Further in 1913, the Constitution was amended to require U.S. Senators to be elected by popular vote. The Founders had arranged for Senators to be chosen by, and beholden to, state governments— and hence inclined to vote against any federal intrusion upon the power of the states. This was part of the elaborate system of checks

---

[1]The last year in which the Consumer Price Index didn't rise was 1954. We have had inflation in 66 of the 80 years since the inception of the Federal Reserve, while there were only 20 years of inflation in the 80 years preceding the Federal Reserve.

and balances designed to keep any element of the government from becoming too powerful.

The passage of the 17th amendment freed Senators to drain power from the states and concentrate it in Washington—so that individuals and companies must court the Senators to obtain favors or to seek exemptions from tyranny.

World War I

In 1917 the United States entered World War I. The government used the war to bring back the draft, impose food rationing, raise the maximum income tax rate to 77%, and interfere with private lives in many other ways.

While many of the impositions were lifted when the war ended, the maximum tax rate never again fell below 24%—a level not even the most fervent income-tax advocate of 1913 had hoped for.

The long-term consequences of World War I were even more tragic. By entering the European war, in which the U.S. had no particular stake, the politicians threw out America's traditional neutrality. They replaced it with a policy that made every foreign conflict America's concern—no matter what the cost in American wealth, freedom, and lives.

The cost in lives has run into the millions. The cost in dollars has run into the trillions. The cost in freedom has been immeasurable.

Regressive

The Progressive Era has been hailed by historians as the time when America came of age. In truth, it was the time when America sacrificed liberty, privacy, stability, and neutrality to be more like the Old World countries immigrants to America were fleeing.

3. THE NEW DEAL, 1929–1945

In the late 1920s the Federal Reserve System put new money into circulation in the U.S. as part of a misguided scheme to bail the British government out of its fiscal problems. When the monetary increase threatened to bring on price inflation, the Federal Reserve stomped on the brakes and pulled money out of circulation— bringing on the crash of 1929 and starting a recession.

The Federal Reserve persisted in its policy, allowing the nation's money supply to shrink by 30% between 1929 and 1933—an unprecedented implosion that devastated the American economy.

Meanwhile, President Herbert Hoover mobilized every avenue of government compulsion to fight the recession. In just four years government spending rose by 65%—to $4.8 billion from $2.9 billion. Income taxes were raised to a range of 4% to 63%, from a span of only 1% to 24%.

The government pressured large companies to keep prices and wages high, even though the general price level was in the process of falling by 27% from 1929 to 1933. The artificially high prices and wages produced a glut of unsold products and mass unemployment.

Previous recessions lasted only a year or so, because the government always stood aside and let the economy recover its balance. But this time, government actively intruded—and transformed the recession into a prolonged depression.[2]

In running for president, Franklin Roosevelt denounced the Hoover administration's misguided policies—saying the government had become too big and too intrusive. He pledged to cut both taxes and the size of government by 25%.

The Second New Deal

But once elected, President Roosevelt expanded the Hoover policies—tripling the size of government within eight years.

With the aid of a compliant Congress, his administration transformed government into the arbiter of nearly all major economic decisions—investigating and regulating every corner of American life and business. It forced farmers to destroy crops, tried to set minimum prices on everything, and set loose new commissions, agencies, and boards on every industry in the land.

The maximum income tax rate rose to 94%. The New Deal also imposed new taxes on cars, tires, phone calls, bank transactions, and a host of other goods and services—taxes you still pay today.

Although historians at government-supported institutions love to say that Franklin Roosevelt saved the country from economic ruin, few mention that in 1939 unemployment was worse than in 1931 and business still hadn't recovered from 10-year-old shocks. And since Americans then had to struggle with the shortages and inflation of World War II, it was the late 1940s (almost two decades after the 1929 crash) before living standards returned to normal.

---

[2]The 1921 recession was potentially far more dangerous than the 1929 recession, because the 1921 recession came after a war and considerable inflation. But because the government stayed out of it, the 1921 recession lasted only 18 months.

Still Paying Today

The New Deal policies of both the Hoover and Roosevelt administrations converted a simple recession into the worst economic disaster in American history.

Even more far-reaching, the disaster allowed government to expand its control over our lives. Since the 1930s, there is no area of American life that is considered off limits to the politicians.

Both Democratic and Republican politicians feel obliged to pay homage to Franklin Roosevelt and the New Deal. They ignore the fact that the New Deal was an economic failure. And they fail to recognize the straight line running from the New Deal to today's meddling government, chronic federal deficits, historically high interest rates, and oppressive taxes.

But, then again, maybe they *do* understand the connection—and *that* is why they pay homage to Franklin Roosevelt.

4. THE GREAT SOCIETY, 1961–1975

The first three eras dismantled the strict limitations the Founders had placed on the federal government.

Although the dismantling diminished our freedoms and prosperity, America survived because the character of the people hadn't changed. Americans still believed they were individually responsible for their own lives and well-being.

However, it won't be so easy to survive the devastation wrought by the Great Society programs of the 1960s and early 1970s. For millions of Americans these programs destroyed the belief that you must earn what you enjoy. Instead, the government is now considered responsible for everything any American might need or want. The loss of self-responsibility has led to a terrible increase in crime and illiteracy, and a trashing of most of the values that blessed our civilization.

Until 1960 the federal government had practically nothing to do with education, crime control, or welfare (except for Social Security). But by 1975, the federal government dominated all three areas.

In each case the pattern was the same: The federal government provided financial subsidies to state and local governments—and, once the governments became dependent on the money from Washington, the federal government imposed conditions for continuing to receive it.

Although the money the federal government gives to a community comes from citizens in that same community, routing it through

Washington allows the Feds to set the rules. Thus the federal government began setting standards for school curricula, school lunches, welfare eligibility, and police procedures and budgets.

By taking control away from communities, the federal government made schools, police, and welfare systems even more remote from the people who pay for them and rely upon them—and made them even more susceptible to fraud and graft, and to meddling by social reformers.

You're Entitled

Welfare is a good example.

Once upon a time, before the 1960s, a person who needed help got it by appealing to a local charity (such as the Salvation Army) or to the town government. The downtrodden individual had to explain how he got into trouble and how he intended to work his way out of it. He was monitored closely to assure that he was telling the truth and that he stuck to his plan to get back on his feet. And he knew that the money he received came from the pockets of his neighbors. Federal welfare, however, requires nothing more ambitious, energetic, or embarrassing than filling out a form.

In former days, you knew that you had to work for what you got. Today you can get a regular check from the federal government if you're willing to undertake the arduous task of walking to your mail box once a month.

The same is true for all sorts of government subsidies. You don't have to be broke or hard up. With minimal qualifications, you can just sign up and receive:

- Unemployment benefits
- Student loans
- Farm subsidies
- Subsidized mortgages
- Subsidized medical insurance
- Disaster relief, and
- Thousands of other giveaways.

Once provided, these benefits become "rights," and anyone who suggests eliminating them is denounced as mean and heartless.

And after a while, a program becomes an apparent necessity. It's assumed that without farm subsidies all small farmers would go bankrupt and the country would starve; without federal loans no one could afford to go to college; and without Medicare no one would live past 65. No one asks how the country survived so well before these things became government's responsibility.

The worst effect of these programs is to separate acts from consequences. They teach people to be careless. Since you don't have to pay for your own mistakes, you have no reason to exercise caution, restraint, or forethought. Whatever goes wrong, the government will take care of you.

So it should be no surprise that Americans save less than they once did, exercise less caution in their business and personal dealings, seem less able to support themselves, and are more dependent on government to survive. This, of course, provides politicians with an excuse for more laws and subsidies.

America has been transformed from the land of enterprise, initiative, and self-reliance into the land of entitlements and dependency.

Lost Virtues

The transformation has devastated our civilization—bringing on terrifying crime rates, the abandonment of educational standards, an epidemic of teenage pregnancies, and the birth of a permanent class of citizens dependent upon the state for support.

As we'll see in Part II, many of the social problems that worry us so much today were virtually unknown before the federal takeovers of the 1960s.

- Crime rates were a fraction of what they are today. Gangs didn't terrorize adults on the street or students in school. No one had seen drive-by shootings since Prohibition ended in 1933.[3]
- Children graduated from high school knowing how to read, write, and add—and knowing a great deal about history, geography, and science. Today many college entrants can't even read the entrance exam. And many students have been told little more about Christopher Columbus than that he was an angry white male who took out his frustrations on the Indians.
- Teenage pregnancies out of wedlock were virtually unknown. In 1950 only one in 79 unmarried teenage girls gave birth to a baby (even before birth-control pills were available). In 1991 the ratio had dropped to one in 22.
- Welfare was rarely discussed, because it wasn't a compelling social issue. "Welfare" as we think of it was a tiny program

---

[3]From 1960 to 1992, the violent crime rate increased by 373%, and the overall crime rate increased by 403%. (Source: Federal Bureau of Investigation: *Crime in the United States.*)

operated by your city or county government. The truly desperate were helped mostly by private charities that took an interest in seeing that anyone in trouble got out of it as quickly as possible. Today welfare is a national scandal, and few politicians have any idea how to end it.

The escalation of "entitlements" in the 1960s and 1970s has led to the devastation of American cities, the decline of American education, and the deterioration of self-reliance. It has turned America into a battleground on which groups fight for the power to dictate who gets to take what from whom, and who gets to impose the rules dictating how everyone must live.

NO LONGER ANYTHING SPECIAL

The four episodes of rapid government growth destroyed the qualities that had made America unique, and transformed it into something like an Old-World nation.

- The Civil War changed the federal government into a national government superior to the states and the people.
- The Progressive Era established the principle that the government was responsible for the economy, and it produced the foreign policy that has kept us in conflict with one country or another for almost all of the past 80 years.
- The New Deal established that no area of American life is off limits to government.
- The Great Society destroyed the self-responsibility that made possible the prosperity and freedoms we once took for granted.

A tragic casualty has been the loss of the system of federalism the Founding Fathers designed. That system empowered local governments to set their own rules. Local tyranny existed sometimes, but people could escape it by moving to another state. Today you can escape only by leaving the country.

The four eras transformed America from a free country into a nation of obedient serfs, paper-pushers, victims, whiners, and antagonists. Now we are just another country in which the citizens live at the sufferance of their rulers.

As Joseph Sobran has said, the land of the free has become the land of the government permit.

Chapter 10

How Much Freedom Is Left?

Since the 1950s government has grown relentlessly. Freedom hasn't a single victory to its credits, and no champions in politics. Some politicians have fought against new government encroachments, but none has taken the offensive to win back any lost liberty.

Liberal politicians keep proposing new programs that further reduce the choices we can make with our money and our lives. Conservative politicians often fight these proposals—objecting that they're too restricting or too expensive. But each year some of the programs pass despite the objections. And they pass permanently—because even when the conservatives have control of the government, they rarely repeal what they once denounced.

And the conservative politicians have programs of their own. They love anti-crime and national security programs even when they reduce the liberties supposedly guaranteed in the Constitution. Liberal politicians often fight such proposals—condemning them as intolerable invasions of our privacy or our freedom. But some of the programs pass. And they too pass permanently—because even when the liberals have control of the government, they rarely repeal the legislation they once denounced.

Thus each big-government program is tolerated, consolidated, respected, and perpetuated even by its most powerful critics.

Politicians who praise "limited government" really mean government limited to what it is *today*.

If it is larger tomorrow, then "limited government" will mean government limited to what it is *tomorrow*. They never mean government limited to what the Constitution allows, or to any other fixed level beyond that.

We Must Undo the Wrongs

Only when we undo the changes made in the four eras of rapid government growth described in the last chapter will America once again be the land of the free.

Pundits like to say we can't go back—that we must live in the present. But the question isn't whether we will live in the present or the past; it is whether we will live free or as wards of the state.

Is it modern or progressive to let government confiscate 47% of the national income—a fatter share than the feudal lords of the Middle Ages demanded of their vassals?

Is it modern to let government enter our homes and businesses at will—in the same way King George's Redcoats violated the privacy of the American colonists?

GOVERNMENT IS EVERYWHERE

Today the Bill of Rights is just a quaint piece of parchment that few in Washington take seriously—lest it interfere with government's power to do what's right for you.

- The 1st Amendment says: *"Congress shall make no law* respecting an establishment of religion, or prohibiting the free exercise thereof; or abridging the freedom of speech, or of the press, or the right of the people peaceably to assemble, and to petition the Government for a redress of grievances."

But the Supreme Court has ruled that Congress can take any of these rights from you if the government claims to have a "compelling" reason.

- The 2nd Amendment says: ". . . the right of the people to keep and bear Arms, *shall not be infringed."*

But Congress routinely passes laws that prevent you from defending yourself. Needless to say, the politicians don't disarm themselves. Members of the Secret Service, the FBI, and other federal agencies charged with protecting politicians are always well armed.

- The 4th Amendment says: "The right of the people to be secure in their persons, houses, papers, and effects, against unreasonable searches and seizures, *shall not be violated."*

But the federal government can knock down your door, seize your property, and dare you to try to get it back—all in the name of fighting drugs—while the IRS routinely demands to see your private records without ever bothering to get a warrant.

- The 5th Amendment says: ". . . nor shall private property be taken for public use, without just compensation."

But federal regulations render much private property worthless with no compensation to the owners.

- The 9th Amendment says: "The enumeration in the Constitution, of certain rights, shall not be construed to deny or disparage others retained by the people."

But in truth the only rights you still have are those the politicians haven't yet bothered to take away. Congress considers every activity of life a fit subject of regulation, and it recognizes no limit on the taxes you must pay.

- The 10th Amendment says: "The powers not delegated to the United States by the Constitution, nor prohibited by it to the States, are reserved to the States respectively, or to the people."

But, although this says the federal government's power is limited to just what's specified in the Constitution, is there a single area of your life the federal government considers off limits?

We have descended from a nation of limited government, individual liberty, and self-responsibility to a nation at the mercy of its politicians.

Don't Tread on Government

The politicians don't tolerate any limits on their ability to "do good." They refuse to let the Constitution get in their way.

For example, on February 7, 1995, Rep. Melvin Watt (D-NC) proposed adding the following amendment to an anti-crime bill, H.R. 666:

> . . . provided that the right of the people to be secure in their persons, houses, papers, and effects, against unreasonable searches and seizures, shall not be violated; and no warrants shall issue, but upon probable cause, supported by oath or affirmation, and particularly describing the place to be searched, and the persons or things to be seized.

The House of Representatives voted down the amendment by 303 to 121. The 303 nay-sayers knew they had just voted against the 4th Amendment to the Constitution, but they considered the

Constitution to be an interference. Of course, *the purpose of the Constitution is to interfere*—to prevent politicians in the heat of a national crusade from going too far.

For another example, on April 24, 1995, the U.S. Supreme Court—in a rare showing of fidelity to the Constitution—ruled that a federal law prohibiting guns within 1,000 feet of a school was unconstitutional, because the Constitution gives the federal government no authority to legislate such a matter. The President of the United States, instead of accepting the Constitutional principle, immediately vowed to circumvent the ruling and find a way to impose the law anyhow.

Taxes Everywhere

Today government at all levels (federal, state, and local) takes 47% of the nation's income. You probably haven't noticed that government's share is so large, because you don't pay that much directly in income tax. But 47% of your earnings are confiscated nonetheless:

- Part of it is taken from you in federal income tax.
- More is taken in Social Security taxes.
- Still more is taken in other federal taxes—excise taxes, gasoline taxes, tariffs, and so on.
- And still more is taken in state and local taxes on income, sales, and property.
- You pay more than you should for products and services because the companies who make, transport, and sell these things pay corporate income taxes and excise tariffs.
- You receive less than you earn because your employer must pay his share of Social Security for you, and pay other taxes that reduce the money available to pay you.

All these taxes together total roughly 47% of your income. How free are you when government takes 47% of your earnings?

As recently as 1950, government's take was only 28%. In 1926, it was only 14%. In 1916, just 7%. And at the beginning of the republic, undoubtedly less than 3% was confiscated by government.

But now you pay taxes on the water and electricity you use, the things you buy in stores, luxury items, necessities, imported goods, gasoline, telephone calls, baby-sitting, airline tickets, snack foods, investment transactions, alcohol, cigarettes, property, gifts, legacies, cable TV, amusements, employment, fuel oil, motor oil, cars, and thousands of other things.

Running Your Life

In addition to the money it takes from you, government regulates what you can buy and sell—and whether you can even go into business. Companies must file endless forms and adhere to thousands of regulations—all of which make it harder for them to provide what you want, in the form you want to receive it, at a price you're willing to pay.

The government even dictates the terms of your job—and deprives you of income you could be receiving. Your employer can spend only so much money to pay for what you do. When the government imposes expensive work rules, the money to obey them comes out of what the employer is willing to pay you.

For example, if the government says your employer must provide "family leave," the cost reduces what he can pay you. So instead of receiving what you've earned, you get only what's left after your employer has paid all the costs government has imposed.

By most estimates, complying with regulations costs companies and individuals at least 10% in the form of higher prices and lower incomes.

Total Cost of Government

Adding the cost of taxes and regulation together, government is soaking up 57% of your economic life.

It means you work 4½ hours out of every 8-hour day for the government, and only 3½ hours for yourself and your family. Or, put another way, you work until around July 27 of each year (6 months, 27 days) for the government, and only the remaining 5 months and 4 days for yourself.

If this is freedom, at what level of confiscation are we no longer free?

What We Get in Return

Of course, you get something in return for all the taxes and regulation. But what is it? Safe cities? Good schooling for your children? Safe and uncongested roads? A harmonious society? A nation secure from attack by terrorists or foreign missiles?

Couldn't you spend that 57% more wisely than government does? Couldn't private companies provide better services at much lower cost than the government's post office, its "insurance" schemes, and its regulation?

WE MUST TURN THIS AROUND

America is no longer the land of the free. And if we don't soon restore individual liberty in America, we may no longer have the chance. The larger government gets, the more power it has to forbid any change in the system—and the more its waste of our resources reduces the chance of getting out of this without national bankruptcy.

We have to reverse the tremendous growth in government. It isn't enough to slow its growth or even freeze government at current levels. A moratorium on new federal regulations isn't the answer, nor is a 7-year plan to balance the budget. Any of these timid measures could be repealed by the next Congress. More important, they leave intact the awesome, oppressive structure already there—the government that is suffocating America with regulation and taxes.

So we must slash government dramatically—and we need to restore the limits set in the Constitution. That won't guarantee freedom forever. But it will at least bind government down by the chains of the Constitution for a generation or two—while we figure out how to protect our freedoms for good.

We must revive the American Republic—and we must do it soon. We have already fallen into the gray world of half-freedoms and stagnant living standards the rest of the world takes for granted. If we continue along this path, it will inevitably become worse; at some point the government will no longer be able to keep its promises—leaving us only two choices:

1. The repudiation of promises made to Social Security recipients and others who have become dependent on the government; or
2. Tax rates of 50%, 60%, 70% or more to pay for all the IOUs the government has signed on your behalf.

These are grim choices. But they will be the *only* choices if we don't act soon to stop the madness.

Chapter 11

Your Innocence
Is No Protection

If you complain that a government plan to fight crime threatens everyone's freedom, you may hear the age-old retort:

"If you aren't guilty, you have nothing to fear."

If only that were so. The truth is that innocence is no protection at all against government agencies with the power to do what they think best—or against a government agent hoping for promotion and willing to do whatever he can get away with.

Tell a businessman he has nothing to fear from the piles of forms he must file to prove he doesn't discriminate. Tell a home owner he has nothing to fear when his property is seized by the government in a mistaken—or contrived—drug raid. Tell a taxpayer he has nothing to fear when the IRS drags him into a "taxpayer compliance" audit that eats up a week of his life, costs him thousands of dollars in accounting fees, and threatens him with unbearable penalties.

It is the innocent who suffer most from government's intrusions. How many times have we seen the following pattern?

1. The press and politicians demand that something be done about violent crime, terrorist acts, drug dealing, tax evasion, or whatever is the Urgent Concern of the Month.
2. A tough, new, take-no-prisoners law or policy is put into place.
3. After the dust settles, the initial "problem" continues unabated, because the guilty continue to slip through the net. But the innocent are left burdened with new chores, ex-

penses, and hazards—more mandatory reports to file, less privacy, reduced access to products and services, higher costs, heavier taxes, and a new set of penalties for those who shirk their duty to fight in the War on _____ (fill in the blank).

4. And, needless to say, the ineffectual law is never repealed.

Being innocent doesn't allow you to ignore the government's demands for reports—or to say "No, thanks" when a government agent wants to search your records, your place of business, or your home—or to refuse to observe regulations that were aimed at the guilty, not you.

When coercion is used to solve social problems, we all suffer. The coercion fails to achieve its stated aims, but it is wondrously effective at harming the innocent.

Even worse, every year a few million innocent people suffer special burdens—greater than those the government places on all of us. The dismantling of the Bill of Rights has allowed the government to disrupt their lives, confiscate their property, or even kill them—even though they've committed no crimes.

I hope you never become one of them.

NOT EVEN MINISTERS ARE SAFE

For example, suppose you're a 75-year-old minister living in Boston. You've worked all your life to console those who are poor in money or spirit.

One afternoon 13 men with sledgehammers break down the door and charge into your apartment. They're wearing helmets, battle fatigues, and boots—and they're armed with shotguns and pistols.

They force you to the floor, pin your legs and arms, and handcuff you. They scare you so badly you suffer a heart attack—and within 45 minutes you're dead.

Who were these criminals?

They weren't "criminals." They were members of a SWAT team searching for drugs and guns. There wasn't anything illegal in your apartment, as you could have told them if they had stopped long enough to ask you.

But they didn't stop and they didn't ask. They didn't have to. They "knew" you were a bad guy, and they weren't going to allow you to escape or to flush your drug inventory down the toilet.

Six weeks after you die, it is revealed that the SWAT team raided the wrong apartment. You have been completely exonerated. But, unfortunately, the government can't bring you back to life.

This isn't fiction. It is the story of the Reverend Acelynne Williams, and how he died on March 26, 1994.

Fatal Attractions

And the tale isn't extraordinary. Donald Scott was shot to death when a task force of 27 men smashed into his house in Malibu, California, on October 2, 1992. They claimed Mr. Scott was growing marijuana—although their only evidence turned out to be a false report from an unidentified informant.

Similar stories can be told of other people who were shot without warning, whose homes were torn apart, or who went to prison for resisting arrest—people like Harry Davis of Fort Washington, Maryland; Charlotte Waters of Los Angeles; David Gordon of Bridgeport, Connecticut; Xavier Bennett, Jr., of Atlanta; Kenneth Baulch of Garland, Texas; Robin Pratt of Everett, Washington; William Grass of Kentucky; Albert Lewin of Boston; Manuel Ramirez of Stockton, California; Charles DiGristine of Titusville, Florida; and Donald Carlson of San Diego.

All of them were innocent. But all of them had plenty to fear from government. And now their families will *always* fear government as much as any Soviet citizen did.

By ignoring the Bill of Rights, acting on anonymous tips and intruding without warrants, government agents have put all of us in jeopardy—the innocent as much as the guilty.

Maybe you haven't been hurt yet by a government agent acting on a malicious report or on his own ambition. So far, a mean-minded office rival or business competitor hasn't stooped to giving a false tip about you to the police or the IRS.

Be thankful. And hope it doesn't happen next year. You might not be given time to prove your innocence.

LIVING THE AMERICAN DREAM

Even if you can prove your innocence, it might not protect your property.

Suppose you work hard, save your money, and finally go into business for yourself.

You start a charter airplane service—flying cargo, making air ambulance runs, transporting businessmen, and giving tours. At age 53, after a long period of going without, you finally achieve some success—and now you own four planes.

Then one day you're contacted by an elegant man who identifies himself as Randy Sullivan, a banker. He asks you to pick him up in

Little Rock and fly him and four boxes of financial records to Las Vegas, for which he'll pay $8,500—your standard fee for such a trip.

On the way to Las Vegas, you stop in Oklahoma City to refuel. When you take off again, he tells you he made a phone call in Oklahoma City, and he now needs to go instead to Ontario—a city near Los Angeles. He pays your $8,500 fee in cash, and adds $200 for the change in route.

When you land at the Ontario airport, U.S. Drug Enforcement Agency (DEA) agents accuse you of drug trafficking, handcuff you, and take you to the local jail. Your bail is set at $1 million. The next day it's lowered to $250,000, then to $10,000.

Three days later, they release you with no indictment. When you go to the airport to get your plane, a DEA agent says the plane and the $8,500 in cash now belong to the federal government. It turns out that "Randy Sullivan" was a previously convicted drug dealer named Albert Wright, and the government claims the boxes of "financial records" contained $2,795,685 in cash—although you're never shown any evidence of that.

The Guilty Escape, the Innocent Suffer

You are innocent; you've broken no law, but you have a lot to fear. You've lost your airplane and $8,500 of your income.

How can this happen?

Since 1970 government agents—federal, state, or local—can seize any of your property they suspect may have been involved—in any way—in a crime.

You don't have to be the one who committed the crime, and it could be that *no one* is ever convicted of a crime—or even charged with one. Government agents don't even have to prove that your property *was* used in a crime. They merely have to assert "probable cause"—a suspicion. In other words there are virtually no limits on their ability to seize your property and keep it.

More than a hundred federal laws contain "asset forfeiture" provisions. They are used by the Drug Enforcement Agency, the IRS, the FBI, the Coast Guard, the Postal Service, the Bureau of Land Management, the Fish and Wildlife Service, the Securities & Exchange Commission, the Department of Health & Human Services, the Food & Drug Administration, the Customs Service, the Immigration & Naturalization Service, and the Department of Housing & Urban Development. And over 3,000 state and local governments have their own forfeiture laws.

These laws were first enacted as weapons against organized crime and large-scale drug operations. But (surprise!) they soon became something else—opportunities for law-enforcement agencies to raise money to supplement their budgets. So now almost anyone can be a target. Potential guilt isn't as important as the salability of the assets to be seized.

Because the laws pretend it's the property that's tainted, not you, the Bill of Rights offers no protection. The rules of evidence are ignored; there's no presumption of innocence, so you have to prove you aren't guilty; you can't demand a jury trial; you can't confront the person who made the accusation against you; there is no court-appointed attorney (even if the government just bankrupted you); and your property can be taken without compensation.

To recover your property, you must file a claim within 10 days of the seizure or give it up forever (no one is obligated to alert you to the deadline); and you must post a bond equal to 10% of the property's value (even if the government has seized all your bank accounts).

The guilty know all these things; so they take steps to keep their property out of reach. The innocent know little about such laws—and are surprised and helpless when the government moves in. *This is why tough new laws aimed at crime always seem to hurt the innocent more than the guilty.*

As Congressman John Conyers put it in 1993, a law designed to give cops the right to confiscate and keep the luxury possessions of major drug dealers mostly ensnares the modest homes, cars, and hard-earned cash of ordinary, law-abiding people.

In many counties of America today, sheriffs' departments have become self-funding empires. They no longer have to beg money from the legislators, because asset forfeiture finances virtually everything they need.

Suing the Government

But back to our story.

The DEA agents confiscate all your business records to search for evidence of your drug dealing.

Eventually, they realize they have no case against you. But they still won't return your plane. They say you should have known who your passenger was and what was in his boxes—even though you have no legal right to search him or his cargo.

Somehow, it's *your* duty to stop the drug trade, even though the government—with over a trillion dollars of tax money at its disposal every year and the legal power to coerce anyone—can't stop it.

The only way you can retrieve your plane is to sue the government—at your own expense. So that's what you do.

The government resists—arguing that it has the right to confiscate your property even if it can't prove your guilt, so long as there is "probable cause." And the fact that your plane flew near Los Angeles, an area known as a center of "illegal drug activity," is probable cause.

You testify that you never saw Albert Wright before in your life. But the government produces someone who claims to have seen you with him in the fall of 1988. He says he recognizes you by your peculiar beard. But you didn't grow the beard until a year after he supposedly saw you, and you produce witnesses who so testify.

After a three-day trial, the government is ordered to return your airplane. But, instead, it asks for another trial—claiming that your witnesses lied about your beard. (The double-jeopardy protection you've seen in all those TV lawyer series doesn't apply to "civil" matters like yours.)

So you produce 51 affidavits from FAA employees, city officials, bankers, U.S. marshals, customers, and other business contacts—all swearing that you didn't have a beard in the fall of 1988. You even submit a videotape from a TV station that shows you clean-shaven in 1989.

But the government still won't return your plane.

You Win, Sort of

Eventually the government offers to let you have the plane back if you'll pay $66,000. Later, the demand is reduced to $30,000.

You inspect the plane and find it's been torn apart in the search for drugs. It will require at least $50,000 in repairs before it can be flown again.

The government lowers the offer again—this time to $6,500.

But by now you've spent $80,000 in legal fees.

You've sold all your assets, lost your business, and filed for bankruptcy. You're working as a truck driver to make enough money just to survive. You don't have $6,500.

But, of course, because you're innocent, you have nothing to fear from the government.

This isn't a fairy tale. It's the true story of Billy Munnerlyn of Las Vegas.

Widespread Looting

And it isn't an exceptional case. A similar fate befell Willie Jones of Nashville, who had $9,600 confiscated because he was a black man paying cash for an airline ticket—which fits the "profile" of a drug dealer. He didn't use drugs, buy them, or sell them. He also didn't have his $9,600 anymore.

Tracy Thomas withdrew cash from his credit union. He used the cash to make bids at a sheriff's auction, and he had $13,000 left over when it was finished. While visiting his godson, police entered the godson's home looking for drugs. They didn't find any and they never charged anyone with a crime. But while they were there, they searched Tracy Thomas and confiscated his $13,000. He sued the police, and a judge ordered them to return the money, but they turned it over to the DEA instead. So Tracy Thomas had to go to court again, this time to fight the federal government.

In 1994 such seizures netted federal, state, and local governments over $2 billion in property. Government agencies sell the confiscated property and use the proceeds to operate their departments—bypassing the normal taxing and appropriation procedures.

Were all the victims criminals? Only 20% of the people who lost their property to seizures were charged with a crime. So we could say that there were at least four innocent people hurt for every one who was guilty—or allegedly guilty.

Perhaps this has already happened to you. If not, hope that it isn't your turn next year. If it is, your innocence will be no defense.

OF MICE AND HUMANS

It isn't just the drug-busters who threaten you.

Suppose you want to build on a piece of property you own, but the U.S. Fish and Wildlife Service says you can't. Why not? Because a marshy area in the lower part of your land is a habitat for the salt marsh harvest mouse—an "endangered species."

Because your rights are far inferior to those of the mouse, you can't build where you want to on your own property. So you alter your plans to avoid the mouse's habitat, and try to build instead on the highlands. But the government says you can't build there either.

Why not?

Because when global warming melts the polar ice caps, the ocean will rise and overflow the lowland habitat—and the salt marsh harvest mouse will run to the highlands to survive. Thus you can't build even on the high area of your property.

Global warming?

Yes, global warming—the fear that the earth is gradually getting warmer and that someday Antarctica will melt and the oceans will overflow the land. Of course, the "someday" may be three centuries from now—if ever. But we need your land now to provide a habitat for the salt marsh harvest mouse in that science-fiction future.

This may sound like a Woody Allen movie, but I assure you it's not a comedy. It's a real-life tragedy. It all happened to John Thorpe of San Francisco.

How can such things occur? Because well-intentioned Americans—like you and me—think the government should use force to bring about good results. But once available, the force is used for purposes beyond the good intentions. And the people who actually use the force don't act by the standards of reason, fairness, and justice that were part of your good intentions.

YOUR LIFE IS AN OPEN BOOK

Your innocence doesn't protect your privacy, either.

Do you ever wonder why banks charge all those service fees?

Maybe it's because they have to spend millions of dollars a year complying with federal orders to provide information about your bank account to the Treasury Department. The T-men go through your bank records and those of other bank customers at will—without a warrant—demanding to know why your banker didn't file a report about that suspicious transfer of money you made. Doesn't he realize you might have been dealing drugs?

You may be innocent, but that doesn't protect your privacy.

OUR VOLUNTARY TAX SYSTEM

And innocence is no protection when the IRS comes calling.

The IRS (Internal Revenue Service) says our system of taxation is based on the willingness of citizens to assess and pay their taxes "voluntarily." How pleasant. How civilized.

But *without a warrant* the IRS can order anyone—your banker, your employer, the stores you deal with—to provide information about your finances.

The IRS can impose penalties on you for any of 150 different reasons. In 1992 it imposed 33 *million* such penalties on taxpayers. Did you get one? If not, maybe your turn will come next year. I hope you can prove your innocence.

You may think a penalty is unlikely because you fill out your tax return so carefully, but *Money* magazine estimated that almost half of all penalty notices the IRS mails are incorrect, and that the IRS collects up to $7 billion in mistaken penalties each year.

In 1992 alone, the IRS seized 3,253,000 pieces of property— bank accounts, paychecks, real estate, and other personal possessions. And the IRS hasn't been deterred by a U.S. General Accounting Office estimate that almost 6% of all IRS levies are mistakes. Was any of *your* property seized in 1992? If not, I hope your luck holds next year.

Of course, you have a legal right to contest IRS actions. But James Payne has estimated the average cost of fighting a tax case to run between $37,265 and $74,530—depending on how far you pursue it before you give up. Even if you win, your chance of having your legal expenses reimbursed is less than one in a hundred.

You may be innocent, but it's still going to cost you. How much can you afford to pay to protect yourself?

BILL OF RIGHTS FOR THE INNOCENT

Every one of the outrages I've mentioned violates the Bill of Rights.

Because our school system doesn't teach much about Constitutional safeguards, many people think the Bill of Rights is just a Get-Out-of-Jail-Free card for criminals. And they wonder why we should protect the rights of killers and thieves.

But the Bill of Rights wasn't written to protect criminals. It was designed to protect *you*:

- To make sure a zealous prosecutor can't take you to court over and over again on the same charge—searching for a jury that will convict you.
- To make sure the police can't break into your home unannounced on the mere chance that you might have some drugs or illegal weapons stashed in your closet.
- To make sure politicians can't confiscate your home or other property to fulfill some dream of social reform.
- To make sure you don't have to answer questions put to you by the police—so a ruthless policeman can't twist your words out of context or browbeat you into confessing something you didn't do.
- To make sure your attorney can cross-examine any accuser or any witness against you.

Of course these safeguards would protect the guilty as well as the innocent. But brushing them aside gives government employees the power to do as they wish—to harass whomever *they* think is guilty.

And these safeguards, which are respected less and less every year, haven't been letting the guilty off. Crime rates haven't skyrocketed because of criminals using the Bill of Rights to their advantage.

Crime is soaring. . .

- Because the government's War on Drugs has transformed a minor social problem into an immensely profitable enterprise for those willing to defy the law;
- Because many of the government's schools have become cess-pools;
- Because the government packs the prisons with non-violent offenders, making it necessary to release the thugs early;
- Because the government diverts law-enforcement resources to fighting victimless crimes—as well as to affirmative action and other social reforms—leaving too little with which to protect your life and property; and
- Because government schools teach young people that inequality of wealth is unjust—providing a moral justification for taking from someone more "fortunate" than oneself.

The government has inspired or abetted a thousand criminals for each one it has freed on a legal technicality.

When Constitutional safeguards are honored, they rescue innocent people far more often than they let the guilty slip away.

Unfortunately, the safeguards are ignored more and more by Congress, the police, federal officials, and the courts. Disregarding the Bill of Rights has done nothing to reduce the crime rate, but it has put your life and mine in jeopardy.

As a result, we have neither physical protection from the guilty nor legal protection for the innocent.

Until the Bill of Rights is a living document again, I hope the government doesn't think you're suspicious or covet your property for one of its programs.

Your innocence probably won't protect you.

Chapter 12

On the Road to a Better World

The dozens of tough-on-crime laws passed in the past few decades, the property seizures, the high taxes, the hundreds of inconveniences imposed by government on the innocent—none of these things has made us safer. The laws always promise to snare the guilty, but it's the innocent who are hurt:

- Gun-control laws don't inhibit criminals, who rarely buy their guns in stores. But the laws do prevent you from defending yourself.
- The anti-privacy laws and door-smashing practices haven't brought victory in the War on Drugs. But they've destroyed the lives of many law-abiding citizens and ruined a lot of doors.
- Abuses of civil liberties by the police, prosecutors, and courts do little to keep criminals off the streets. But they could turn your life into a nightmare.

Social reformers and crime-busters try to beg off responsibility for the destruction by saying these invasions are the price we pay to create a better world, a better nation, or a better community. After all, "you can't make an omelet without breaking a few eggs."

But, somehow it's always someone else's eggs that get broken—never theirs.

And the omelet never materializes—only cracked shells and broken lives.

Their better world never materializes because it depends upon coercion to succeed. And coercion never improves society. So government is always promising to do something that's impossible—

64

such as coercing people to stop taking drugs or abandon their prejudices.

When the coercion doesn't work, the politicians must impose harsher and harsher measures in order to show they're "serious" about the problem and, inevitably, we come to the abuses we saw in the preceding chapter—such as property seizures and "no-knock" invasions of your home.

These aren't legal mistakes in need of reform. They are the inevitable result of asking government to use coercion to create a better world.

Escalation

Each increase in coercion is easier to justify. If it's right to force banks to report your finances to the government, then it's right to force you to justify the cash in your pocket at the airport. If it's right to take property from the rich to give to the poor, then it's right to take your property for the salt marsh harvest mouse.

As each government program fails, it becomes "necessary" to move another step closer to complete control over our lives. As one thing leads to another—as coercion leads to more coercion—what can we look forward to?

- Will it become necessary to force you to justify everything you do to any government agent who thinks you might be a threat to society?
- Will it become necessary to force your children to report your personal habits to their teachers or the police?
- Will it become necessary to force your neighbors to monitor your activities?
- Will it become necessary to force you to attend a reeducation program to learn how to be more sensitive, or how not to discriminate, or how to avoid being lured into taking drugs, or how to recognize suspicious behavior?
- Will it become necessary to prohibit some of your favorite foods and ban other pleasures, so you don't fall ill or have an accident—putting a burden on America's health-care system?

Some of these things—such as getting children to snitch on their parents or ordering people into reeducation programs—already are happening in America. The others have been proposed and are being considered seriously. History has shown that each was an important step in the evolution of the world's worst tyrannies.

We move step by step further along the road to oppression

because each step seems like such a small one. And because we're told that each step will give us something alluring in return—less crime, cheaper health care, safety from terrorists, an end to discrimination—even if none of the previous steps delivered on its promise. And because the people who promote these steps are well-meaning reformers who would use force only to build a better world.

WHERE THE ROAD LEADS

The reformers of the Cambodian revolution claimed to be building a better world. They forced people into reeducation programs to make them better citizens. Then they used force to regulate every aspect of commercial life. Then they forced office workers and intellectuals to give up their jobs and harvest rice, to round out their education. When people resisted having their lives turned upside down, the reformers had to use more and more force.

By the time they were done, *they had killed a third of the country's population*, destroyed the lives of almost everyone still alive, and devastated a nation. It all began with using force for the best of intentions—to create a better world.

The Soviet leaders used coercion to provide economic security and to build a "New Man"—a human being who would put his fellow man ahead of himself. At least 10 million people died to help build the New Man and the Workers' Paradise. But human nature never changed—and the workers' lives were always Hell, not Paradise.

In the 1930s many Germans gladly traded civil liberties for the economic revival and national pride Adolf Hitler promised them. But like every other grand dream to improve society by force, it ended in a nightmare of devastation and death.

Professor R. J. Rummel has calculated that 119 million people have been killed *by their own governments* in this century. Were these people criminals? No, they were people who simply didn't fit into the New Order—people who preferred their own dreams to those of the reformers.

Every time you allow government to use force to make society better, you move another step closer to the nightmares of Cambodia, the Soviet Union, and Nazi Germany. We've already moved so far that our own government can perform with impunity the outrages described in the preceding chapters.

These examples aren't cases of government gone wrong; they are examples of government—period. They are what governments do—just as chasing cats is what dogs do.

They are the natural consequence of letting government use

force to bring about a drug-free nation, to tax someone else to better your life, to guarantee your economic security, to assure that no one can mistreat you or hurt your feelings, and to cover up the damage of all the failed government programs that came before.

A BETTER WAY TO A BETTER WORLD

Coercion can't produce a better world. But *you* might help produce a better one—if you're free to act on your dreams, free to use your talents, and free to invite others to enjoy what you learn and build.

Coercion doesn't work. Government doesn't work. But you do, and I do, and so do millions of people who manage to get what they want without threatening to draw a gun.

The only reliable and productive endeavors are what people undertake voluntarily—and to which they *willingly* give or trade their time and other resources. Only when we turn to free individuals and voluntary endeavors—and away from government and force—will we recover the American dream.

Part II will show how we can do that—how we can get what we want without force.

How we can bring back the American dream.

PART TWO

SOLVING TODAY'S SOCIAL & POLITICAL PROBLEMS

Chapter 13

Fixing America's Problems

I want to live in a city where crime is an exception, rather than a daily terror. I want to be free to walk the streets at night—confident that I won't be accosted, threatened, or mugged. But I can't, because government policies have converted large parts of our cities into war zones.

I want children to come out of schools knowing how to read, write, and do simple arithmetic—and knowing a great deal about American and world history, geography, science, and civilization. But government schools are more interested in teaching political theories, sex education, selected tales of American injustice, prejudice against business and industry, and horror stories of environmental catastrophe.

I want to live in a country where people are independent, proud of themselves, and responsible for their own lives. But government is breeding a nation of welfare dependents, victims, litigants, thumb-suckers, and buck-passers.

I want to live in a community where people are civil to one another, where they say "please" for the help they need and offer something in return. But government has set group against group, each demanding privileges at the expense of others.

I want to live in a nation that's secure against foreign threats. But government has exposed us to danger by looking for trouble all over the world, choosing sides in foreign disputes, and leaving us defenseless against attack by any one-missile dictator.

I want to live in a country with clean air, clean rivers, and clean streets. But government has allowed its property to be polluted, and it subverts our rights of private property—leaving us less incentive to preserve the purity of what we own.

I want to live in a nation where parents can raise their children according to their own values of civility, self-reliance, and virtue. But government's massive taxes have forced many families to send both parents into the job market—leaving their children to learn about life from government employees.

I want to live in a country where people can use the money they earn to care for their families, to seek their dreams, and to build for the future. But government takes so much of our earnings that the average person can't get out of debt—let alone build for the future or make his dreams come true.

IDENTIFYING THE REAL PROBLEMS

This part will look at today's leading social problems and identify the cause of each.

It's easy to believe that some problems cry out for more government—tougher laws to deal with crime, tougher enforcement to stop the flow of immigrants or the flow of drugs, new laws to stop lobbyists from influencing legislation, an end to the easy-going attitude that seems to have let moral standards decline.

But these are problems because government has made them so.

- Crime wasn't America's #1 social problem until the federal government moved into the crime-fighting business in the 1960s.
- Immigration became a problem only after government began offering immigrants free schooling, free welfare, free privileges of all kinds.
- Lobbyists became a problem only when government became big enough to provide attractive rewards for effective lobbying.
- Family values haven't declined because government is too lax, but for precisely the opposite reason—because government has grabbed responsibility for everything, leaving many individuals no reason to exercise self-responsibility, and because government taxes away our ability to care for our own, teach our children our own values, or live our lives in the ways that make sense to us.

So instead of suggesting the usual solutions—more government, more control over our lives, and higher taxes—I'll show how we can correct these ills by reducing government and taxes, and by expanding personal freedom.

FEDERALISM

Problems in many areas—such as crime, education, and welfare—were small when handled at the local level, but became crises when the federal government moved in during the 1960s and 1970s. To apply real solutions we have to get the federal government out of those areas.

The Constitution gave the federal government no power to deal with common crimes, or to regulate individual conduct, or to take care of people in need. The Founding Fathers knew that politicians could use such power to reward their friends, punish their enemies, and gain control over your life.

So all these matters were left to the individual states to deal with.

Did the Founding Fathers trust state politicians more than federal politicians? Of course not. But they knew the states would compete with one another. Any state that went too far could lose population (and tax sources) to its neighbors. People could move easily from state to state without leaving America.

The federal system didn't guarantee that no state would get out of line. But the Founding Fathers knew it was better to let one or two states go too far than to give the national government the power to go too far.

They created the best protection against centralized government any country has ever enjoyed. But it wasn't perfect: over the years, the decades, and the centuries, the federal government has pushed further and further beyond the boundaries the Founding Fathers set for it.

Most of today's social problems result from the federal government's intrusions into areas where it has no Constitutional authority and no competence. It is imperative that we change this—and, as Thomas Jefferson said, bind down the politicians from mischief by the chains of the Constitution.

Functions Performed More Efficiently

This means getting the federal government out of welfare, education, crime control, housing, transportation, labor relations, regulation of business and the economy, and much else.

That won't mean these areas will be forsaken.

In some cases, state or local governments will take them over—and perform them at less cost to the taxpayer. And citizens in each state will have more power to reform or abolish the programs as they choose.

In other cases, individuals and private organizations (companies and non-profit groups) will pick up what the federal government abandons. In a free society private companies are always looking for unfulfilled needs—hoping to profit by helping people do what they can't do themselves. And when government doesn't interfere, competition drives those companies to improve their services continually—making them more convenient, less expensive, and more efficient.

And in some cases, a federal program simply will disappear because it's no longer needed—like lamp-lighting. Politicians may say, "See, if the free market won't take care of this, government has to do so." But the free market's "failure" to handle it is a sure sign that only politicians want it.

Whatever *needs* to be done *will* be done—and done better—when we get the federal government out of the way.

WHAT DO WE WANT?

We have to decide what kind of America we want.

Do we want an America in which individuals are proud of themselves—confident they can handle their own problems?

Or do we want a country in which everyone is responsible for everyone else but no one is responsible for himself, where groups dislike each other because each gains only at the expense of others, and where we are dependent upon the favors of politicians to survive? Do we want a society in which government takes half our income from us and then doles it back to us as though we were children on an allowance?

We no longer are proud, self-reliant Americans. Government has turned too many of us into whiners, dependents, people clamoring for favors from the state.

Fortunately, it isn't too late to change this.

But the changes have to come soon. We are fast reaching the point where government will be so insolvent from over-promising that we can no longer unravel the mess without shortchanging and hurting millions of people.

The changes have to be quick and decisive. Government doesn't keep its promises. So we can't depend on it for 5-year plans to phase out wasteful and destructive agencies—or 7-year plans to balance the budget. Like the famous Soviet 5-year plans, Congressional multi-year promises are never fulfilled.

And each reduction in government has to be complete. Reducing an agency to a small fraction of its current size leaves intact the mechanism by which it can grow again. Like a weed it has to be pulled out by the roots—not cut back.

In each case, there are only two realistic choices:

1. Get rid of the program and get rid of it quickly.
2. Or resign ourselves to living with it forever.

There is no middle ground.

Chapter 14

Why Freedom Brings Prosperity

Most people know how to handle their own affairs. They understand they have only so much money to spend—and that nothing becomes affordable just by wanting it. They know that buying one thing means they can't buy something else.

But when people think about the country as a whole, they may forget what they understand so clearly about their own budget. And so they find it easy to say "Yes" when politicians make something sound attractive—and they forget that it can be paid for only by giving up something else.

All the public problems that trouble us—including dismal schools, crippled families, the welfare mentality—are aggravated by the government's bad economic policies. So we need to understand how the marketplace works—and how governments, when they try to overrule the activities of the marketplace, nurture small problems so that they grow into big ones.

We need to realize that government can no more make us prosperous than it can deliver the mail on time.

The Ability to Do Damage

If government stuck to the few simple functions authorized in the Constitution, the national economy would flourish, and we could focus on our own lives. But politicians now promote government economic policies that affect us intimately. They seduce us with thoughtless, grandstanding laws that are supposed to improve our lot but actually destroy jobs—and even lives.

- They make unskilled teenagers unemployable by raising the minimum wage. They make it hard for married men and women to find jobs by passing "family leave" bills. They put almost everyone's job at risk with unrealistic "safety" regulations. And they do all these things while posing as friends of the working man.
- They kill thousands of people by imposing gas-mileage standards that force auto makers to build flimsy, lightweight cars—or by withholding life-saving medicines from the market—or by passing health-care legislation that makes it harder for doctors and hospitals to attend to their patients. And they do all those things while masquerading as compassionate, vigilant guardians of your welfare.

Every law that forbids people from peaceably pursuing their own happiness and well-being eventually hurts thousands or millions of people. Some of them die.

Government doesn't work, but freedom does. Free people, working in the hope of profit, worry about what you want—and strive to help you get it. Politicians and bureaucrats worry about what their political backers want.

Understanding Economics

We can't cover all of today's economic issues here. But even if we did, tomorrow the politicians would be back with new schemes and new promises. To see through them all, ask yourself one question: When has any government program ever delivered the benefits that were promised for it?

GETTING WHAT YOU WANT

Nearly everything you treasure was produced and delivered to you without the coercion of government. The car you drive was built by people who willingly produced it in exchange for your money. The house you live in was built by people who willingly constructed it in exchange for your money.

You bought those things because you wanted them. They built them because they wanted what you were willing to pay. This is the essence of economic freedom, and it's what makes society work—what makes it peaceful and prosperous.

Whatever is most important to you, some company will work to provide it.

Do you want a safe product? Then the company that demonstrates that it meets your safety standards will get your business.

Do you want an inexpensive product? Then the company that can keep prices low will get your business.

Do you want a reliable product? Then the company that proves how durable its product is will get your business.

Do you want extra features? Then the company that includes the extras you value will get your business.

Do you want good service? Then the company catering to your desires has a chance to sell to you again and again.

No company will satisfy you perfectly. (Only politicians promise perfection.) But some company will give you the best that's possible today.

The five desires listed above—safety, low price, high quality, special features, good service—can be incompatible. In fact, they usually are. Extra safety, quality, features, or service all work against the lowest possible price. And new features raise safety questions—simply because they are new.

Which of the five goals should be foremost?

It might seem obvious that safety should be most important. But *how* important? Should no car be sold unless it's absolutely accident-proof? If such a car is possible today (I don't know that it is), it might cost $500,000 or more. Should government use coercion to prevent you from buying any car that has the slightest chance of causing an accident? If it did, only the wealthiest people would have automobiles. The rest of us would have to walk.

Should good quality be the first consideration? To prohibit the sale of any VCR that might someday break down would in effect prohibit the sale of VCRs that cost less than $10,000 to produce. Would that be a good thing?

Should good service be primary? Any company wants to keep its customers happy, and so it will always try to improve service—but it has to consider price as well. A fast-food restaurant knows you might like table service—and maybe a singing waiter as well—but it doesn't want to charge too much for a hamburger. Should government require Burger King to deliver your Whopper on a silver platter and your Coke in a crystal goblet—with your own personal waiter to pick up your napkin if it falls to the floor? Would we all be willing to pay $30 per hamburger for such service?

Weighing the Factors

Safety, quality, features, and service all have to be weighed against price. Why? *Because there's a limit to what you can and will pay.* No consumer—not even the wealthiest—has an unlimited budget.

There's always a limit to what a customer will pay for a particular product. The limit varies between any two people, because each person must weigh:

- How much money he has.
- How much he wants the product.
- Other attractive uses for the money.

No matter who he is, his resources are limited. And so he must weigh a product's price against the product's value to *him*, in light of the money he has to spend and all the other things he could spend it on.

In the marketplace, each person makes his own choices—the compromises he judges to be the best possible for himself—without forcing his choices on his neighbors.

How to Handle Diverse Desires

But if each person has his own standards, how can the needs and wants of different people all be served?

The marketplace takes care of that automatically.

Most companies offer products that are a little different from those of their competitors—in order to catch the consumers who prefer those differences. That's why there are so many different car models to choose from. That's why there are so many different computers and computer programs. That's why there are so many different kinds of mustard in the supermarket, and so many different dresses in the department store.

In the marketplace, you get to weigh safety, quality, service, features, and price by *your* standards—and pick the product that's closest to what you want. And your choices don't keep anyone else from choosing what he wants. Everyone can make his own choice without preventing others from getting what they want.

And the opportunity to choose isn't limited to products. It applies as well to the services you require—to such things as safety information, guaranteed repair service, special help in making a selection, instruction in how to operate a product, a cheaper alternative, shopping without leaving your home, or almost anything else. If a sufficient number of people want it, someone will see that desire as an opportunity to profit, and will make the service available.

It isn't necessary to muster a majority to make something available—as it is in political matters. Many a company prospers by serving only 1% of its market—because it provides the features the 1% want. For example, there are hundreds of magazines, each with a devoted readership. There are thousands of furniture manufacturers, each producing the kinds of chairs that *some* people want.

There are millions of businesses, each offering something a little different that *some* people want. And even when an industry, such as breakfast cereal, is dominated by a few giant companies, each competes by offering dozens of choices.

How Can You Know Everything?

But are all those choices a blessing?

How can you judge them? How can you test and rate such things as safety or quality? For example, how can you know whether a particular car is safe or reliable?

Perhaps you can't. But there are people who can. They work for insurance companies that have to decide how much to charge you for auto insurance. They work for large leasing companies that need to know the long-term effects of buying one model over another. They work for magazines like *Consumer Reports* or *Motor Trend* that want you to rely on them for guidance. And millions more of them—the amateurs—work for free, and will gladly tell you about their experience with the products of a given manufacturer.

All these experts are willing to help you. And if there were no experts, the makers of safe cars would devise ways to *prove* their products are safe. Otherwise, you'd be afraid to buy a car—and they'd go out of business.

PROSPERITY

Freedom brings prosperity because it allows every manufacturer and seller to respond to what his customers want. Freedom allows every employer to work out mutually agreeable conditions with his employees.

The marketplace conveys vital information to all of us. When the price of something goes up, it says there's a shortage—so producers can profit by making more of it to cure the shortage, and consumers can save money by using it more sparingly. When the price of something falls, it says there's a glut—so producers should switch to making something people want more, and consumers who like this product should take the opportunity to use more of it.

Anything that intrudes upon this arrangement—by forcing prices upward or downward, or by preventing producers from making what consumers want—hurts all of us. It reduces the bounty the marketplace offers, it reduces the menu from which we can choose, and it means we have to work harder for less.

The marketplace is a wondrous institution. It harnesses the self-interest of each of us and puts it to work for the benefit of all. And it does so without intruding upon our desires, our privacy, or our freedom. It is regulation by reality, not by coercion.

Chapter 15

How Your Life Is Regulated

QUESTION #1: If you had a package that absolutely had to be delivered 1,000 miles away tomorrow morning, would you send it by:

(a) The U.S. Post Office, a government agency, or
(b) Federal Express, a private company whose success depends on being more reliable than its competitors?

Most likely, you'd choose Federal Express. You've learned through the years not to rely on the Post Office for prompt service.

You know that Federal Express will respond immediately if the package doesn't arrive on time—and track it down and make special arrangements to get it to its destination quickly. But the Post Office will tell you to submit a written complaint—which will do nothing to solve your immediate problem.

Federal Express has to be good. It has to keep finding new ways to make its service more affordable, easier to use, and more reliable. If it doesn't, it will lose business to UPS, Airborne, or another private carrier.

But the Post Office is a government agency. It has to please Congress, not you—so you can wait in line. No postal employee will worry about missing a raise if your package doesn't arrive on time, or if you get tired of waiting and go somewhere else. No one will lose his job if your package is lost or stolen. No matter how many reforms are promised, the Post Office remains a government agency—and you know what that means.

So, if you had a package that absolutely had to be delivered tomorrow morning, you wouldn't depend on the Post Office. You'd turn to Federal Express or one of its competitors.

QUESTIONS #2: If your life depended on a medicine's reliability, would you want it tested by:

(a) A government agency, or
(b) A private company whose profits depend on being more reliable than its competitors?

The answer should be the same as for Question #1, but many people would say "government agency."

They All Work for the Same Company

Almost every real-life experience you've had with government has been a burden. When you deal with the Post Office, Motor Vehicles Department, the IRS, or any other government agency face to face, you see how government operates. And you'd gladly deal with almost any private company instead—if only you could choose.

Still, you've been told by teachers, journalists, and politicians that the government is there to protect us, to be impartial, to care only for the public good. So it's not surprising if you believe the Food and Drug Administration (FDA), the Federal Aviation Agency (FAA), the Environmental Protection Agency (EPA), and other government agencies—*with whom you've never had firsthand contact*—are different from the Post Office.

But *all* government agencies are run by bureaucrats whose advancement has nothing to do with satisfying customers. They are there to put in their time. The FDA is simply the Post Office for medical progress—with *very* long waiting lines.

Because we don't deal with most government agencies personally, we don't know how they operate. So when you read that the Securities & Exchange Commission (SEC) has fined a company for fraudulent activities, you may not suspect that the company's only sin was to file a particular report two days late, or to violate Interpretation 17 of Ambiguous Rule 89546(e)1(D)4.

When you hear that the FDA has been testing a new medicine for five years, you may think the FDA is making sure you don't take something unsafe. But, in fact, the FDA may be wasting four of those five years on routine procedures that aren't needed, but that no FDA employee has a motive to bypass—just as no postal employee has a reason to break his routine to keep your letter from taking two weeks to get across town. Or an FDA executive may have decided it's safer—for him—to let thousands of people die while the medicine undergoes further tests, rather than take a chance on being blamed for one death from an unanticipated side effect.

A private company goes bankrupt if it's wrong too many times. But government agencies don't disappear when they make mistakes—so people who work for them have no compelling reason to be sure what they do helps anyone.

POLITICAL REGULATION

As we saw in the preceding chapter, the marketplace allows each person wide freedom to choose what is best for himself. But political regulation does away with personal choice. We all must bow to the judgments of the individuals in Washington who decide what we can buy, what we can sell, what we can eat and smoke, how we must deal with our employer or employees, and what we can do with our own property.

Can government help by supervising people who provide things for you—by forcing products to be safer, by forcing quality to be higher, by forcing companies to charge less and be more polite?

How can it? To get your business, every company already wants to produce what you and other consumers have decided you want the most.

But when government produces or regulates a product, bureaucrats and politicians overrule those decisions—and no one is allowed to provide what you might prefer. Everyone must abide by the same standard. How is that an improvement?

It isn't.

When "public interest" groups pressure Congress to mandate higher gas mileage in all cars, they are overruling your desire for safety or lower prices. You're expected to take better gas mileage and bless them for it.

When the federal government forced aspirin makers to use only child-proof containers, they also forced millions of older, childless people with arthritis to give up convenience. If you have trouble opening the bottle, buy a pair of pliers.

Whether the product is a car, a computer, food, clothing, or anything else, the principles are the same:

- The marketplace gives you a long string of alternatives and lets you pick the one that most closely matches your desires. You can buy your own regulation—from a laboratory, an insurance company, a consumer advocate, a magazine, a personal consultant, or some other advisor—for much less than what the regulators charge you, and without giving up freedom of choice. And if you don't trust the verdict, you can always switch to a different regulator.

- Government services or regulation give you one choice—selected by those with the greatest political influence—and make you accept it. One size fits all—no matter how uncomfortably.

With government, you sometimes get more safety in a given product than you want to pay for. Or you may get *less* safety than you want because political pressure has made price or energy efficiency paramount.

But in either case you pay more than you should, because government, not businessmen, have designed the product. And some products you might want—such as a medicine for a rare disease or a car strong enough to survive the worst crash—aren't available at all because government has prohibited them or made them unprofitable to produce.

And even when government does make a particular product safer, it makes *you* less safe—because the product's high cost leaves you with less money to spend on safety in other areas.

Government has nothing to offer that you couldn't get for yourself in the free market. If there's something you need urgently or something you're afraid of, someone out there knows how to take care of the problem and he wants to handle it for you—for a price. He's going to be more reliable than the government, because his profits depend on making you happy.

POLITICIANS LOVE REGULATION

Politicians don't see it this way, however. A regulatory agency is useful to them because it gives them power over individual companies.

Imagine for a moment that you're a U.S. Senator who chairs an important Senate committee. Suppose a big financial supporter heads a company that makes an alternative fuel that can be used, however inefficiently, in automobiles. Think how indebted he would be if you could get the EPA to force auto makers to allocate 10% of their production to cars that use alternative fuels—justifying the rule as a way to make the air cleaner, or to make America energy sufficient, or to bring about some other nice-sounding goal.

As chairman, you decide what bills your committee will consider. All Senators are beholden to you, because they have bills that must pass through your committee. So, unless it is conspicuously stupid, whatever you want the EPA to do is likely to be written into law.

It doesn't matter that the fuel you're promoting makes cars less efficient and wastes precious resources. Who's going to stop you?

•

When car makers protest, you can say the car makers are putting profits ahead of the environment—and the press will probably agree with you.

When the TV discussion shows debate the issue, the auto makers will be represented by a public relations flak from General Motors. But the pro-legislation side will be presented by someone from a non-profit, non-partisan, non-political, scientific, scholarly, consumer-advocacy, unbiased, public-interest organization that has studied the matter carefully and concluded the alternative fuel would make our air cleaner or make the Arabs lose business.

Of course, the TV host (or the journalist who reports the opposing viewpoints) won't mention that the "unbiased" expert works for an organization that's funded by the alternative-fuel company, or even funded by the government itself, or that the expert once predicted the world would run out of oil by the year 1980, or that he makes a larger salary than the public relations flak, or that he once worked for the Senate committee chairman who is now pushing the EPA bill.

The journalist has been taught, just as we have, that private companies are motivated by greed to do bad things to the country—while politicians, bureaucrats, and members of non-profit organizations were somehow born without a self-interest gene, and live only to serve us. In truth, the non-profit organizations are often in business solely to promote government programs—while private companies that don't rely on the government profit only by doing what the public wants.

TAKING SIDES

The idea that government is our protector, and that business is the enemy, is widespread. All our lives we've been told the government is there to help us, and that private companies would shortchange us if the government didn't stop them.

This point of view is found in history books, school textbooks, the press, TV news, political speeches, movies, and TV stories—almost everywhere that business is discussed. We are shown two warring sides:

US		**THEM**
Consumers		Manufacturers
Employees	**vs.**	Sellers
Government		Employers
Press		

The people who sell us products and employ us are pictured as our enemies—against whom we supposedly would be helpless if it weren't for the noble government regulators, and for the fearless journalistic reformers blowing the whistle on corporate misdeeds.

But companies succeed only when they please you. So, obviously, they care what you want. They have to be on your side or they'll go out of business.

On the other hand, the only objective of a government agency is to get bigger. And it gets bigger by showing Congressmen that it's doing something to help them get reelected. Congressmen will be particularly supportive if a government agency is helping their political friends and punishing the competitors of their friends—including competitors that are providing what you want. By reducing your choices, government works against your interest.

Despite this, the press usually assumes the government to be right in any conflict with business. Journalists generally are reformers, and reformers generally assume that people won't do what's right unless they're forced to. So newspapers and TV newscasters often make statements like:

"Consumers won a victory today when Congress passed a bill to tighten regulation over cable TV companies."

"Congress gave workers a present today when it passed legislation to force employers to provide a number of fringe benefits."

Journalists fail to realize that whatever manufacturers or employers are forced to provide will prevent them from providing what consumers or employees want more. By siding with the government, reporters also work against your interests.

So the two warring sides really should be represented as:

US		**THEM**
Consumers		Government
Manufacturers		Press
Sellers	**vs.**	
Employees		
Employers		

HOW PROGRESS IS MADE

We've been taught that all progress has been driven by government forcing business to do what's right. We've heard frequently that government saved us from the robber barons in the 19th century, for example.

Someday the history books may tell us how government protected consumers against computer companies that tried to make it hard to operate computers. The story might go like this:

> Once upon a time, to operate a personal computer you had to learn a mysterious language of cryptic commands. Using this language was slow, tedious, and error prone. Fortunately, public-spirited politicians and zealous regulators forced computer companies to make their products so easy to use that you could get your work done merely by pointing to your choices on the computer screen.

Of course, this story is nonsense. The truth is otherwise. When IBM introduced the first of the modern personal computers (PCs) in 1981, Microsoft furnished the operating system—known as MS-DOS (Microsoft Disk Operating System). MS-DOS was a simplified version of the operating systems that had run larger computers.

It was a big improvement, but still too technical for most people to handle easily. You had to love computers to want to own a PC.

So Apple Computer saw a chance to profit by offering potential buyers an easier way. It introduced the revolutionary Macintosh computer in 1984. This allowed you to point to your choice on a screen full of pictures and labeled buttons—without learning those cryptic MS-DOS commands.

Not to be outdone, Microsoft developed a competing system, called Windows, with many of the same benefits as the Macintosh system, plus a few more. And IBM offered another pictorial system, called OS/2, that had still more benefits.

It was *competition* among profit-seeking companies, not regulation, that made computers easier to use.

It was *competition*, not regulation, that cut computer prices by over 95% between 1981 and 1995.

It was *competition*, not regulation, that made computers faster and more powerful.

It was *competition*, not regulation, that made them more reliable.

Is the computer market exceptional? Yes, it is. It is one of the least regulated markets in America. If other industries don't progress at such a fast clip, it's not because they're older and more settled. It's because they're more heavily regulated.

REGULATION, THE INVISIBLE DESTROYER

Still, you might think we must give government the power to do good—to protect those less sophisticated than us, and to be a referee between competing interests. But when government referees, it always favors the team with the most political influence.

And when you give regulators any power at all, you give them the power to terrorize businessmen—to demand that they change their products or the way they make them, or that they spend all their time filling out forms to prove they don't discriminate, don't pollute, and don't beat their wives anymore. And you pay the bill for all this—in increased prices, in reduced choices, and in slower service.

Regulation leads to a multitude of social ills. Many of the public problems hotly discussed by political pundits exist only because of government regulation. And yet regulation is rarely identified as the culprit.

For example, a corporation's decision to build a plant outside the U.S. may be attributed to the lower wages some foreign workers will accept. So politicians call for new laws to penalize companies for relocating, or for high tariffs that would make it harder for U.S. companies to sell their foreign-made goods in the U.S.

In fact, the wage differences have existed throughout this century, but companies didn't find it attractive to move abroad until the last couple of decades.

Whenever everyone in an industry seems to be doing the same thing, it's usually because of a technological breakthrough (as in the rise of computers during the past decade or so) or because of government pressures (as in the case of companies fleeing the U.S. or the litigation explosion).

The dominant cause of company relocations has been the regulatory load piled on American business. This, combined with ever-increasing taxes, has created burdens that many companies find unbearable—which forces them to move abroad or go out of business.

Driving a Company Out

For example, Intel Corporation of California is the world's leading maker of computer chips. It got that way by being intensely competitive, fast on its feet to make changes as quickly as necessary to stay ahead in its market, and by correctly foreseeing what its customers will need and want next.

Intel is now considering moving all its manufacturing operations out of America. Why?

Because the Environmental Protection Agency (EPA) is using Title V of the 1990 Clean Water Act as justification to demand that every factory like Intel's apply for a new permit every time it makes *any* change in its operating procedures.

Intel doesn't pollute the environment, but it has the "potential" to do so—as defined in the EPA's regulations. So the EPA won't let Intel make any changes without the EPA judging the effect on the environment. And since Intel continually changes its operations in order to be competitive, each Intel factory may have to make scores of these applications every year.

Each permit application runs several hundred pages. The slightest mistake in these book-length applications could subject a company officer to prosecution for fraud or perjury.

After the application is filed, the company must wait 30 days for public comment, another 45 days for the EPA to respond, 90 days for revisions to be considered, and then 60 days for citizens to petition for changes. In other words, instead of responding quickly to its customers' needs—a key factor in Intel's success—the company will have to wait months for the EPA to approve its applications.

Every time Intel applies for a new permit, anyone who doesn't like the company—for any reason—can file a protest. The Clean Air Act even allows organizations to sue a company whose environmental policies displease them. A company may have to pay the complainer's legal expenses, pay fines to the U.S. Treasury, and even help fund the organizations' own projects as penance for its alleged "misdeeds."

There is enormous pressure on companies to settle such suits out of court—as the only way to keep moving ahead. So organizations can file nuisance suits as a way to finance their own projects. Even competitors or disgruntled employees can use the courts to tie up the companies under this "environmental" law.

No wonder the lawyers are busy.

And it's no wonder that Intel finds the grass greener in foreign lands.

But the politicians don't generally attribute such wanderlust to the laws they wrote. Instead, they propose new laws and tariffs in response to the mistakes caused by their own policies.

Any thinking person could have foreseen the bad consequences of the Clean Air Act when it was passed in 1990. Of course, Congressmen are busy people and it was a long bill. So who can blame them if they didn't have time to read the fine print?

REGULATION & SAFETY

No matter how many problems such regulation causes, politicians will still claim we need it in order to be safe. But federal regulation is the enemy of safety.

As we'll see on page 95, FDA regulation is responsible for far more deaths than it prevents. The same is true for many other agencies. As I mentioned earlier, the EPA forces carmakers to obey unrealistic fuel-economy standards that lead to smaller, more dangerous cars. And almost all regulations stifle economic growth—which is the single most important factor contributing to longer lives.

We are rightly enraged by such events as the killing of innocent people in the Oklahoma City bombing in 1995, or the Waco massacre of 1993. And we mourn for the victims in a plane crash or a natural disaster. But the FDA kills many times more innocent people each year than a dozen such tragedies.

When will those who shed such tears and lavish such compassion over the welfare mother or the baby seals or an endangered species show some compassion for the victims of regulation—the suffering cancer victim who is denied the relief of marijuana, or the dying AIDS patient who is prohibited from trying an experimental drug that might save his life?

HOW THE BURDEN AFFECTS YOU

What does all this regulation cost you?

A study by Thomas D. Hopkins of the Rochester Institute of Technology estimated the cost of federal regulation at $600 billion annually, which is 11% of the $5,599 billion national income for 1994. A 1992 study for the Heritage Foundation by William G. Laffer, III, and Nancy A. Bord estimated the net cost of regulation (after allowing for the benefits regulation might produce) to be between 16% and 32% of the national income.

It is impossible to calculate precisely the cost of regulation, but it's obvious that it exacts an enormous cost from us—and that it eats up at least 10% of the national income. Add that to the 47% that federal, state, and local governments tax away from us, and at least 57% of your earnings are diverted to satisfy government before you get to spend anything on yourself.

The graph on page 91 shows the average annual income per U.S. household since the turn of the century. After World War II, incomes rose at a prosperous clip. But with all the additional regulation piled on the economy in the late 1960s and early 1970s, together with the taxes needed to pay for all the federal programs begun in the 1960s, the burden on the economy was too much. There has been virtually no growth in household incomes for two

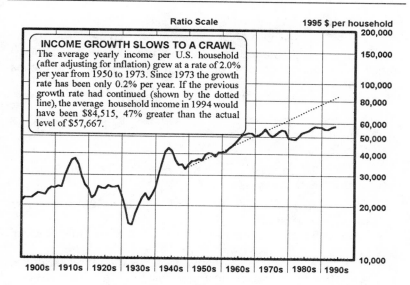

Ratio Scale

1995 $ per household

INCOME GROWTH SLOWS TO A CRAWL
The average yearly income per U.S. household (after adjusting for inflation) grew at a rate of 2.0% per year from 1950 to 1973. Since 1973 the growth rate has been only 0.2% per year. If the previous growth rate had continued (shown by the dotted line), the average household income in 1994 would have been $84,515, 47% greater than the actual level of $57,667.

1900s | 1910s | 1920s | 1930s | 1940s | 1950s | 1960s | 1970s | 1980s | 1990s

decades. In fact, adjusted for inflation, household income in 1994 was only 4% greater than in 1973.

Had the previous growth rate continued, household incomes would be about 47% greater today. Think how much better your life would be if your family income were half again as large as it is now. That difference is the price we've paid for increased government regulation and spending. So if we could do away with just the additions since 1973, our incomes might jump by one half.

Reforming the Regulators

It has reached the point where many people—even some politicians—are outraged by regulation gone mad.

The new Republican Congress promised to do something about the problem. But, unfortunately, its "solutions" won't accomplish anything. For example, there are proposals to require regulatory agencies to make a "cost-benefit analysis" for each new regulation—to determine whether it will cost the economy more than the benefits it supposedly provides.

But this is a weak reform. Bureaucrats will almost always find a way to conclude that their new rules will do more good than harm.

Other proposals attempt to curtail the budgets of some regulatory agencies. But whatever is cut can be restored quickly by the next Congress.

WHAT TO DO

Lost in all this is the realization that the Constitution doesn't authorize the federal government to regulate individuals or companies in any way.

Article 1, Section 8 of the Constitution says:

> The Congress shall have Power . . . to regulate Commerce with foreign Nations, and among the several States, and with the Indian Tribes; . . .

Thus, the federal government was given the power to regulate commerce in three areas:

- With foreign Nations—that is, to impose tariffs or other restrictions on imports.
- Among the several States—that is, to tell States they couldn't put up trade barriers against other States.
- With the Indian Tribes—that is, to act as the representative of the nation in making commercial treaties with Indian Tribes.

There is no authorization to regulate companies or individuals—and there was no such federal regulation in America for almost 100 years until the Interstate Commerce Commission was established in 1887.

The answer to the problem of too much regulation is to return to the Constitution and get the federal government completely out of regulation.

People within each state could then decide for themselves whether they want their state or city governments to perform some of the regulation. People in states that choose not to regulate would finally be free to buy what they want, free to try to sell what they want, and free to work out voluntary arrangements between employer and employee.

In such an atmosphere, everyone could have more than he has today.

And each of us could choose for himself whether he wants to rely for safety on a government agency or a company whose future depends on being right.

Chapter 16

Health Care—The Problem

If the road to Hell is paved with good intentions, the road to big government is paved with small steps—each of which seems harmless in itself.

The pattern rarely changes.

1. There is widespread publicity about a crisis.
2. Politicians float a drastic proposal to solve the problem with a new, far-reaching, bureaucratic program.
3. "Moderates" in Congress and the public mount opposition to the government takeover.
4. Eventually the politicians arrive at a compromise—to fix the problem without radical overhaul.
5. Although the moderates congratulate themselves on holding the line against big government, the compromise makes government bigger, more powerful, and more damaging—making the next crisis inevitable.

Because politicians refuse to recognize that government doesn't work, they never blame the current problem on the program they passed earlier. Instead, while professing their undying faith in free enterprise, they note regretfully that the market has failed to work in this instance. So they propose to fix it with a larger, more bureaucratic system—and the cycle continues with a compromise, more government, more damage, and another proposal.

Health care is an excellent example. From the passage of Medicare in 1965 to a health-care system run completely by the government a few years from now, the politicians have led us along step by innocuous step. Although each step has been presented as the end of the journey, each has added to the problem and made the next step seem necessary.

In this chapter we'll see how the current health-care problem has developed. The next chapter will show how politicians are using this problem to lead us to a health-care system run totally by government. And we'll also see how we could fix the problem almost overnight.

DR. GOVERNMENT

Government has been involved in medicine since before any of us was born. And over the past 30 years its involvement has grown rapidly. Its policies are the cause of medical care's high cost and the difficulty of obtaining health insurance—the two problems the politicians now propose to cure with more government.

Here are 18 ways the state of your health, the quality of medical service you receive, and the price you pay are affected by federal or state government interference.

Physicians

1. Licensing: Government restricts your access to health care by forbidding you to seek advice and treatment from an unlicensed physician. And laws forbid nurses and other experienced health-care specialists from performing many services—even though they may be qualified to do so and would charge less than a doctor.

So you must go to a licensed physician for almost any care at all. If his fees seem high, it may be partly because the government limits the competition he must face, and partly because he has to charge you for the costs he pays to stay in good standing with state and federal regulators.

2. Restricted access to care: Today "telemedicine" makes it possible for your doctor to transmit tests and X-rays to non-local physicians who have more experience or more sophisticated equipment for analyzing a particular problem. This increases your chance of being cured—and cured quickly. It also can be cheaper, because it bypasses trial-and-error treatment and eliminates the need to travel long distances for consultation and treatment. But many states prohibit you and your doctor from consulting a doctor who isn't licensed in your state.

3. Litigation costs: Government courts have fostered a litigation explosion that makes malpractice insurance extremely expensive for your doctor. To limit this expense, many doctors won't take on new customers, and some have left the profession altogether. This reduces the supply of doctors and lifts medical costs even higher.

Doctors have to guard against any possibility of a lawsuit. So your doctor may order expensive tests for you—to assure that later you won't complain in court that he failed to explore every possibility.

If you could agree in advance that you wouldn't sue for malpractice except in certain specified circumstances, the doctor could afford to charge you less. And if he could refuse to treat anyone who didn't sign such an agreement, he could charge you a lot less. Unfortunately, government courts in most states refuse to honor such an agreement. And physicians can be sued just for turning down a patient.

Medicines & Medical Devices

4. FDA approval: Government keeps you from obtaining any medicine that it hasn't yet approved. Getting a new drug approved from the FDA (Food and Drug Administration) costs a company on average $300 million—and can take as long as 10 years. By the time the drug finally gets approval, it may have been available for years in other countries—while you were stuck with a less effective, more expensive alternative.

5. Foreign products: And because drug companies in other countries don't have to run the FDA gauntlet, medicines often cost much less overseas—and in some cases are available *only* overseas. It would be nice if you could order these medicines, which would save money and allow you more choices. But you can't, because the government usually won't let you. And if you get caught trying, they may even put you in jail—even if the drug you were buying is the only known cure for a fatal disease.

6. Cost in lives: The FDA claims to save lives by keeping unsafe drugs off the market. But the drugs banned here don't cause bodies to pile up in countries where the drugs are legal. On the contrary, *Americans die because the FDA forcibly prevents them from taking the drugs they need.*

For example, the FDA approved propranolol for limited use in 1968, but refused to allow it to be used for angina or hypertension. Then it reversed itself and approved the drug for angina in 1973—and then for hypertension in 1976. A study by Arthur D. Little, Inc. estimated that roughly 10,000 Americans died for lack of propranolol every year the FDA prevented their doctors from treating them with it. Dr. Mary J. Ruwart, a scientist with Upjohn Co., says more Americans may have been killed by being denied access to this *one* drug than by the use of *all unsafe drugs in the 20th century*.

Robert Goldberg (a senior research fellow at Brandeis University's Gordon Public Policy Center) has pointed out that, in the same way, "the FDA has sat on or rejected drugs for depression, schizophrenia, kidney cancer, and epilepsy—not because they were unsafe, but because in the final analysis the agency didn't think the drug was so important or effective."

If someone dies from taking an FDA-approved drug, Congress holds lengthy hearings to see how FDA approval can be made even more difficult. But if thousands of people die while the FDA strings along the pharmaceutical companies, there are no hearings, no TV soundbites, no one-liners for the press, no grim-faced TV anchormen, no outraged editorials, no attention whatsoever—just a lot of prematurely dead people whose families have no political pull. If you were an FDA decision-maker, which way would you lean?

7. Prescriptions: Even after the FDA approves a drug, you can't buy it without written permission from a government-licensed doctor—even if you've used it many times before. And because government has made it so easy to sue a doctor—and collect—many doctors won't approve prescription refills without an office visit. The drug itself may cost only $20, but it might cost you $120 to get it.

8. Non-prescriptions: Some ailments can be treated effectively, and sometimes more cheaply, by non-prescription means—such as over-the-counter medicines, vitamins, selected foods, and even red wine (in the case of potential heart conditions). But despite the first amendment, the FDA won't let the sellers of many of these products advertise their health benefits—even those that are widely accepted in the medical profession. The FDA has actually conducted armed attacks on health-food stores to confiscate offending vitamins and other nutrients.

Even aspirin makers are forbidden to tell you that almost all doctors and heart specialists believe a daily aspirin reduces the chance of your having a heart attack. How many deaths and expensive bypass surgeries would be avoided if more people knew about the preventive power of aspirin?

The government's own Center for Disease Control has asserted that folic acid supplements help pregnant women prevent spina bifida and other birth defects, but the FDA forbids vitamin makers from putting this information on their labels.

9. Litigation: Government courts also have driven many surgical devices off the market. Ingredients such as Teflon and silicone are disappearing from the market because of lawsuits against chemical companies. E. I. Du Pont, for example, decided to stop selling polyester for medical devices. Total annual sales of polyester amount to only $200,000 for Du Pont, but potential lawsuits can run into the millions, so the reward is just not worth the risk. This trend will make it harder to obtain such things as heart pacemakers, artificial grafts, and other devices.

Hospitals

10. Non-payers: Federal law dictates that all private or government hospitals that receive any payments from Medicare must treat anyone who shows up at their emergency rooms. This affects almost every hospital in the U.S. because each one has at least one patient covered by Medicare. If the patient can't pay, you and other paying patients have to make up the difference.

Research

11. Political influence: Government subsidies keep researchers busy on projects chosen by politicians for their most-favored backers—even if more lives could be saved with other projects.

12. Loss of medicines: Research on rare diseases has come almost to a halt because the demand for potential drugs won't be large enough to recoup the enormous cost of getting them through the FDA.

Insurance

13. Tax policy: You can't deduct medical expenses from your taxable income unless you're self-employed, in which case you can deduct only a small part of them.

But an employer can deduct all the cost of the medical benefits he provides for employees. So your employer pays you less and provides health insurance instead—which is tax-free for you.

Further, the tax incentives encourage your employer to reward you with additional fringe benefits rather than raises. So he's likely to provide "first dollar" insurance—wherein all medical expenses are covered, rather than just catastrophic illnesses or accidents.

Since you don't have to pay *any* of the bills, you have no incentive to economize. Neither do the millions of others with similar plans. Together, they push up the demand for medical services—and its cost.

In a true free market, rising costs discourage demand for a product—allowing prices to ease back down. But the tax system has separated the consumer from the price—the patient from the cost—so demand continues to rise, even as prices are rising.

14. State mandates: Almost every state has laws that force insurance companies to cover certain conditions and procedures in every medical policy—regardless of the consumer's needs. These add-ons include such things as psychiatric care, birth services, teeth-whitening, abortions, toupees, chiropractic services, cosmetic surgery, alcohol and drug rehabilitation, sex therapy, acupuncture, and marriage counseling.

Obviously, the add-ons run up the cost of your policy—and the state won't let you buy a cheaper one, even if you want to. So it's not surprising that many people feel health insurance is too expensive, and choose to go without it.

15. Community rating: Some states force insurance companies to set premium rates that don't "discriminate" by age, gender, or other factors. Since the cost of insuring a healthy 25-year-old is about one third of that for a normal 60-year-old, the single, one-size-fits-all mandated rates make insurance prohibitive for most young people. Not surprisingly, a lot of them join the ranks of the "uninsured"—the folks the politicians believe the free market has failed.

Government Insurance (Don't Call It Socialized Medicine)

16. Medicare & Medicaid: The tremendous runup in health-care costs started in 1965 when Congress created Medicare—which put the government squarely in the health insurance business—and Medicaid.

Medicare is a health insurance program for the elderly, with compulsory "premiums." Medicaid is a program by which state governments use federal money to pay for health care for low-income people.

When Medicare was passed in 1965, Congress projected its costs into the future, and estimated it would cost $3 billion for 1990, the equivalent (after adjusting for inflation) of $12 billion in 1990 dollars. The actual cost in 1990 was $98 billion—further evidence that no government program stands still.

The payroll tax in 1967 was a modest 0.9% (divided between employer and employee). It has risen steadily and is now 2.9%. And the amount of your earnings that can be taxed has risen as well. In 1993 Congress removed the ceiling entirely, so that all earnings are taxed now.

But despite these tax increases, Medicare will be bankrupt by the year 2002 if the tax isn't raised further. The program's actuaries project that the rate has to rise to 4.3% by 2000. But, of course, any projection will be revised upward before its target date arrives.

Because the politicians consistently underestimate Medicare's costs (refusing to recognize that coercion distorts supply and demand), Medicare tax increases never catch up with ever-rising expenses, and so the tax increases just keep coming.

Every year or two, with great fanfare Congress passes a 5-year or 7-year deficit-reduction package that includes large cuts in Medicare and Medicaid spending. Always the actual cuts are scheduled for the later years of the plan, with the details to be worked out by some future Congress. Meanwhile, the current Congress holds a press conference and congratulates itself for cutting spending and reducing the deficit.

But when the later years arrive, there are no cuts—just more increases. The big tax increase and deficit-reduction package in 1990, for example, assumed that Medicare cuts would save $60 billion over five years. Instead, *additional* Medicare spending over the next five years amounted to $166 billion.

In the mid-1980s, Congress introduced a series of cost-control provisions in Medicare. But since then, costs have risen at twice the rate of health-care costs in general.

The pattern is virtually the same for Medicaid. When Congress passed it in 1965, it cost $1 billion per year. By 1993 it was up to $76 billion per year. In the 1980s alone, Congress expanded Medicaid services 24 times—adding about $20 billion per year to its cost.

Because these programs impose so many requirements, the health-care system now has far more administrators per patient and far fewer doctors and nurses per patient. Those big medical bills aren't paying your doctor's country club dues; they're financing a bigger and bigger health-care bureaucracy.

17. Shifting costs to you: Medicare often pays only a third or so of the actual cost of a hospital stay. The American Hospital Association estimates that hospitals lose an average of $900 on every Medicare patient treated, amounting to $9 billion a year in losses. Hospitals have to pass the unpaid remainder on to you, other paying patients, and insurance companies—making hospital stays and insurance more expensive than they should be.

18. Government driving health care: By 1992, Medicare and Medicaid accounted for 31% of all medical spending in the U.S. Health care can hardly be called a "free market."

More money is spent on medical care now by governments than by all private companies and individuals. This table shows how health-care expenses were paid during the 1992 federal fiscal year:

WHO CONTROLS THE HEALTH-CARE DOLLARS?

Billions of $	Amount	Percentage
Government		
Medicare	$ 128	17%
Medicaid	109	14%
Federal subsidies	63	8%
State subsidies	12	2%
Other	78	10%
Total government:	**$ 390**	**51%**
Private		
Patients	$ 151	20%
Group insurance	149	19%
Individual insurance	57	7%
Other	21	3%
Total private:	**$ 378**	**49%**
Overall Total:	**$ 768**	**100%**

WHO'S TO BLAME?

Despite all we've seen in this chapter, the politicians blame "greedy" doctors, hospitals, insurance companies, and pharmaceutical companies for today's health-care problems.

They say the free market has failed to provide proper health care for everyone. But that's an absurdity.

It is government that has failed. It has taken over health care—dominating every aspect of it—and is therefore responsible for every problem the politicians now complain about.

Government doesn't work. And so it isn't to government that we should look for remedies.

Chapter 17

Health Care—The Solution

In the health-care debate of 1992–94, words like *compassion, right, need,* and *fairness* showed up frequently. But a number of relevant words were ignored.

For example, I never heard the words *force* or *coercion* in public discussion about the issue. And yet the Health Security Act, the President's 1993 proposal for universal health insurance, had a great deal to do with force. There are some revealing terms in the proposal—such as *prison* (which shows up 7 times), *penalty* (111 times), *fine* (6), *enforce* (83), *prohibit* (47), *mandatory* (24), *limit* (231), *obligation* (51), *require* (901), and so on. For example, a person withholding information about his medical history could go to prison for five years.

That was the Democrats' proposal. But lest you think the Republicans don't believe in forcing people to do the right thing, their principal proposal included the terms *prison* (1 time), *enforce* (37), *penalty* (64), *fine* (12), *prohibit* (19), and *require* (482).

Even the plan publicized as the most "free market" of the eight major proposals contains the words *penalty* (5 times), *prohibit* (5), *require* (54), *enforce* (1), and so on.

But coercion is nothing new in government-run health care. Medicare already has plenty of fines and penalties. For example, a doctor is fined merely for filing the wrong form—or failing to file a form for every visit by a patient.

Is It Compassion or Force?

The health-care debate has ignored the most important factor: government involvement in health care means forcing people and institutions—doctors, patients, hospitals, insurance companies—to do what they don't want to do. And such plans never work out as promised.

Ignoring the coercion lets the health-care advocates seem compassionate—as attempting to help people get insurance or better medical care. But if there were no brass knuckles inside the velvet glove, the government wouldn't be wearing it.

Coercion is there, and that means the outcome will differ considerably from the rosy future the politicians describe.

SOLVING THE PROBLEMS

We saw in the preceding chapter that government already is very busy in the health-care industry—where it eats up the time and resources of doctors and hospitals, pushes up medical prices, and slows new medicines from coming to market, thereby causing needless deaths.

If medical prices are too high, it is because government has inflated demand and restricted supply. If too few people have health insurance, it is because government rules have priced too many young people and too many healthy people out of the insurance market.

If doctors' waiting rooms are crowded and service is skimpy, it is because government has restricted the supply of physicians, driven others out of the profession, overloaded the remaining physicians with paperwork, and prevented patients from getting low-cost help from other qualified health-care professionals.

Two Roads

So what should be done?

There are only two choices.

1. You can imagine the perfect solution and try to force people to carry it out for you. Or . . .
2. You can get government out of the way, so people can handle their problems as *they* see fit.

We know which road the politicians prefer to take.

In 1995 a bipartisan bill was introduced in the U.S. Senate to reform health care. Politicians and journalists greeted the bill with approval—calling it realistic and non-controversial, compared to the far-reaching plan the President introduced two years earlier. The common description of the new bill is that it contains the "few simple reforms everyone agrees on,'' instead of pushing to re-create the health-care system entirely.

Here are the bill's ''few simple reforms'':

- It prohibits an insurance company from denying coverage to an individual with a pre-existing condition—such as cancer, diabetes, or a heart condition. Insurance companies could charge him higher premiums for the first year of the policy, but thereafter must charge him the same rate as someone without such a condition.
- It forces insurance companies to allow a worker who leaves a job to convert his group coverage to an individual policy and take it with him.
- It forces employers to provide insurance coverage for all employees, including those with chronic conditions, if they provide coverage for any employee.
- It includes a list of benefits that every health-insurance policy must include.

Proponents say these reforms don't place an undue burden on insurance companies, and they will make health insurance available to millions of people who don't have it.

Now, what's wrong with this picture?

It ignores the obvious:

1. Insurance companies are in business to make profits.
2. Insurance companies make profits by selling health insurance to as many people as possible.

So companies already do everything they can think of to get everyone covered. If there were a realistic way to insure people with pre-existing conditions, wouldn't they do it? If they could keep as customers the people who are changing jobs, wouldn't they do it?

If people who spend every working moment trying to expand the insurance market don't know a way to do these things at an affordable cost, why should we believe career politicians—who can't even balance the federal checkbook—know the answer?

What the politicians plan to do, which they carefully avoid identifying, is to point a gun at the insurance industry and force it to lose money.

Are social problems that simple—that all you have to do is imagine a perfect world, point a gun at someone or some industry, issue some orders, and the problem is solved?

If you pin them down, the politicians will acknowledge that, yes, they plan to force insurance companies to make changes they don't want. But they will be such harmless, simple changes. And we all have to make some sacrifices to solve this problem.

And thus we start on the final leg of the journey to the total government takeover of the health-care system.

WHERE ROAD #1 LEADS

If government forces insurance companies to accept applicants regardless of existing medical problems (called "guaranteed issue"), many people won't bother to buy health insurance until they contract a chronic illness. They'll have to pay a higher premium the first year, but the price will still seem small considering all the premium-free years that preceded it.

Many other people, who already have insurance, will no longer fear being without it—and will let their policies lapse until they need them.

It's as though you didn't need to buy fire insurance on your house until you smelled smoke.

The insurance companies will be overwhelmed with claims from new customers—and will have to raise their rates dramatically.

When New York adopted such a plan in 1993, the dollar amount of the average claim doubled—as did the price of insurance for a healthy 25-year-old. So large numbers of young people dropped their insurance. Overall, the number of individuals with insurance declined 12% within nine months after the program began.

Washington State's 1993 health-care plan forced insurance companies to accept all new applicants, regardless of pre-existing conditions, during a 3-month "amnesty" in 1994. Families with chronic medical problems, who hadn't obtained insurance coverage before contracting their conditions, moved into the state—running up insurance prices for Washington residents. And 19 insurance companies moved out—leaving fewer choices for Washington consumers.

A study by the American Society of Actuaries found that claim costs have risen by an average of 38% wherever a guaranteed-issue rule has been imposed. Other studies have produced similar estimates.

The other "simple reforms" in the 1995 Senate proposal will beget other undesirable consequences. For example, one reform requires employers to cover all employees—even those with hefty claims—if any one employee is covered. Obviously, some employers will find this prohibitively expensive, and decide they can stay in business only by canceling insurance for all employees. Other employers may cancel their insurance because of the higher overall premiums created by the guaranteed-issue rule and other mandates.

Imagine the surprise when politicians discover that their plan to expand insurance coverage actually reduces it. Who would have thought that human beings would pursue their own self-interest—just as politicians pursue theirs? The free market fails again.[1]

The same law would force insurance companies to let employees keep their policies on their own, but could employees afford the higher rates?

The Next Crisis

When insurance premiums go through the roof, government edicts won't be blamed, any more than they are now. The politicians will accuse the insurance companies of price-gouging, declare another crisis, and "reluctantly" decide to impose price controls on insurance policies.

When insurance companies can no longer charge adequate premiums, they will have to reduce benefits. This will lead to detailed regulations that dictate how every policy must work. It won't be long until every insurance company either gets out of medical coverage or goes bankrupt.

And that will leave only one alternative: a health-insurance system run completely by the government. Many politicians will say that's the last thing they want, but they'll vote for it—because, once again, "the free market has failed."

We will have arrived at our destination—a destination that became almost inevitable the day Congress passed the original Medicare Act in 1965.

We will have a single-payer (meaning government) insurance system, just as the Canadians and British do.

And just like the Canadians, when a personal medical crisis hits, you may have to go south of the border to get immediate care. Those Tijuana clinics are going to be very, very busy.

The Joys of a Government Program

But that won't be the end of the road.

The government insurance system will dictate how much it will

---

[1]Of course, it isn't the "free market" that will have failed the politicians. It will be human nature. Every such program assumes that individuals and companies will sacrifice their lives or well-being for the sake of the politicians' grandstanding. But human beings don't exist to please politicians.

pay for doctors' services, hospital stays, and medicines. And those prices won't be set by supply and demand. They'll be set by what politicians and bureaucrats consider "fair."

Cost containment will be the mantra for everyone working in the system. Medicines will be dispensed reluctantly—with cheaper, and not equivalent, substitutes being used in many cases. The flow of new drugs will dwindle.

The fee schedule for doctors won't recognize different levels of attention or care; one price will fit all. With below-market fees, doctors will have to skimp on service. Many doctors will quit altogether and become stockbrokers, land developers, or pro golfers. Young people who might have been good doctors will enter other fields instead. The reduced supply of doctors will lengthen the waiting lines.

Lower payments eventually will make hospitals unprofitable, and the federal government will be required to take over that business as well.

U.S. medical care will begin to resemble that of the Soviet Union.

And while you're being wheeled into the operating room, your doctor may be on the phone pleading with the local health-care commissar to authorize the tests you need.

Good for the Political Business

The sad state of American medical care will be a constant concern of the very Senators who caused it. They'll hold hearings that lay the blame on heavy-handed bureaucrats—instead of the government system itself. No matter how bad it gets, the idea of ending the government system will seem as absurd to the politicians as getting rid of Medicare, Medicaid, or Social Security does now.

And why shouldn't it seem absurd? After all, politicians will still get first-class treatment—no matter how the people in their districts suffer.

They'll get other benefits as well, because everything connected with medical care will become politicized:

- Research centers and hospitals will be built in the Congressional districts and states of committee chairmen.
- Associations of doctors, nurses, pharmacists, chiropractors, radiologists, abortionists, paramedics, ambulance companies, Christian Science practitioners, and everyone else in the health-care business will fawn over Congressmen to maintain their positions in the pecking order when Congress conducts its annual check-up on the nation's health-care system.

No incumbent Congressman will want for political contributions. If you're a major donor, your Congressman should be able to move you to the front of those long waiting lines. If you aren't a major donor, don't expect to get anything considered a "luxury"—such as cosmetic surgery (even after an accident) or breast reconstruction after a mastectomy.

Shutting People Out

As costs continue to escalate, it will become necessary to limit medical research, the types of patients who can be treated, and the procedures that will be covered.

Research will take a back seat to immediate care, because neglected research doesn't lead to exposés on television—the way people dying in a waiting room do.

But eventually it will no longer be either/or—since the scarce resources available for medical care will require rationing in every area. This means bureaucrats will decide—literally—who will get treatment and who won't. In other words, who will live and who will die.

The first purge will end treatment for older people—who are the heaviest drain on the system, and who produce nothing to help support it.

Then the retarded, the physically handicapped, and others whose "quality of life" is judged to be too low will be pushed to the back of the line.

All this will be considered regrettable but, after all, *someone* will have to go without. Of course, before government took over, *no one* had to go without—even those who didn't have health insurance.

The limited resources will severely curtail the variety of medical procedures available, and those still on the approved list will have long waiting lines—which will lead to bribes, as patients try to jump up the list for surgery or access to some overworked machine.

Cost Containment

Despite the falling levels of service, the rationing, and the apparent heartlessness, costs still will rise—just as the Post Office continues to raise prices in the face of falling service. This will mean higher and higher payroll taxes.

It won't take long for people to realize they're paying for other people's ailments—some of which could have been avoided.

So we'll start looking at our neighbors' habits and resenting the burdens they place on the health-care system—and on us, through our taxes.

The politicians will respond by outlawing unhealthy behavior.

Smoking is an obvious target. It will have to be prohibited to keep "medical care affordable for everyone."

If you're a non-smoker, you may applaud the prohibition. But don't expect the witch hunt to stop there. As medical costs continue to rise and care becomes scarcer, motorcycle riding and skiing might be added to the list of taboos. And then perhaps football and other high-injury sports.

Then heavy health taxes could be imposed on fatty foods—hot dogs, cheese, ice cream, pizza, fried chicken. Or they might be prohibited altogether if the government mounts a War on Fat. I hope we don't read in the paper someday that the Health Enforcement Agency found a french fry in the glove compartment of your car and you were sentenced to 25 years in prison.

Your Future

If you think these projections are just scare stories, you should be aware that similar situations already exist in Veterans Administration hospitals, and in countries that have the government health-care systems the reformers are trying to push on us. And they have their counterparts in the Post Office, the War on Drugs, the Defense Department, and virtually every government bureaucracy today. You may not realize it, but today the indigent receive better care in U.S. emergency rooms than many people in government-run systems in Europe.

And that is the Brave New World that awaits us. When we arrive there, will we remember how it all started? Will we recall those politicians who in 1995 urged a few simple reforms "we could all agree on" as the way to avoid the President's bureaucratic nightmare? We probably won't. But the most fanatical socialist couldn't have done more than they did to assure such a Big-Brother future.

A little government involvement is just as dangerous as a lot— because the first leads inevitably to the second.

HOW TO SOLVE THE PROBLEMS

Fortunately, that doesn't have to be our future.

There's a second road—one that leads to better care than we get now, to lower prices, to freedom.

What should the government do to get us there?

Nothing—except to get out of the way.

The answer isn't insurance "reforms," employer mandates, the encouragement of managed care, means-testing Medicare or reducing its benefits, or tax increases.

Government can help the health-care system only by getting out of it. It has no more ability to make us well than it does to make us rich.

Here's a laundry list of things to be washed out:

1. *Abolish the FDA.* Let people decide for themselves, with the help of their doctors and private testing agencies they choose for themselves, which medicines are safe enough for them. Let people decide for themselves what risks they're willing to take. Let people with fatal illnesses choose any therapy they want in hope of beating the odds.

No one will be left on his own unless he wants to be. You and your doctor can use any testing and certification company you want—including one staffed by former employees of the FDA. Let drug manufacturers prove to you and your doctor the safety of their drugs. That way they won't have to run up the cost of the medicine—as they do now to get the FDA to act.

2. *Save Medicare by turning it over to private companies.* Then, like any other service in the marketplace, it will be completely voluntary. Let seniors pick their own policies. Let them make as much money as they want without losing benefits. Get government out of the health insurance business.

3. *Abolish Medicaid.* The answer to the Medicaid funding problems, the corruption, and the scandals is to end the program. Don't string taxpayers along with more "reforms" that don't reform anything. End federal grants and federal tax-collecting on behalf of states. Get the federal government out of it entirely. Let each state's citizens decide for themselves whether they want a government program to provide health care to the needy—and, if so, what kind.

And let's hope most states stay out of health care as well. State government programs are still government programs. Far fewer people will ask for help if they know it's not available just for the asking. The small numbers who would actually *need* assistance would get it from private charities financed by the donations of people who care. I'm sure there will be many compassionate politicians among them.

4. *Solve the portability problem by making all medical expenses totally deductible from taxable income.* Then employers won't have to provide health insurance instead of pay raises. Employees will own their own policies. They can choose the policies that suit them, and they can take them wherever they want.

Let individuals decide for themselves how to use the money

they've earned. Let *them*—not some omniscient politicians or bureaucrats—be responsible for their lives.

Better yet, get rid of the income tax entirely—so that tax advantages no longer influence any economic decision. But we'll come back to that in chapter 24.

5. *Get state governments to stop imposing conditions on health insurance.* Don't require individuals to pay for benefits they don't want. Don't force insurance companies to take customers they don't want—a practice that prices healthy people out of the insurance market.

If a politician thinks an insurance company should accept everyone who applies, then he can start his own company and operate it that way. If it's as easy as he thinks, he'll make a fortune. Of course, no politician will do that—because it's much easier to give orders than to cope with the real dilemmas of life.

Anyone who cares—really cares—about people who can't get insurance because of pre-existing conditions can contribute to a private charity that would cover such people by providing either insurance or medical care.

Benefits

There is more that could be done to get government out of health care, but those five steps would improve the system enormously.

These are real reforms—not more bureaucratic dictation. They will lead to better medical care at lower cost:

- You will be able to select the insurance policy that's most appropriate and most economical for your family.
- You'll be free to deal with the doctor of your choice.
- You won't be priced out of insurance because of government mandates.
- Life-saving medicines will be on the market sooner. Prescription drugs will cost less.

And who knows what other benefits will flow? So much of what we put up with now results from government policies. With government out of health care, we will see benefits we can't even imagine now.

Maybe—just maybe—doctors will start making house calls again.

TO THIS WE'VE COME

I can't help but wonder what Thomas Jefferson would think of the current health-care debate. He and his colleagues fought a war to rid themselves of a king who made their decisions for them. They fought to establish the first nation whose guiding principle was *freedom from government*.

But today your "protectors" in Washington are busily scheming to take away your freedom to bargain with your employer or employees, the freedom to choose your own doctor, the freedom of doctors to set their own fees (just as politicians do), the freedom to obtain the kind of insurance you need, and the freedom to live your own life and be responsible for yourself.

I'm sure the politicians think Thomas Jefferson is looking down upon them with approval. After all, it was he who wrote the immortal words:

> We hold these Truths to be self-evident, that all Men are created equal, that they are endowed by their Creator with certain unalienable Rights, that among these are Life, Liberty, and Health Insurance You Can Never Lose.

Chapter 18

Improving Education

The federal government's takeover of education followed the usual pattern. First, politicians complained that local school districts didn't have enough money. They decided the federal government could help in a "limited" way—without interfering with local educational policies.

From the end of World War II, federal aid to education increased gradually until the mid-1960s. Then it rose sharply. Since the late 1970s, its growth has slowed to about the rate of inflation.

As with every other area they touch, politicians become alarmed when federal education money isn't spent in the way they want. So the federal government has long since attached rules to its subsidies—even though only about 6% of the money spent on education comes from the federal government.

Have federal money and federal control helped American students learn more?

Hardly. As the graph on the next page shows, learning, as measured by Scholastic Aptitude Test (SAT) scores, steadily declined throughout the 1960s and 1970s.

The federal government's heavy hand transformed the public schools and the private schools that became dependent upon it. Yesterday's schools focused on reading, writing, arithmetic, history, and geography. Today's schools spend much more time teaching children:

- To be citizens of the world,
- To be sensitive to people who are different from themselves,
- To pester their parents to recycle cans and bottles,
- To understand how western civilization destroyed a peaceful North American continent,
- To report their parents if they catch them using drugs, and
- To practice safe sex.

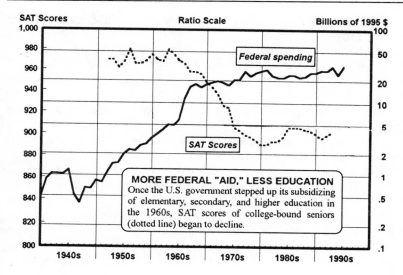

MORE FEDERAL "AID," LESS EDUCATION
Once the U.S. government stepped up its subsidizing of elementary, secondary, and higher education in the 1960s, SAT scores of college-bound seniors (dotted line) began to decline.

Since none of those subjects shows up in the SAT tests, it's not surprising that SAT scores declined so much.

Money Not the Problem

No matter how much the federal government appropriates for education, no matter how many bond issues your school district approves, you hear over and over that there isn't enough money for schools.

But education has declined as the money spent on it has increased dramatically. The graph on the next page shows the amount spent per pupil after adjusting for inflation. Obviously, lack of money isn't the problem.

Why Hasn't Education Improved?

Many explanations are offered for the decline in education. But by focusing on the decline, we may have the issue upside-down. The correct question should be: Why hasn't education improved?

Look at the tremendous progress made in computers, audio equipment, TV sets, VCRs, telephones, fax machines, and many other tools of communication. Such things are ten to twenty times more efficient today than they were 40 years ago. Computers, in fact, are literally thousands of times more powerful than they were in the 1950s.

With the advancements made in communication technology, children should be learning much *more* than their parents and grandparents did. Literacy levels should be much *higher* than they were, and so should SAT scores.

But just the opposite has occurred. Today's children know far less than their parents did.

Why has schooling deteriorated when the ability to communicate has improved so much?

The reason isn't hard to discover. Computers, audio/visual products, and telecommunications are all provided by private companies.

But education is dominated by government. And so long as it is, no significant improvement is possible.

Even without the federal government's intrusions, local schools are fighting a losing battle simply because they're government institutions.

But why must schools be run by the government?

Is it because education is so important? If so, all the more reason to keep it away from government. The U.S. Postal Service wastes only our time and money. But we suffer a much greater loss

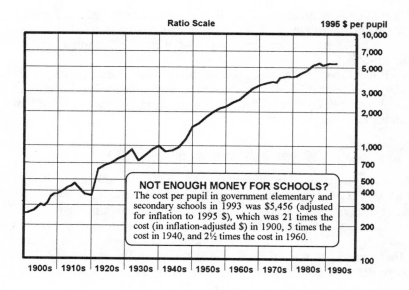

Ratio Scale   **1995 $ per pupil**

NOT ENOUGH MONEY FOR SCHOOLS?
The cost per pupil in government elementary and secondary schools in 1993 was $5,456 (adjusted for inflation to 1995 $), which was 21 times the cost (in inflation-adjusted $) in 1900, 5 times the cost in 1940, and 2½ times the cost in 1960.

1900s | 1910s | 1920s | 1930s | 1940s | 1950s | 1960s | 1970s | 1980s | 1990s

when so many children graduate from high school with little more than an elementary school education.

If Only Government Would Feed Us

And if important things must be handled by government, why doesn't government provide free food for everyone—as it provides free schooling for every child?

One could live without knowing how to read—as many public school graduates manage to do—but no one can live without food. So why doesn't government operate the supermarkets?

Imagine what it would be like. The food stores would become what the schools have become.

Political battles would decide which foods are available. If you didn't like the choices, you'd have to attend "food board" meetings and lobby state legislators to change the menu.

Food would become more and more expensive, even as the quality deteriorated. Wilted vegetables, stale bread, and inferior meat would be the norm. So would vandalism and gangs.

And don't get caught praying in a supermarket.

A Better Dream

Now let's reverse the picture. Imagine instead that schools were operated like today's supermarkets.

Most school systems would offer a variety of approaches to any one subject—just as a supermarket offers a variety of brands for any one food item. And if you didn't like what one school offered, or if you didn't like the way you or your child were treated, you could patronize another school.

If you wanted prayer in the school, you wouldn't have to pray to Congress to get it. You'd just take your child to a school that permitted it. If you didn't want prayer, you'd find a school that didn't have it.

You'd be able to choose between science or social engineering, calculus or condom use. If you wanted, you might even find a school that would teach your children how to nag you about recycling, or that had other special programs to undermine parental authority and encourage moral smugness.

Some schools would offer inexpensive, no-frills education. Others would offer additional (gourmet) classes in music, art, accelerated mathematics, physical education, and other subjects that public schools like to cut when taxpayers say "No" to demands for more money.

If there were violence or drug-trafficking at your child's school, you wouldn't have to complain endlessly and in vain. You'd simply move him to a school where such things don't happen. And with competition, any school that tolerated such problems probably would go out of business.

How would poor children get an education? Most likely the same way many of them get private educations now—through scholarships, church schools, foundation grants, and outright charity. Today many inner-city children get good elementary-school educations at low-cost parochial schools and through scholarships at nonreligious schools. And if government no longer levied heavy property taxes for schools, the poor would be less poor and the donors would have more to donate.

Choices

The success of private schools—even private schools on skimpy budgets—has inspired the idea of "school choice" or "vouchers." This plan has the government giving the parents of each child a voucher to be spent at a school of the parents' choosing—government or private.

I understand very well the attraction of this approach. And it might be an improvement over today's poor schooling.

But government doesn't work. And giving government control over education—in any form—is dangerous. A voucher program requires a government bureaucracy to administer it and government "experts" to decide which schools are "qualified" to accept the vouchers.

It is especially dangerous to have the federal government administer such a program or set the rules for it. The Feds are too far removed from local school issues to have any competence in education.

It is far better to lower the tax burden so that parents are financially able to buy the education they want—with no rules imposed by government.

Then each family could send its children to a government school, a church school, or a non-religious private school—or even teach them at home. When there's no subsidy from the government, there are no government strings attached. Parents could do what they think best.

Are Parents Competent?

Would all parents make the best choices for their children?

Of course not. We don't live in a perfect world. But we should live in a free country—one in which each of us is free to make his own choices, good or bad.

And those parents who *are* capable of making good choices shouldn't have their children held hostage in government schools because other parents are less competent.

WHAT MUST BE DONE

Lowering the tax burden to leave parents with enough money to pay for a good education for their children is the subject of chapter 24. Here, let me point out the two important changes that must be made to improve education:

1. The federal government must get completely out of education. It has made a bad situation much worse. And it has no Constitutional authority to meddle in education in any way—even if it *were* capable of helping.
2. Federal taxes must be lowered dramatically so that parents have the ability to finance their children's education directly, without having to depend on the kindness of strangers—or strange bureaucrats.

Once we make these reforms, it will be up to the people in each state to decide what educational system is best.

- Some states will revert to the kind of education provided before the federal government took over—with public schools that reflect local values and circumstances.
- Some states will adopt a voucher system, in order to enhance freedom of choice and lessen dependence on government.
- And maybe some states will withdraw from education entirely—reducing taxes accordingly so that parents have the funds to buy whatever education they want for their children, and making education completely insulated from government interference.

In the states in the third group, schools would become truly "public"—responsive to the choices of their customers, the parents. They would necessarily be economical, and yet effective, places of learning. And you would never have to endure a school that was bent on indoctrinating your child in an alien philosophy.

Schools would compete to acquire the best teachers from today's public and private schools. Good teachers could finally teach—instead of having to quell violence and obey politically correct rules.

Education is one of the most important things we give to our children—much too important to allow government to tamper with it.

Chapter 19

Welfare

The U.S. welfare system is a mess.

Fortunately, the President has a plan to reform the system from top to bottom. He has promised to rid the system of perverse incentives that split up families, that encourage teenage girls to get pregnant, and that invite teenage boys to get into trouble—while at the same time making sure the truly needy aren't forgotten.

As the President put it:

> The goals of our public welfare program must be positive and constructive. . . . [The welfare program] must stress the integrity and preservation of the family unit. It must contribute to the attack on dependency, juvenile delinquency, family breakdown, illegitimacy, ill health, and disability. It must reduce the incidence of these problems, prevent their occurrence and recurrence, and strengthen and protect the vulnerable in a highly competitive world.

A *New York Times* editorial hailed this overhaul, pointing out that spending more now to retrain and reunite families will pay off in lower welfare bills later:

> [The President's] welfare message to Congress yesterday stems from a recognition that no lasting solution to the problem can be bought with a welfare check. The initial cost will actually be higher than the mere continuation of handouts. The dividends will come in the restoration of individual dignity and in the long-term reduction of the need for government help.

Perhaps it isn't overstating the point to say, as the President did, "The days of the dole in this country are numbered."

Maybe—at last—the welfare mess will be solved.

Meanwhile, Back in the Real World . . .

Unfortunately, this isn't the 1990s welfare system I'm talking about. It's the welfare system in place in the 1960s.

The President who introduced the new program was John F. Kennedy, in 1962. And it was Lyndon B. Johnson who, as he signed the first War on Poverty bill in August 1964, said, "The days of the dole in this country are numbered."

The welfare "mess" that those presidents promised to clean up was one we would gladly settle for today.

THE FEDERAL NOSE IN WELFARE

President Kennedy's reforms were meant to fix the problems created by 30 years of federal welfare. The New Deal had stuck the federal government's metaphorical nose into what had historically been a local issue—social welfare. During those 30 years, federal policies had given incentives to the poor to weaken their ambition and to destroy their families.

Traditionally, welfare had always been considered a temporary expedient—something to take care of a widow until her children were old enough to support her, or something to tide a worker over until he found a new job. It was never meant to be a way of life.

Someone close to the welfare recipient monitored his situation—the someone being a representative of a private charity or of the local government's welfare department.

But the entry of the federal government made welfare impersonal—like banking by mail. In some cases federal welfare workers monitored the "clients," but the rules were set hundreds or thousands of miles away, and the checks were dispensed automatically from Washington.

Depersonalized welfare was less successful in rescuing people from their misfortunes. Fewer lives were rehabilitated. And many people were subverted as welfare became an opportunity, rather than a source of stigma.

Still, as of 1962, the federal government was only a minor participant in the ugly business of demoralizing the poor, and the problems were minuscule compared to today's. In 1962 the federal government spent only $31 billion on social welfare and insurance programs, while state and local governments spent $32 billion.

And the number of poor people in America had been shrinking rapidly. The graph below shows the percentage of the U.S. population that was considered by the federal government to be living below the "poverty level." Although the government's statistics don't track this trend prior to 1950, the trend away from poverty had persisted throughout the 20th century. Except during the Great Depression years, America was becoming steadily more prosperous—and almost everyone was benefiting.

How It All Changed

Shortly after the U.S. government declared War on Poverty, the downward trend in poverty came to a halt. It became obvious—or should have been obvious—that the more money the government gave to the poor, the less people would strive to avoid qualifying for help.

The federal government's biggest contribution to welfare was to make enrollment permanent, rather than a temporary expedient. Welfare became a right—one to which you're entitled if most other people make more money than you do. No more monitoring, no more pressure to get back on your feet, no more need to change the habits or way of living that pulled you into poverty. Your only duty is to walk to the mailbox once a month to pick up your check.

By the 1990s the welfare system was a shambles. In 1991 the

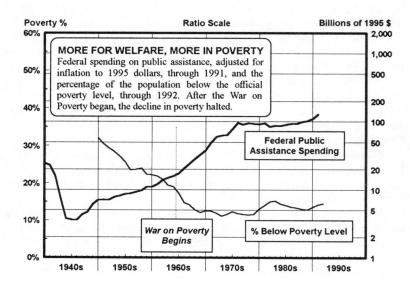

federal government spent $676 billion on social welfare of one kind or another—20 times the 1962 level—and state and local governments spent $489 billion, largely to qualify for federal welfare programs.

Social welfare spending by all levels of government had increased to $1,165 billion ($1.1 trillion) in 1991, from $63 billion in 1962.

The money spent for public assistance (what we think of as pure welfare) by all levels of government increased to $180 billion in 1991 from $5 billion in 1962—the year President Kennedy promised to reform the system.

HOW WELFARE HURTS

With so much money being thrown around, we shouldn't be surprised to hear stories of waste, fraud, and corruption. But far more tragic and dangerous were the accompanying explosions in teenage pregnancies, one-parent families, and teenage crime.

Welfare costs us plenty. But it also destroys lives. It perverts the natural incentives of everyone who is touched by it. Here are some examples:

- AFDC (Aid to Families with Dependent Children) pays money to Mom only if there's no Dad at home, so—surprise!—Dad goes away.
- A teenage girl can become independent of her parents by getting pregnant; otherwise, she must live off her parents and obey their rules. Which life is more attractive to most teenagers?
- Federal job-training for welfare recipients circumvents the need for a teenager to stay in school and learn how to make a living.
- The income test for welfare makes a low-paying job seem pointless. This eliminates the incentive for a young person to get the all-important first job, and so he never gains the experience needed to get a job that would pay more than welfare.
- Medicaid reduces the incentive, especially among the young, to avoid injury and disease.
- The availability of welfare reduces the incentive to save for emergencies. And once people don't have savings, what else can they do but go on welfare when trouble strikes?

The people who have been seduced by welfare have become wards of the state, unable to fend for themselves, with no self-respect and no self-confidence.

Is this compassion?

EVERYBODY IN THE POOL

The table on the facing page lists the federal programs in place as far back as 1974, as compiled by the Joint Economic Committee in its report on the welfare system. Merritt Ierley made a perceptive observation about the report:

> . . . it would seem . . . that nearly every citizen ought now to be eligible for something, at some time or another. And indeed, there is statistical justification for suggesting that income security or social welfare (what started out as public charity) is for all.
>
> The report of the Joint Economic Committee included an estimate of beneficiaries, program by program. If those estimates are added together, the total comes to 201,089,614. The estimated 1974 population of the United States was 211,389,000.
>
> To be sure, there are a great many duplications, a great many among the 201 million who were recipients of public support under different categories, and a great many among the 211 million who never required or never received any form of public assistance. Yet the sheer numbers make their point.

The 1974 inquiry into welfare led to more reforms, which led to more programs, which led to more money, which led to more welfare recipients.

The Cost

The one constant during the 30 years of the War on Poverty has been the drain on the taxpayer. It never stops. Here are some of the costs run up on your behalf between 1965 and 1991:

- Federal public assistance (welfare) spending has totaled $1.1 trillion (equivalent in 1995 dollars to $2.0 trillion).
- Total public assistance spending by all levels of government amounted to $1.7 trillion ($3.1 trillion in 1995 dollars).
- Federal spending for all forms of social welfare (education, social insurance, and so on) has totaled $7.5 trillion ($13.7 trillion in 1995 dollars).
- Spending by all levels of government for all forms of social welfare has totaled $12.6 trillion ($23.3 trillion in 1995 dollars).
- Your family's share of the public assistance bill came to $31,360 (in 1995 dollars).
- Your family's share of the bill for all social welfare came to $232,750 (in 1995 dollars).

Do you think it might be time to put a stop to this?

"THE DAYS OF THE DOLE ARE NUMBERED"

In 1974 the Joint Economic Committee of Congress compiled a list of federally funded Income Security Programs, which included:

Disability & Unemployment

Black Lung Disability and Survivors' Benefits
Black Lung Survivors' Benefits
Disability Insurance
Federal Employees' Compensation (Job-Related Illness and Injury)
Federal-State Unemployment Insurance
Railroad Unemployment Insurance
Trade Readjustment Allowances (for Workers Displaced by Imports)

Education

Basic Educational Opportunity Grants
College Work-Study
"Follow Through"
"Head Start"
Interest-Free Guaranteed Loans
Medical Education Loans and Grants
National Direct Student Loans
Nursing Education Loans
Special Services for Low-Income and Physically Handicapped Students in Post-Secondary Schools
Supplemental Educational Opportunity Grants
"Talent Search"
"Upward Bound"
Vocational Education Work-Study

Food Benefits

Food Commodities (for Families, School Children and Needy in Institutions)
Food Stamps
School Lunches
School Milk
Special Supplemental Feeding (For Pregnant and Lactating Mothers)
Special Supplemental Feeding for Women, Infants, and Children

Health Benefits

Comprehensive Health Services
Crippled Children's Services
Dental Health of Children
Health Care of Children and Youth
Intensive Infant Care Project
Maternity and Infant Care Projects
Medicaid
Medicare

Housing

Appalachian Housing Program
Farm Labor Housing
Home-Ownership for Tenants of Public Housing ("Sweat Equity" Accrued through Tenant Doing Maintenance)
Home-Ownership Loans
Indian Housing Improvement Program
Indian Housing Technical Assistance
Interest Subsidies for Rental Housing
Low-Income Housing Repair Loans
Low-Rent Public Housing
Mortgage Insurance for Families Who Are Special Credit Risks
Mortgage Insurance for Low and Moderate-Income Families
Mortgage Insurance for Low and Moderate-Income Families (Condominiums)
Rent Supplements
Rural Housing Loans
Rural Housing Site Loans
Rural Rental Housing Insured Loans
Rural Self-Help Housing Technical Assistance

Jobs, Training, & Business

Career Opportunities Program
Concentrated Employment Programs (Job Referral in Poor Neighborhoods)
Economic Opportunity Loans
Foster Grandparents
Job Corporations
Job Opportunities in the Business Sector ("JOBS")
Manpower Development and Training
Neighborhood Youth Corporations
Operation Mainstream
Public Service Careers (On-the-Job Training)
Senior Community Service Employment
Senior Companions
Vocational Rehabilitation Services
Work Incentive Projects

Retirement Programs

Federal Civil Service Retirement
Old-Age Insurance
Railroad Retirement, Disability, and Survivors' Benefits
Social Security Special Benefits for Persons Age 72 and Over
Survivor's Insurance

Social Services

Aid to Families with Dependent Children
Assistance to Cuban Refugees
Emergency Assistance
General Assistance to Indians
Legal Services for the Poor
Meals for the Elderly
Services to Needy Aged, Blind, or Disabled (Counseling, Day Care, Homemaker Services, Health Care)
Services to Needy Families on Welfare (Counseling, Day Care, Homemaker Services, Health Care)
Supplement Security Income

Veterans Programs

Compensation to Veterans for Service-Connected Disability
Death Compensation for Survivors of Veterans (Service-Connected Death)
Dependency and Indemnity Compensation to Veterans' Dependents (Service-Connected Death)
Military Retirement
Pensions for Survivors of Veterans (Non-Service-Connected Death)
Pensions for Veterans
Veterans' Educational Assistance
Veterans' Hospital, Domiciliary and Medical Care
Veterans' Hospital, Domiciliary, and Medical Care (Non-Service-Connected Death)
Veterans' Housing Loans
Vocational Rehabilitation for Veterans
War Orphans' & Widows' Educational Assistance

Reprinted in *With Charity for All* by Merritt Ierley (Praeger Publishers, 1984), pages 188-191.

REFORM WELFARE?

Of course, in the 1990s both the Democrats and the Republicans have plans to reform welfare. We hear about "two years and out," block grants, "workfare," no-strings funding, and other supposedly innovative ways of making a bad system work well.

Fool me once, shame on you; fool me 35 times, shame on me 34 times.

Over and over during the past 30 years, the politicians have claimed they've learned how to fix the welfare system. We've seen one reform after another. We've been treated to recurring news stories of the success of federal programs—complete with anecdotes of former welfare recipients whose lives were turned around when government job-training made them self-sufficient at last.

But despite all the new programs, the good news, and the anecdotes, the numbers of welfare recipients don't seem to shrink—and the epidemic of pregnancies, family breakups, and crime continues.

A 1988 reform, implemented in 1990, was aimed particularly at reducing the number of people on the rolls of Aid to Families with Dependent Children (AFDC). But over the next four years, the ranks of AFDC grew 29%—to 14.2 million from 11.0 million.

After the reporters have published their success stories and gone home, the cold hard truth is that new programs just make things worse. Government doesn't work. It is no more competent to administer charity than it is to deliver the mail. And the next welfare reform isn't going to make a silk purse out of a sow's ear.

I don't think we should bite on this hook again.

The only answer is to get the federal government out of welfare—and leave local governments to return to the "temporary expedient" view of welfare or turn it over to private charities.

Compassion

Would it be hard-hearted to do away with welfare entirely?

Perhaps the question should be: Is it compassionate to teach people they can't survive without government help?

Was it compassionate to run up bills of $232,750 for *your* family to pay? Is it compassionate to leave no one responsible for himself, and make everyone responsible for everyone else?

It isn't compassionate to force people to pay for projects one thinks are good.

Those who truly can't help themselves will get better care from people who help voluntarily. The genuine compassion of volunteers has the best chance of leading the needy out of dependency—rather than deeper into it.

And for those who *can* help themselves, but who may have lost the habit, the best we can do is to set them free. For their sake, we should get the government out of the economy, to open more opportunities for the unskilled and inexperienced.

Transition

Would a transition program ease the move from today's welfare system to a completely private, voluntary system?

We have to remind ourselves over and over that government doesn't work. So any government program to ease people off welfare—by retraining them or educating them—won't work any better than the current welfare system works.

If you demand a transition period of a couple of years or so, you may as well resign yourself to eternal welfare—to another trillion dollars or more in bills run up in your name—because multi-year government programs never lead to the results promised. The politicians will go back on their promise to terminate a program as soon as public attention turns elsewhere.

The next President will be concerned with the budget for the 1998 fiscal year that begins in October 1997. He will address the nation shortly after taking office in January 1997. He should announce to all people receiving welfare checks from the federal government:

> If I have my way, your federal welfare payments will end in eight months. So you have eight months to turn your life around, to find a job, to learn how to take care of yourself.
>
> We expect to pay you for those eight months. So if you get a job tomorrow morning, you can get two checks each month for those eight months. Or you can wait until the last moment to change things. But even if you haven't found a job in eight months, your checks from the federal government will end.
>
> So what are you going to do?

WHAT KIND OF AMERICA DO WE WANT?

We have to decide what kind of country we want to live in.

1. Do we want to live where everyone is dependent on the government? In such a country, everyone pretty much works under compulsion—because most of what he earns is taken

from him—and then receives his pittance from the government, doled out to him as though he were a child on an allowance.

2. Or do we want to live where people are self-reliant, proud of their ability to take care of themselves—in a country where people get to keep what they earn, and so produce far more of value to society.

The Soviet Union showed us where the first system leads. America used to be an example of where the second one leads.

Today we are halfway between the two systems, moving gradually toward the Soviet system, in which the state controls everything. The so-called "middle way" is really a transition from freedom to slavery.

It isn't possible to give government just a little control over the economy and our lives. Once we cede that power to government, it uses the power to take more from us. That's why every year the government controls more of our lives.

We've already gone so far that it will require a tremendous effort to recapture our lives. If we wait another few years, it may be too late. By then we may not have the resources, the power, or the freedom to reclaim our country and our liberty.

Chapter 20

Fighting Crime
or Playing Games?

Crime isn't just one more problem. It is one that can kill you.

Today, after all the "get tough" policies and all the "wars on crime," our streets and homes aren't safe, nor are our children. Insurance rates in many areas are sky-high, to compensate for the billions of dollars paid on claims for vandalism and theft.

To combat all this, the politicians offer only the same useless remedy: more government.

To you, crime is a curse. To them, crime is a blessing—another chance to show they're more outraged than their opponents. They propose mandatory sentences, more money for police, bigger prisons, more wire-tapping, more bond issues, and more invasions of our privacy. And, of course, they need higher taxes to pay for all this toughness. Each one wants to propose the toughest "tough on crime" program:

"I say three strikes and you're out—three felonies and we lock you up for life and throw away the key."

"See how my opponent loves to coddle criminals. I say *two* strikes and you're out."

"What a namby-pamby, soft-on-crime, bleeding-heart liberal attitude. *One* strike is enough. If you can't do the time, don't do the crime."

"No, that's too lenient. Drug-pushers should get the death penalty."

They're in a bidding war—bidding for the status as "toughest on crime"—and paying with your money and your freedom.

WHAT'S THE SOLUTION?

At first glance, crime seems to be a rare problem of too *little* government, instead of too much. After all, you have to use force to stop crime.

But there are far more prisons today than there were 40 years ago, far more police, far tougher laws, far more control of guns, far tougher sentencing, far more money spent by the federal government. This ever-increasing toughness has done nothing to make you safer. As the graph below shows, the crime rate has risen sharply since the 1950s. Obviously, more government hasn't worked.

When a politician makes some new government program sound plausible, please remember that dozens of "tough on crime" federal laws have been passed in recent decades—laws that obviously made no improvement. Here are some examples from the long-running War on Drugs:

- The 1970 Comprehensive Drug Abuse Prevention and Control Act;
- The 1978 Psychotropic Substances Act;
- The 1981 Posse Comitatus Act;
- The 1982 Tax Reform Act (which allowed the IRS to pass on "confidential" information from your tax return to other government crime-fighting agencies);

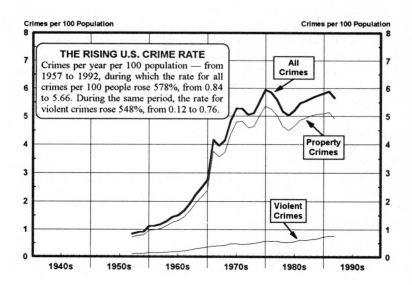

THE RISING U.S. CRIME RATE
Crimes per year per 100 population — from 1957 to 1992, during which the rate for all crimes per 100 people rose 578%, from 0.84 to 5.66. During the same period, the rate for violent crimes rose 548%, from 0.12 to 0.76.

- The 1983 Organized Crime Drug Enforcement Task Force program;
- The 1984 Comprehensive Crime Control Act;
- The 1986 Anti-Drug Abuse Act;
- The 1990 amendments to the Anti-Drug Abuse Act.

The crime wave of the past 30 years isn't a result of soft-on-crime attitudes.

I believe there are five steps needed to lower the crime rate substantially and bring back the peaceful society America had 35 years ago. All five call for *less* government.

1. STOP LOCKING UP NON-VIOLENT OFFENDERS

The first step is to clear the prisons of non-violent offenders. They are no threat to society, but locking them up diverts prison cells, police resources, and court time from the violent thugs who are terrorizing us.

Prison facilities should be reserved for those who murder, rape, assault, and rob.

No one should be in prison for prostitution, gambling, buying or selling handguns, pornography, or possessing drugs. As much as you may disapprove of these activities, all of government's high-cost huffing and puffing hasn't slowed them, and it won't. Government is incapable of stopping these enterprises.

People who are guilty of fraud, embezzlement, or other white-collar crimes shouldn't be locked up either, if there is any reasonable prospect that they can make restitution—to their victims, not to the government. Prison time should be reserved for repeat offenders who don't make restitution.

Possession of a weapon (of any kind) should be considered a crime only if it's used to injure or threaten someone.

Victimless Crimes

Crime rates have skyrocketed because too much of the criminal justice system has been diverted to combating what are called "victimless crimes"—prostitution, gambling, drugs, pornography, and other activities that participants enter voluntarily. No coercion or threat of coercion is involved. (When coercion *is* involved, a crime isn't victimless.)

A victimless crime is one in which:

- No one has been assaulted.
- No one's property has been invaded.

- No one has been cheated by fraud or broken promises.
- There is no victim making a complaint.

Someone might say there *is* a victim—the person who harms himself by, for example, taking drugs. Or the members of his family.

But someone might harm himself or his family by buying a car he can't afford, or marrying the wrong person, or choosing the wrong career. Should government try to stop such things? Should we lock up the car dealer or the ill-chosen spouse or the personnel officer?

Should we have a War on Thoughtless Budgeting? A War on Misguided Marriages? A War on Vocational Ineptitude?

For as long as I've been alive, government has been trying to stop people from gambling, taking drugs, and patronizing prostitutes. But all these activities have flourished.

Why Violence Thrives

And since it is impossible for the federal government to stop these activities, pretending to do so by escalating a "War on Crime" will require more and more resources—leaving less and less to deal with violent criminals.

The police are too busy pursuing vice instead of violence. The court system is clogged—leaving it receptive to the plea bargains of violent criminals. And the prisons are overflowing with non-violent offenders, which opens the door to the early release of violent criminals.

Every marijuana smoker or pimp in prison uses a cell that could have been occupied by a mugger, rapist, or child molester.

Drug violators comprised 60% of the individuals sentenced to federal prisons in 1993 (the latest year for which there are statistics). And 26% of all prisoners in state and federal prisons combined in 1993 were there for drug violations.

At the same time, state prisons held from 17% to 29% more prisoners than their intended capacity, and federal prisons were operating at 25% over capacity. In other words, if it weren't for the drug prisoners, there would be plenty of room for murderers, rapists, and child molesters, and they wouldn't be getting out early.

Understand that a drug violation isn't a gang shoot-out over a drug territory. It is a peaceable, non-violent purchase, sale, or possession of a narcotic.

2. END WASHINGTON'S WAR ON DRUGS

The crusade against victimless crimes reaches the apex of absurdity in the War on Drugs. It is the quintessential example that government doesn't work.

Government has failed completely to stop people from taking

drugs. It can't stop drugs from coming into the country. *It can't even stop drugs from getting into its own prisons.* And yet the politicians keep telling us that the next freedom taken from us will be the price that finally pays off in getting drugs off the streets and away from our children.

It ought to be obvious by now that this War will never be won. Government can't stop the supply, it can't reduce the demand, and its strong-arm tactics don't work.

Drug use is more prevalent today than it was 35 years ago. And we have paid for this fruitless crusade in hundreds of billions of dollars in taxes, the corruption of police forces, the loss of civil liberties, soaring crime rates, and gang warfare.

The past 30 years have seen a steady flow of tougher federal laws, formation of new task forces, expansion of powers for agencies like the CIA or FBI, spectacular drug busts, confiscation of a mountain of cocaine and heroin, and gleeful news of increases in arrests and convictions.

Still the War is further than ever from victory. The War has served only to undermine our protections against reckless law enforcement—and to make life easier for violent criminals. Warrantless searches, uncharged detentions, property seizures, mistaken arrests and shootings have become the rule—all in violation of the Bill of Rights.

But the federal government continues to send optimistic dispatches from the War front.

Who Will Supply the Drugs?

There has always been a demand for mind-altering drugs, and there always will be. This demand will be met by someone. When drugs are legal—as are alcohol and tobacco—demand is met by legitimate companies operating a conventional business in merchandise. When drugs are illegal (or even sharply regulated, as when cigarettes are heavily taxed), the demand is met by criminals who are willing to risk capture and imprisonment.

The need to circumvent the law drives up the prices of drugs a hundredfold. A dose that in a legalized environment might cost $2 can cost $200. Many addicts can support their habits only through crime.

All normal ethics are discarded in a business dominated by criminals. Jim Beam doesn't send pushers into schoolyards to hook children on whiskey, and it doesn't conduct drive-by shootings at Seagrams dealers. But its forerunners during the Prohibition of alcohol did do these things, and so do the criminals running the drug trade today.

Prohibiting drugs means that someone will have a monopoly on drug sales. So gangs who finance their activities with drug sales battle each other to determine who the someone will be. Innocent people get shot in the crossfire and in drive-by shootings. It's the Prohibition era all over again. And the winner, if he understands the process, says, "Thank you, government, for making all this possible."

The similarity between alcohol Prohibition and the War on Drugs shows up in the graph below. Ending Prohibition also ended a rising trend in homicide rates. Starting the War on Drugs in the 1960s started a new uptrend in homicide rates.

If drugs were legal, there would be no drive-by shootings, few judges and policemen on the take, and no unjust entries, arrests, and property seizures—and no pushers hanging around school-yards. Drugs wouldn't be the scandal they are today. We would hear much less about addicts (less than we hear about alcoholics today), the streets would be much safer, gang members would have no prize to fight over, and the country would once again enjoy the domestic peace it experienced from 1933 (the end of Prohibition) to the early 1960s (the start of the War on Drugs).

Truth Is a Casualty in the War on Drugs

Because they're in a losing battle, the Drug Warriors grow progressively more hysterical in trying to justify their activities. It has become impossible to discuss calmly any issue concerning drugs.

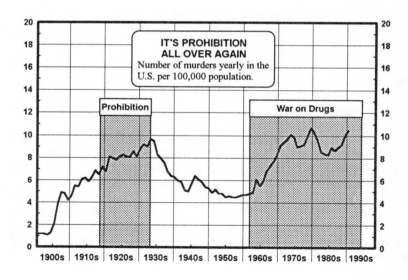

IT'S PROHIBITION ALL OVER AGAIN
Number of murders yearly in the U.S. per 100,000 population.

For example, marijuana is very effective in relieving chronic pain; alleviating nausea for cancer patients undergoing chemotherapy; and treating glaucoma, multiple sclerosis, epilepsy, and other medical conditions. But the Drug Warriors prefer to let patients suffer, rather than acknowledge that marijuana isn't an unconditional evil.

Lost in the hysteria are a few simple facts:

- No one has ever been known to die from smoking marijuana.
- No scientific study has indicated that smoking marijuana leads inevitably to heavier drugs.
- More people use mind-altering stimulants, sedatives, tranquilizers, or analgesics than use cocaine or crack.
- Fewer people die from illegal drugs than die from accidental poisoning by legal drugs and medicines.

Much of the misery coming from illegal drugs occurs because they are illegal. People sometimes die or become very sick from poorly formulated illegal drugs or from overdoses of them, because the law prevents reputable companies from providing a safe product in standard dosages.

If drugs were completely legal, probably a few well-known companies would produce them. Prices would be a fraction of what they are today, so addicts wouldn't need to steal to support their habits. Profits would be at a normal level, so there would be no reason for turf wars.

Would legalization and lower prices lead to more drug users? Possibly. But those who did use drugs would probably have fewer problems than drug users do today, because the drug companies would have to compete on the basis of safety—just as the makers of cars and airplanes do now.

Myths of Legalization

To warn us against drug legalization, Drug Warriors point to crack babies, or to someone whose life was ruined by cocaine, or to some other drug mishap. These tragedies are very real. But they weren't caused by drug legalization; they occurred with drugs outlawed. So they shouldn't be considered warnings against legalization unless you believe such events would increase with legalization. And I've seen no evidence that they would.

Some people say that legalizing drugs would send the wrong message about drugs to children. But that's true only in a society where government is the arbiter of all right and wrong, where whatever isn't forbidden is mandatory—or at least encouraged.

We need to teach young people not to look to government for moral guidance.

Drug legalization sends no "message" at all—no more than the freedom to say bad things about people sends the wrong message about free speech, or the freedom to buy unhealthy things from abroad sends the wrong message about free trade.

President Clinton once said he wouldn't support the legalizing of drugs because his brother wouldn't be alive today if drugs had been legal. I'm glad he cares about his brother. But he's saying, in effect, that the life of his brother is worth more than the lives of all the innocent children who are terrorized by drug dealers in school or killed in drive-by shootings, and worth more than the safety of the millions of people who have been assaulted by muggers trying to support a drug habit at prices inflated by the War on Drugs.

If you want to stop drug use, don't waste your time asking the government to do it. It can't. And this country may not be able to survive another 35 years of the War on Drugs.

If we really want to reduce crime, the quickest and most effective step we could take would be to end the War on Drugs.

3. END PROPERTY SEIZURES

Another necessary step to reduce crime is to repeal all laws that authorize asset-forfeiture.

These laws invite law-enforcement agencies to finance their activities by taking property on flimsy pretexts. This diverts the agencies' attention from their real purpose—to protect citizens from violent criminals.

Donald Scott (described on page 56) was killed by police during a drug raid motivated by a desire to seize his ranch. Government agents had investigated the market value of the property before the raid.

In 1992 the FBI projected that the value of its property seizures would increase by 25% each year over the succeeding three years—a statement indicating that the seizures are a goal, rather than the byproduct of law-enforcement.

Former New York City police commissioner Patrick Murphy said, "the large monetary value of forfeitures . . . has created a great temptation for state and local police departments to target assets rather than criminal activity."

We need to get rid of these laws, so that existing law-enforcement resources can be aimed at violent crime, not at innocent citizens who possess tempting property.

4. REPEAL GUN-CONTROL LAWS

The fourth needed step is to get rid of all federal gun-control laws.

As with most crime-control attempts, these laws inconvenience the innocent while providing no deterrent to criminals. The latter rarely patronize gun shops, endure waiting periods, or register their firearms. They buy their guns in the underworld, or they simply steal them.

But innocent citizens who obey the laws are left defenseless— and become safe targets for criminals.

States like New Hampshire place very few restrictions on firearm ownership and have relatively low crime rates—while Washington, D.C., and California, with stringent gun-control laws, have relatively high crime rates.

Gun-control laws don't reduce crime, but passing them gives politicians another soap-box opportunity to pose as crime-fighters. Conservative politicians act tough by repealing the Bill of Rights, while liberal politicians act tough by outlawing weapons. Neither action reduces the crime rate. But both allow politicians to feel self-righteous, and both undermine our freedoms.

Gun-control laws show how risky it is to let the government take even an inch unless you're prepared to grant it a mile. The laws start by banning something no reasonable person is likely to want— and then become more and more restrictive, until the ban is total.

In the case of guns, assault weapons came first, and it was emphasized that no one needed an assault weapon for hunting or defending his home from burglars. But a Los Angeles store-owner could certainly have used one when confronted by a mob of looters during the Rodney King riots of 1992. A revolver was inadequate protection, and the police were nowhere to be found. And since many of the store-owners were uninsured (since they were located in high-crime areas), the lack of an assault weapon caused many store-owners to lose their life savings and their livelihoods.

If guns kill people, so do knives, automobiles, baseball bats, choking hands, and icicles. None of these things should be outlawed. But more of the people who misuse them to commit crimes would be prosecuted if the police, the courts, and the prisons weren't overloaded dealing with victimless crimes—including gun-control violations.

The Founding Fathers

The 2nd Amendment to the Constitution says, " . . . the right of the people to keep and bear Arms, shall not be infringed." This right was important to the Founding Fathers, because an armed citizenry was considered to be one way to keep government from overstepping its bounds. In that sense, they considered the 2nd Amendment to be the most important part of the Bill of Rights.

Politicians will use any event as an excuse to take away more of your rights. But the 2nd Amendment doesn't say, " . . . the right of the people to keep and bear Arms shall not be infringed until some crazed postal worker kills his fellow employees." It is absolute.

Repealing federal gun-control laws will help deter criminals from harassing citizens or breaking into homes in the middle of the night.

5. KEEP THE FEDERAL GOVERNMENT OUT

Lastly, we must get the federal government out of crime control. There is no reason for the politicians in Washington to collect money from the citizens of the states, tie strings around the money, and then send a portion of it back to the states.

All crime is local. Whether it be a violent crime (such as murder, kidnapping, rape, or a mugging) or a crime of property (such as burglary, trespass, or fraud), it occurs in the jurisdiction of some police department or sheriff's department.

The Constitution specifies only three federal crimes—treason, piracy, and the counterfeiting of government bonds and coins. And yet Congress has passed federal laws against kidnapping, gun ownership, drug use, "hate crimes," discrimination, fraud, carjacking, vandalism, pornography, obstruction, and dozens of other activities that have no national significance.

Federal laws interfere with local police work and violate the Constitution. They also allow government to circumvent the Bill of Rights and subject citizens to double jeopardy. If a jury acquits someone of violating a state gun-control law, for example, he can be retried for violating a federal gun-control law—even though the second trial is for the same act.

In addition, the federal government hinders law-enforcement by its "assistance" programs that impose federal standards on local police.

Crossing State Lines

The federal government's criminal work doesn't make us safer.

Local law-enforcement agencies often need outside help in solving crimes and pursuing fugitives. But they could set up an agency of their own to do research, keep a fingerprint bank, do special forensic work, act as a clearinghouse for criminal records, or perform any other function the federal government does now.

In fact, there could be more than one such agency. Private companies could compete to provide needed services to local governments. One company might excel at one kind of task, while another specializes in another.

Private companies already track down fugitives. Unlike government agencies, these companies aren't above the law—and thus are liable for damages if they trespass on private property, make false arrests, or otherwise hurt innocent people. And they can be fired if they are inefficient or corrupt.

Keep the Feds Out

The federal government has no special wisdom, no special authority, and no special ability to fight crime. The Founding Fathers thought that would be a terrible idea.

The past 35 years have confirmed their wisdom. The federal government's involvement in local law-enforcement has helped the guilty and hurt the innocent.

SAFE STREETS

I want to live in a city where it's safe to walk the streets night and day, and where there's no special need to lock my doors.

That's the way it used to be in America just 40 years ago. But the federal government has taken that away from us by meddling in areas where it has no authority and no competence.

To restore a peaceful society, we need to stop government from policing morals and prosecuting victimless crimes, end the War on Drugs, stop law-enforcement agencies from seizing property, get rid of gun-control laws, and keep the federal government out of crime-fighting.

It's time to stop playing political games with crime.

Chapter 21

A Weak National Defense

I want to be certain America won't be attacked by any foreign power. But we don't have that certainty today. To achieve it will require an entirely new approach to national defense.

With the current system, our government has spent lavish sums, and yet it has left us vulnerable to attack by any petty dictator who can get his hands on a missile. And our government has exposed us to danger by looking for trouble in all the wrong places and making itself the judge of disputes among foreign nations—so that half the world is angry at us and most of the rest have little respect for us.

We Are Fortunate

Two oceans separate us from the turmoils of Europe and Asia. In over 200 years, no one has ever started a war by invading America. If ever a people were blessed with the opportunity to live in peace just by minding their own business, we are the ones.

And yet over a million Americans have died in wars, another million have been wounded, and *trillions* of dollars have been spent on the military.

Instead of defending our borders and people, the government has drafted Americans and sent them to die in the trenches of France and the jungles of Asia. Instead of focusing on defense, the government has seized on minor incidents to jump into wars that didn't threaten America.

And it has embroiled all Americans in conflicts that may have been the concern of only a few people. Governments are superb at amplifying the distress and tragedies of a few people into national catastrophes that kill tens of thousands. Any petty dispute that harms an American—even one that's no business of government—provides an excuse to rattle the sabre or even wield it.

Politicians know that war—even just the threat of it—stirs the passions. So they use it to divert attention from their failures at home, to enhance their own importance, to secure a place in history, or to gratify some group that has an interest in a conflict or has a grievance against a foreign nation.

It's unfortunate that the founding fathers didn't find a way to limit the government's war-making powers when they drafted the Constitution.

HISTORY OF U.S. WARS

It didn't take long after the birth of America for politicians to find a way to use war to their advantage.

In 1812 British naval ships confiscated some American merchant ships and drafted their crews into the British Navy. American politicians were outraged. And so America went to war.

Why? Certainly it was a terrible crime to enslave American seamen. But why was it the U.S. government's business? Private companies had chosen to send those ships into foreign waters, and were responsible for the safety of their employees. If they couldn't provide safe passage (either by arming the ships or by negotiating with the British), they should have stayed out of the area. Left to their own devices, innovative businessmen will find ways to get the job done; but let them depend on government and the results will generally be disastrous.

In this case, 286,730 Americans were sent into a 2½-year war against Great Britain—during which an estimated 2,260 Americans were killed and 4,505 wounded.

Did the freeing of the seamen justify sacrificing the lives of 2,260 other Americans? Did the honor of the new country depend on rushing off to war at the slightest provocation? Was America's reputation so fragile it had to be upheld no matter what the price? Was it worth the burning of Washington, D.C., and the destruction of vast amounts of American property?

Nothing Ever Settled

The war supposedly was fought to affirm the freedom of American commercial ships and American citizens to go anywhere in the world. A noble sentiment.

But in fact the war established nothing. American ships continued to be harassed—by pirates or other governments—for decades afterward.

The same pattern has continued throughout American history:

- The Mexican War didn't end hostilities along the Mexican border. It did add to the territory of the U.S. But was that territory worth 13,283 American lives? Wouldn't it have been cheaper to buy it with money, instead of lives?
- The Civil War (which took 498,332 American lives) didn't bring the reconciliation among the states that Abraham Lincoln promised. Instead, it produced nearly a century of regional animosity and amplified racial hostility.
- World War I (116,708 American lives) wasn't "the war to end all wars" as promised. It caused such devastation and bitterness that it made Adolf Hitler and World War II all but inevitable.
- World War II (407,316 American lives) didn't make the world safe for democracy, it made the world safe for Joseph Stalin and the Soviet Union to launch the Cold War.
- The Korean War (33,651 American lives) left Korea as divided as before.
- Despite 58,168 American deaths in Vietnam, the dominoes continued to fall and the Communists took over all of Indochina.
- Even the supposedly successful 1991 Gulf War (296 American lives) produced no resolution—other than to return the Emir of Kuwait and his 70 wives to their palace.

The death figures cited above don't include the tens of millions of foreigners, military and civilian, who wanted to live in peace and who wanted no part of the conflicts between governments—but who died, were wounded, or saw all they had worked for destroyed in American bombing raids.

The politicians always justify the human tragedies as being necessary for the greater good. They speak movingly of giving one's life for one's country. But it's always someone else's life they're talking about.

Small-Scale Wars

In between the big wars, the U.S. government has conducted little ones—footnotes in history. In the 1800s, the Marines landed in such faraway places as China, Panama, Uruguay, Egypt, Greenland, the

Philippines, and Samoa. In the first few decades of this century, it was Cuba, Mexico, Haiti, Nicaragua, and others.

In the 50 years since World War II, the U.S. government has had no trouble finding provocations wherever it looked—claiming to see threats to freedom and peace in virtually every corner of the Earth. It has shipped money, weapons, and soldiers to *nearly a hundred nations*.

There have been U.S. military campaigns in Greece, Cuba, the Dominican Republic, Cambodia, Grenada, Lebanon, Libya, Panama, Somalia, Haiti, and Bosnia—and I've probably forgotten a few other countries. In addition, there has been meddling in Nicaragua, El Salvador, the Philippines, and dozens and dozens of other countries.

Is this what a free country should be doing?

Solving Problems Through Government

In every incident the cause is just, and the issue is a clear-cut, black-and-white case of Good vs. Evil. Each crusade has a limited and specific goal—which will be achieved quickly and at very little cost.

Always we're promised that the magic touch of our government is just what's needed—and *all* that's needed—to resolve this problem once and for all. This will bring "peace in our time," a "new world order," a "world safe for democracy," "nations united in peace," the opportunity to let the "peace process" continue.

But in fact nothing is ever settled.

The problem "goes away" only when the politicians stop ranting and raving about it. They turn instead to some domestic crisis—to welfare reform or health care or urban violence. Or their attention wanders to another foreign crisis. So we go from Iran to Grenada to Lebanon to Libya to Panama to Iraq to Somalia to Haiti to Bosnia and to who-knows-where next.

Perpetual War

And thus we are almost always at war—cold or hot, but a conflict nevertheless—a war in which Americans will die, or a war that Americans will be taxed for, or a war that could easily erupt into wholesale destruction.

And what is the object of all this war? Why, peace, of course. We are always fighting to bring peace to the world. We will have peace even if we have to kill thousands to get it.

So we have what historian Charles Beard called the "perpetual war for perpetual peace"—the nonstop conflict always justified by the peace just around the corner.

Alternative Strategies

I'm not saying there are never provocations. But such things can be handled without war—without sending Americans to die, without taxing Americans to the breaking point, and without bombing innocent foreigners.

Politicians always claim to seek peaceful solutions first. They enter into negotiations and make treaties. But the negotiations almost always lead to unrealistic demands, and the treaties make us more vulnerable by linking our fate to other countries.

Most of the diplomatic endeavors are window-dressing because, no matter how much a politician professes peace, he can't resist war. It enhances his personal power as nothing else can. So a politician like Abraham Lincoln, Woodrow Wilson, Franklin Roosevelt, or Lyndon Johnson may promise peace, but sooner or later he'll tell us war is unavoidable.

As Randolph Bourne said, "War is the health of the state." But for the rest of us, war is a game we can't win.

POPULARITY OF WAR

Still, war is popular with many people—not just politicians.

These people assume the next conflict will settle things once and for all. They truly believe an aggressive military force can bring peace to the world.

They don't realize, as Joseph Sobran put it, that war is just one more government program.

The War on Poverty has been raging for 30 years, but now there are more people on the relief rolls than ever. For almost as long, our privacy, civil liberties, and money have been sacrificed to wage the War on Drugs, but not one city has been liberated. There are hundreds of federal and state gun-control laws, but murders with firearms continue to increase. The government provides mediocre education, it can't bring peace to the cities, it certainly hasn't done much for the environment, and it doesn't deliver the mail on time.

And yet, many people who recognize all these things believe this same government will achieve its next foreign objective perfectly—that, somehow, the government will succeed overseas even though it invariably fails at home—that, by some miracle, the government that can't balance a checkbook will achieve its military objectives precisely, and without igniting the fuse for World War III or Police Action #79.

Why don't they understand?

There's a good reason.

Walk into an IRS office, the Motor Vehicle Department, or almost any Post Office—and you see immediately that it isn't operated the same way as your favorite restaurant or almost any company you do business with. All the trappings of a government bureaucracy are in plain sight. We know how inefficient these agencies are.

But how many times have you visited the Pentagon? How many years did you serve in battle?

If the answer to both questions is zero, you can be forgiven for not realizing the military is simply the Post Office in battle fatigues.

But every veteran knows the military is a government program. He's seen the bureaucracy, the pettiness of superiors, the snafus, the forms in quadruplicate, the men sleeping on guard duty, the bug-outs, the resentments, the time spent listening to social-reform lectures.

Government doesn't work. We can't expect it to fight efficiently any more than we can expect it to eradicate poverty or drugs or alcoholism. If it wins a war, it's only because it's fighting another government.

So we shouldn't be surprised that foreign disputes have cost us so much in lives and taxes. And we shouldn't be amazed that none of them produced the peace that was promised or resolved the problems that started the conflict.

Lovely Words

But the politicians go on talking as though it's obvious that government and the military achieve great successes, and that we must continue to lavish great sums of money on them.

As soon as the Soviet Union fell, they started chanting, "It's still a dangerous world out there"—as though government could make it less so. And they continue to dress up their pleas for military spending with phrases such as "national interest," "America's role in the world," "leader of the free world," "repelling aggression," "a new world order," and "mutual security."

But the terms are devoid of substance. Have you seen anyone following the leader of the free world lately? Where can we find world order or mutual security? (Can you imagine anyone running to *our* defense if *we* were attacked?) Our national interests aren't served by killing, dying, or by piling up enormous debts for our children to pay. And aggression is just as widespread today as it was before we started repelling it.

Government doesn't work. War doesn't work. Every war leaves America and the world as insecure as they were before—with new enemies to face or with old enemies threatening to get even.

WHAT IS WAR?

The politicians' stirring phrases are meant to keep our eyes averted from the reality of war—to make us imagine heroic young men marching in parades, winning glorious battles, and bringing peace and democracy to the world.

But war is something quite different from that.

It is your children or your grandchildren dying before they're even fully adults, or being maimed or mentally scarred for life. It is your brothers and sisters being taught to kill other people—and to hate people who are just like themselves and who don't want to kill anyone either. It is your children seeing their buddies' limbs blown off their bodies.

It is hundreds of thousands of human beings dying years before their time. It is millions of people separated forever from the ones they loved.

It is the destruction of homes for which people worked for decades. It is the end of careers that meant as much to others as your career means to you.

It is the imposition of heavy taxes on you and on other Americans and on people in other countries—taxes that remain long after the war is over. It is the suppression of free speech and the jailing of people who criticize the government.

It is the imposition of slavery by forcing young men to serve in the military.

It is goading the public to hate foreign people and races—whether Arabs or Japanese or Cubans or Serbs. It is numbing our sensibilities to cruelties inflicted on foreigners.

It is cheering at the news of enemy pilots killed in their planes, of young men blown to bits while trapped inside tanks, of sailors drowned at sea.

Other tragedies inevitably trail in the wake of war. Politicians lie even more than usual. Secrecy and cover-ups become the rule rather than the exception. The press become even less reliable.

War is genocide, torture, cruelty, propaganda, and slavery.

War is the worst cruelty government can inflict upon its subjects. It makes every other political crime—corruption, bribery, favoritism, vote-buying, graft, dishonesty—seem petty.

Government's Role

If government has a role to play in foreign affairs, it *isn't* to win wars, to assure that the right people run foreign countries, to protect innocent foreigners from guilty aggressors, or to make the world safe for democracy—or even a safer place at all.

If government has a role, it can be only to *keep us out of wars*—to make sure no one will ever attack us, to make certain you can live your life in peace, to assure you the freedom to ignore who is right and who is wrong in foreign conflicts.

The only reason for military power is to discourage attackers, and—if they come anyway—to repel them at our borders. Such things as stationing troops in far-off lands, meddling in foreign disputes, and sending our children to foreign countries as "peace-keepers" only encourage war.

To make America safer and to assure that we stay at peace, we don't need to put more weapons in the hands of government employees, or to make more treaties with other governments, or to increase the military budget.

In fact, we need just the opposite of these things. We need to make it as hard as possible for politicians to involve us in war. And we need to create a defense system that relies as little as possible on the normal workings of government.

Chapter 22

An Effective National Defense

We're not nearly as safe as we could be. Three major contradictions have kept us vulnerable to the dangers of the world:

1. Our government wants to bring peace to the entire world, even though it can't keep the peace on the streets of its own capital.
2. The government is ready to bomb innocent civilians by the thousands, but it won't assassinate a foreign dictator who is actively threatening the United States.
3. Our government has developed the ability to rain nuclear bombs on any country in the world, but it has deliberately avoided developing any ability to defend us from incoming missiles.

These policies have stirred anti-American feelings throughout the world and left us naked before a nuclear attack. Correcting them would finally make America secure.

WORLD BUSYBODY

The U.S. government has no business in alliances, treaties, world organizations, or joint efforts to pacify the planet.

No treaty protects us from attack, but many treaties increase the risk that an attack on another country will drag us into war.

Arms Sales

Politicians rail against the right of American citizens to own guns. But the U.S. government is the biggest arms dealer in the world.

Over the past 30 years the United States sold or gave weapons to at least 102 foreign governments.

This has to stop.

Foreign Aid

American citizens should never be prohibited from making gifts to any government, organization, or individual in the world.

Nor should they be *forced* to make contributions—as they have been for the past 50 years. Since 1946 the U.S. government has sent $343 billion of our money (equivalent to $909 billion in 1995 dollars) to foreign governments and international agencies for military and economic assistance.

Even as our own government was going more deeply into debt:

- It has sent money to foreign governments, allowing them to pay off their own debts;
- It has given foreign dictators the money to sustain oppressive regimes;
- It has given money to third-world governments to keep bankrupt socialist economies afloat;
- In some wars in Southeast Asia and the Middle East, it has helped finance both sides;
- It has built tennis courts in Rwanda, sent sewing machines to areas without electricity, constructed hospitals in areas that already had empty hospitals; and
- It has provided a steady flow of money to U.S. companies that sell goods to the foreign aid system—companies that readily finance the politicians who vote for foreign aid.

Some politicians complain about these absurdities, but vote for foreign aid anyway—because they hope to reform the program to make it help only friendly governments.

But you can't reform a government program; the only way to fix it is to get rid of it. If you only reduce its size, the next Congress will pump it back up.

And foreign aid doesn't help a foreign country; putting its government on the dole weakens it. The aid subsidizes and prolongs all the problems a government causes. Many countries might have found prosperity decades ago if U.S. foreign aid hadn't enabled their governments to persist with devastating socialist policies.

Israel is a good example. It's populated by some of the finest minds and hardest-working people in the world. Their determination to resist invasion has saved them from extinction. Such a country obviously has what it takes to be self-supporting. But it has been dependent on U.S. military and economic aid since its founding.

Why?

Because the U.S. government subsidizes Israel's enemies—selling arms and providing foreign aid to almost every country in the Middle East at one time or another. And because the U.S. government has subsidized Israel's socialist economy—removing any incentive for Israel to turn to free markets.

If it's wrong to encourage drug addicts, if it's wrong to furnish liquor to an alcoholic, how can we expect to help a country by paying its government to continue with unworkable socialist policies?

The Beacon of Freedom

Is it negative and isolationist to stay out of world affairs—to shun alliances and foreign aid?

Certainly not. Such a policy would do more for world peace and freedom than any form of aggressive diplomacy or sabre-rattling, more than any alliance or treaty, more than any program of foreign aid or arms sales.

An America of freedom, small government, free trade, nonintervention in foreign affairs, and goodwill toward all would be an inspiration to the world's people—one country that is safe, secure, and at peace with the world. If America could achieve this, it could inspire people elsewhere to demand the same for themselves.

As Thomas Jefferson said, "Peace, commerce and honest friendship with all nations; entangling alliances with none."

FREE TRADE

The greatest guarantor of peace isn't a strong military or an international organization. It is free trade among countries.

When people can buy and sell freely with people in another country, they have a good reason to discourage their leaders from going to war with that country. This interdependence is a far more reliable guarantor of peace than foreign aid, arms sales, and treaties.

Winston Churchill put it very well back in 1903:

> . . . the fact that this great trade exists between nations binds them together in spite of themselves, and has in the last thirty years done more to preserve the peace of the world than all the Ambassadors, Prime Ministers, and Foreign Secretaries and Colonial Secretaries put together.

When a government excludes other countries from sources of raw materials or from markets for their wares, it undermines the economic motives for maintaining peace.

Lost Jobs?

Free trade doesn't cost jobs, it improves them.

Money spent on foreign products doesn't disappear from the American economy. It's true that an American company loses a sale when an American buys a Japanese car. And if it loses enough sales to foreign competitors, it will stop hiring for a while—or even lay people off (just as it would if it lost sales to an American competitor). But the total number of American jobs doesn't decline, because the money spent abroad will come back here in one form or another.

When an American buys a foreign car (or any other foreign product), the foreign seller receives dollars. He (or some other foreigner to whom he trades the dollars) will use the money to buy an American product. Or he'll buy an American investment—which also puts the money into circulation in America. Or he'll leave it in a bank—which will lend it to someone who will spend it in America. One way or another, the money creates jobs somewhere in the American economy.

When a foreign industry outsells an American industry, the lost American jobs are highly visible. But the new American jobs aren't so easy to see, because they're spread out over many different industries. So politicians can score points railing against foreign competitors—even though their arguments have no basis in reality.

Trade Aggression?

Politicians describe foreign trade as though it were a war between countries—with winners and losers. Here, for example, is a statement by one of the 1996 presidential candidates:

> The Japanese in the last 25 years have bought 400,000 American cars and sold us 40 million. Now if that is not trade aggression, I don't know what is. You've got to wake up and start defending the national interest of the United States and of American workers, American businesses, and American auto workers.

But every one of those 40 million Japanese cars was bought by an American who wanted it. Providing what someone wants isn't aggression.

Barring Japanese companies from selling cars in America is forcibly preventing Americans from getting what they want—which *is* aggression.

And if someone thinks Japanese sales here are aggression, what are American sales in Japan? Here are a few areas in which U.S. companies "aggressed" rather aggressively in 1994:

U.S. TRADE WITH JAPAN, 1994

Item	U.S. sales to Japan	Japan sales to U.S.	U.S. Surplus
Aircraft & spacecraft	$ 3,428	$ 442	$ 2,986
Aluminum	496	158	338
Cereals	2,380	110	2,270
Douglas fir	1,164	0	1,164
Chemicals, inorganic	1,127	309	818
Meat	2,160	482	1,678
Oil Seeds & oleaginous fruits	1,171	26	1,145
Tobacco products	1,805	6	1,799

(billions of dollars)

Was this trade aggression? Should American companies be forcibly prevented from selling products they can make better than foreign companies?

Most politicians miss the whole point of international trade. It isn't a game or a battle or a war. Each transaction benefits both sides.

To quote Winston Churchill again:

. . . both the selling and the buying of these things were profitable to us; that what we sold, we sold at a good profit, for a natural and sufficient return; that what we bought, we bought because we thought it worth our while to buy, and thought we could turn it to advantage.

And in this way commerce is utterly different from war, so that the ideas and the phraseology of the one should never be applied to the other; for in war both sides lose whoever wins the victory, but the transactions of trade, like the quality of mercy, are twice blessed, and confer a benefit on both parties.

Punishing the Innocent

But what about American companies that are shut out by foreign governments?

Just as the sale of foreign goods in this country blesses both buyers and sellers, a foreign government that prevents its citizens from buying American goods injures both the would-be buyer and seller.

But our government's response to such wasteful policies is to double the harm by imitating them. If the Japanese government interferes with American car companies, our government wants to forcibly reduce the number of Japanese cars sold here. But why should American car-buyers be punished for the sins of the Japanese government? The politicians don't address that point because they don't care about the American buyer.

But if pressed for an answer, they'd probably say it's the only way to pressure the Japanese government to open its trade doors. Hurting innocent people in order to make someone else bend to one's will is the tactic of a terrorist. Governments have been using this tactic for centuries—which it why there still are so many trade barriers.

Again, Winston Churchill in 1903 had something to say to those today who believe we can open foreign markets by closing our own:

> There's a feeling that England has only to retaliate and foreign tariff walls will immediately collapse. But all the great nations of the world are Protectionist; they have been for 100 years past, and perhaps for many years before that, endeavoring by every dodge of reciprocity or negotiation to force each other to reduce their tariffs in each other's respective interests.
>
> Where have they come to? Have they reached Free Trade? On the contrary, their tariffs have risen higher and higher, and at this moment Free-trade England, which does nothing, Free-trade England, with masterly inactivity, occupies in regard to the nations of the world so far as tariffs are concerned, a position of advantage to which few of the Protectionist countries have attained and which none of them has surpassed.

With virtually no tariffs of its own, England had become the world's leading exporter—while governments that used trade barriers to jockey for advantage did more harm than good to their own exporters. Too bad England eventually fell off the Free Trade wagon.

Treaties & Trade Blocs

America doesn't need to belong to GATT, NAFTA, the World Trade Organization, or any other trade alliance. Our government doesn't need to negotiate trade treaties with other governments. It needs only to reduce our own trade barriers and tariffs.

- Simple free trade will give Americans the widest possible choice of products and services at the lowest available prices.

- Simple free trade will give American manufacturers access to the best and least expensive raw materials in the world.
- The prosperity achieved will make us the envy of foreign people, who will pressure their own governments to reduce trade barriers.
- Powerful people in every country will profit from our open markets—and will work to prevent their governments from drawing us into war.

We don't need to negotiate trade with anyone. We don't need to sign treaties, to join world organizations, or pressure any government. We need only look out for American consumers and open our markets to everyone.

Let me quote Winston Churchill one last time:

> Our free trade plan is quite simple. We say that every [citizen] shall have the right to buy whatever he wants, wherever he wants, at his own good pleasure, without restriction or discouragement from the State.

Such a plan is one of the most important ways we can preserve peace.

THE GUILTY & THE INNOCENT

Another folly that keeps the world dangerous for us is punishing the innocent for the sins of the guilty.

At the time of the Gulf War, our president railed against Saddam Hussein—calling him a modern Hitler and claiming he was a threat to world peace. So how did the President deal with him? He ordered the deaths of thousands of innocent Iraqi citizens in bombing raids and ground attacks—and left Saddam Hussein in power.[1]

This is what usually happens when our government sallies forth to make the world safe for democracy. The bombing of Libya in 1986, for example, did nothing to harm Muammar Qaddafi, but it killed 15 innocent people.

As Robert Higgs has pointed out, this is "equivalent to bombing a prison because one has a grievance against its sadistic warden."

If Saddam Hussein was a threat to the United States and world peace, what then was Syria—which at that very time was destroying Lebanon? A government's indignation toward aggression is always selective.

But assume Saddam Hussein *was* a threat. Is that a reason to

---

[1]Dan Shaw called this "professional courtesy."

kill innocent people and expose thousands of Americans to danger? Isn't there a better way for a President to deal with a potential enemy?

Yes, there are many options available. One would be to publicly deliver a message to Mr. Hussein:

> We bear no hostility toward the people of your country. We sympathize with the hardships they bear because of you. Our quarrel is with you alone.
>
> If you carry out the plan you have threatened, we will pledge $20 million—to be given as a reward to the person who assassinates you.
>
> Everyone in the world is eligible for the reward: American citizens, citizens of other countries, Iraqi citizens, members of your Palace Guard, your cabinet—even your wives.

There are brave, daring, ingenious, ambitious people in the world who would love to try for such a reward. At least one of them probably would be successful. But, what is more important, the *potential* for such success should dissuade anyone from threatening us.

Would the President be condoning cold-blooded killing? Yes—but of just one guilty person, rather than of the thousands of innocents that die in bombing raids.

Would this cause some people to resent us? Probably, but it wouldn't upset nearly as many people as bombs and missiles would.

OFFENSE & DEFENSE

A final folly we must correct is our vulnerability to missile attack.

In 1995 there are 14 governments that are known to have the ability to fire nuclear missiles at the United States, are suspected of having the capability, or are expected to have it soon—including Russia, Belarus, Kazakhstan, Ukraine, China, India, France, Britain, Israel, Pakistan, Iran, Libya, Iraq, and North Korea.

Any single missile could destroy an entire American city—killing hundreds of thousands, if not millions, of people. It might be fired as an act of war or by accident.

To prevent attacks, our government has signed non-aggression and disarmament treaties, mostly with the Soviet Union. But these treaties have no power over governments that don't sign them. And a treaty provides no recourse if a nation cheats on it.[2]

---

[2] One President said, "We must trust, but verify." But he didn't say what he could do if verification revealed the treaty had been violated.

If a nuclear missile were fired at America, what defense has our government provided for us?

Amazingly, the answer is *none*.

Consider this:

- The U.S. government in 1995 spent $270 billion on the military—equivalent to roughly $1,000 for each American, or $4,000 for each family of four.
- Since 1945 it has spent $6 *trillion* on the military—equivalent to roughly $23,000 for every American alive today, or $91,000 for each family of four. Adjusted for inflation, the 50-year total is equal to $14 trillion in 1995 dollars—or $204,000 for every family of four.

But despite these colossal expenditures, *America has no missile defense whatsoever—no ability to shoot down incoming missiles.* We are completely helpless in the face of any petulant dictator.

Of course, the American government can respond with overwhelming nuclear power of its own—annihilating entire cities in the dictator's country. But killing other innocent people won't bring back the Americans who died.

America's ability to counterattack is supposed to be a deterrent—discouraging any foreign aggressor from ever launching an attack against us. But if, for example, Saddam Hussein is the madman described in our government's 1991 propaganda, why would *any* deterrent stop him?

And how can we be sure no missile will ever be launched against us by accident?

We can't. We are vulnerable, and we will continue to be vulnerable until America has a missile defense.

Unhistory of the Missile Defense

Since the 1960s, the United States and the Soviet Union (and now Russia) have each had the ability to deliver a nuclear missile to the other's territory.

Our politicians decided this was a good thing. Supposedly, as long as each leader knew the other could respond with a rain of missiles, neither would be willing to start a nuclear war. This method of securing peace was called the MAD doctrine (Mutually Assured Destruction).

You may think this is a scary way to protect the country. So do I.

The MAD doctrine assumes that every foreign dictator cares as much about the lives of his subjects as you care about your fellow Americans. But Leonid Brezhnev and Mao Tse-tung had already proven they were willing to sacrifice the lives of their subjects in pursuit of more power.

High-speed computers made an automatic missile defense possible by the 1960s—which should have caused rejoicing. We no longer needed to rely on the good sense of dictators.

But the politicians didn't see it that way. In 1972 the U.S. and the Soviet Union signed the Anti-Ballistic Missile (ABM) treaty—*pledging that neither country would build a missile defense.*

They said a missile defense would be "destabilizing." A country invulnerable to incoming missiles could attack another country without fear of retaliation. This would frighten the undefended nation into striking first. And so we have continued to live under the cloud of Mutually Assured Destruction—a quarter century after it became possible to remove it.

History of No Missile Defense

In 1983 Ronald Reagan decided to ignore the ABM treaty, and he announced the Strategic Defense Initiative (SDI)—a plan to build a system to intercept and destroy incoming missiles. Part of the defensive system would be based on the ground and part in orbit.

Unfortunately, he turned the project over to the Department of Defense—a government agency. After a dozen years and $30 billion, we still don't have a missile defense.

Meanwhile, in 1987 the Soviet leaders acknowledged that they had broken the ABM treaty years before and were developing their own anti-missile system. Where that program stands now, I don't know.

But it's obvious that the breakup of the Soviet Union wipes out any argument for honoring the treaty.

Can It Be Done?

Many politicians and pundits have ridiculed the very concept of a missile defense—calling it "Star Wars" and saying it can't be built. They claim SDI is just an expensive boondoggle.

Is a missile defense possible? Definitely. It is possible now to detect the launching of a missile anywhere in the world; it's possible to track its course; and it's possible to intercept one missile with another one. The task is to combine the three capabilities into one operation.

The only important question is how much it would cost.

Most estimates for a working defense—made by both friends and foes of the idea—range between $200 billion and $1 trillion.

Many people might think the system would be worthwhile even if it did cost $1 trillion—but many others wouldn't agree.

Fortunately, we don't have to speculate on the cost of building a reliable system—or throw tax money up in the air and hope it lands somewhere useful. Someone else can be persuaded to risk the money to find out.

How to Get Things Done

Before I explain how, let me pose a hypothetical problem.

Suppose in 1980 the Defense Department determined that an important weapon needed to be improved dramatically. So the Department ordered a task force to increase the weapon's efficiency 100 times over within ten years—while cutting its cost by 90%.

Aside from the Manhattan Project that built the first atomic bomb during World War II, I'm not aware of any government program achieving such success.

But in fact similar achievements occur all the time—outside of government. They are so commonplace that we usually don't even notice them.

Perhaps the best example is the personal computer (PC). The PC of 1990 was at least 100 times as fast, generally could hold 100 times as much data, and could perform 100 times as many functions as its 1980 counterpart, which was clumsy by comparison. And the 1990 model sold for a fraction of the 1980 PC.

What caused computers to progress so rapidly while weapons systems improved only marginally?

The hope for profit. People needed and wanted the computers and would reward those who produced faster, more powerful machines. Firms like Microsoft, Lotus, Adobe, Dell, Intel, and others grew spectacularly during the 1980s and 1990s by responding to public needs—making their founders and shareholders fabulously wealthy.

Hundreds of other companies tried and failed. Some people risked their life savings but couldn't turn out a product that enough people would pay for. But it was their *own* savings they risked—not yours. And many who failed on the first try succeeded on the second.

Today the Department of Defense uses tens of thousands of fast, powerful personal computers. But it wouldn't have them if it had tried to develop them itself.

How to Build a Missile Defense

The only way to build a missile defense quickly, inexpensively, and effectively is to harness the same thirst for profit.

No, I'm not suggesting—as some people do—that government should be run like a business. It can't be done. A business operates efficiently by gaining the willing cooperation of everyone involved— financial backers, managers, employees, customers, and suppliers— and thus it can survive only by providing what people want.

But government runs on coercion. Inefficiency can continue indefinitely because no one can choose to stop supporting it—no matter how poorly a program operates. And a government program has no fear of competition.

Nor am I suggesting that the government award a contract to the lowest private bidder. That has its own problems—underbidding, cost overruns, and so on. And if the company that wins the bid fails to deliver, a great deal of time has been lost.

Instead, the government should post a reward of $50 billion (or some such sum) for the first company that produces a working missile defense. Not an idea, not a plan—but an actual demonstration that meets the performance and cost standards the government has set.

This way we might have a working system within three or four years—rather than the dozen years the government has already spent without success.

Drawbacks?

Objections might be raised to this plan—questions of national security, politicizing the rules of the contest, oversight of the systems operation by government employees, and so on.

But these aren't problems with *this* system. They're problems with *any* defense system—whether designed by the government or a private company.

A missile defense won't stop terrorists or foreign agents from smuggling a bomb into the U.S. But Stealth bombers or aircraft carriers or tanks don't protect against those things either. A missile defense can't make you a tuna sandwich, but that's no reason to leave the country defenseless against the principal threat—nuclear missiles launched from outside America.

With a Proper Defense

Once a defense is in place, America finally will be secure. We will know that no madman, no accident, no provocation can rain nuclear missiles on American cities.

MAKING AMERICA SAFE

By interfering in foreign affairs, by spending too much on purely offensive weapons, and by forgoing a missile defense, America today is vulnerable—and that makes it seem that we need all sorts of policies and expensive armaments.

But we don't need those things. We don't need troops overseas. We don't need the ability to attack faraway countries. We don't need to buy the support of foreign dictators. And we don't need to spend $270 billion a year on the military.

We need only to protect ourselves.

There is much we can do to avoid war—to assure that America's youth never go to war again, and that our lives and homes are secure against foreign attack:

1. End all loans and giveaways to foreign governments and international agencies. U.S. taxpayers shouldn't be drained to help foreign governments grow. And stopping the give-aways keeps our government from taking sides in foreign disputes, thereby reducing the resentment of other govern-ments and foreign terrorists.

2. Get the American government out of all alliances, treaties, and international organizations. America doesn't need to be a joiner to have good relations with the rest of the world.

3. End all arms sales by the government. There are few things our government does to provoke more hostility among foreign people than selling arms to their enemies. (This doesn't rule out unsubsidized arms sales by private firms.)

4. Open our markets to goods and services from all over the world. Nothing could do more to give foreign people a vested interest in keeping the peace with us, and such a policy costs us nothing in taxes or jobs. To the contrary, it makes us far more prosperous.

5. When a foreign leader threatens the United States, announce that carrying out any warlike act against us will lead to a multi-million-dollar reward for his assassination.

6. Establish a defense that protects against missiles launched from anywhere in the world—a system built on speculation by private companies competing for a reward.

By staying out of the perpetual wars of Europe, the Middle East, and Asia, we will be safer and more prosperous.

This isn't isolationism. It is the best kind of internationalism—relationships between people, not between governments. This kind of internationalism breeds common interests, goodwill, and friendship.

And, most of all, it breeds peace.

Chapter 23

How to Fix Social Security Once and for All

I know a dandy way you can make a lot of money.

Here's the idea: Offer a retirement plan that pays a pension more generous than people can get elsewhere. Every payday each customer will pay you a small portion of his paycheck—say, 2%. You promise that when he reaches age 62 you'll send him a monthly check equal to what he was making when he retired.

As the money comes in from your first customers, spend it all and live a lush life. You don't need to keep money in reserve for your customers' retirement. When the time comes, just pay them with money you receive from new, younger customers. So long as you keep attracting new customers to pay into the plan, you'll be okay.

If you ever have trouble attracting enough new money to keep your promises, just change the rules. Raise the retirement age to 65. Or lower the promised benefits. Or raise the amounts deducted from your customers' paychecks—from 2% to 5% to 10% to 15%, however much you need.

It's a sweet deal.

Back in the Real World

So what's to prevent you from doing this?

Well, for one thing, it's illegal. Try it and the government will shut you down, haul you into court, and send you off to prison.

You'd be operating a Ponzi Scheme—named after Charles Ponzi, who set up a similar plan in Boston in 1920. He promised to pay investors 50% profit on their money in just 45 days. Gullible people poured money into his plan. But he couldn't possibly earn enough on the money to deliver the rate of return he promised. So when someone wanted to withdraw his principal and interest, Ponzi simply paid him from money received from new investors.

Eventually he couldn't meet the demands for repayment, and his scheme collapsed. He ended up going to jail for 3½ years.

The Double Standard

Another such scheme was started in 1935, and this one is still going.

It's called Social Security. It, too, is a Ponzi plan.

When Social Security was established in 1935, a trust fund was set up—to keep the money collected in taxes, so it could be returned with interest to the taxpayer when he retired. This is called a "fully funded" system—one in which the full amount of money promised for the future is kept in a fund drawing interest.

But it took politicians only four years to change the rules. After all, you can't expect them to keep their hands off a large sum of money. So in 1939 Social Security was transformed into a "pay as you go" system—one in which the amounts paid to beneficiaries come from taxes collected the same year.

The Social Security tax you pay isn't put aside as a nest egg for you. It is paid out to others older than you. The money your grandmother receives from Social Security comes from your paycheck. And if *you* receive anything from Social Security, even if you've been paying into it for 40 years, what you get will be taken from the paychecks of younger people.

The system is a Ponzi scheme pure and simple. However, it differs from a private Ponzi scheme in two ways: (1) the government can't go to jail, and (2) the government can change the rules at any time to keep the scheme going.

And, in fact, the rules are changed almost yearly. The tax rate is increased about once every three years. The amount of your wages that can be taxed has risen twenty times over—from an original maximum of $3,000 to the current $60,600. And the benefit schedules are changed frequently. In other words, the government does whatever it needs to buy a little more time for the system.

Crises

But the game is getting tougher. As life expectancy rises, a larger and larger share of the population is retired. That means each person still working has to support more people who are collecting.

In addition, there is continual pressure on politicians to sweeten the benefits.

This leads to a Social Security crisis every few years. Each time, it becomes apparent that at current rates of taxation and benefits, the system will be insolvent within a few years. To fix this, a bipartisan commission is appointed, some reforms are enacted, and Social Security is pronounced completely safe and secure for another 50 years.

But time seems to go by rather quickly in the political world. The 50 years seem to last only four or five years—until it becomes apparent that at current rates of taxation and benefits, the system will be insolvent within a few years. So another bipartisan commission is appointed, more reforms are enacted, and Social Security is again pronounced completely sound and secure for another 50 years.

But then four or five years later . . . Well, you get the point.

The latest expectation is that Social Security will be in the red in 2012 if it isn't fixed soon.

Of course, part of the fix always is to raise taxes. The tax rate has risen sevenfold since Social Security's founding in 1935.

Today your employer must deduct 7.65% from the first $60,600 of your income each year. In addition, he has to match that dollar for dollar. So roughly 15% of the first $60,600 of your employment earnings is lost to Social Security.[1]

YOU PAY IT ALL

Although it may seem that you pay only 7.65% in Social Security tax, you actually pay the entire 15.30%—the 7.65% deduction you see and the 7.65% your employer seems to pay.

This is such an important point that we need to digress for a moment.

An employer hires you because he expects to derive a certain value from your work. Based on what he expects to gain, he calculates a price he can pay for your services.

Let's say that price is $50,000 per year. If you demand more than that, he can't afford to hire you.

There are expenses attached to your job you might not notice—the cost of your working area, tools or supplies needed to do your job, regulations your employer must obey in order to employ you, a health plan, state taxes such as unemployment insurance, and so on. If all

---

[1]Also you and your employer each pay a Medicare tax of 1.45% on all your earnings, but that's a different subject.

those items together cost, say, $10,000 a year, they reduce to $40,000 the amount he can pay you.

Then we come to the Social Security tax. He has to reduce his offer still further to accommodate what he must pay to Social Security. If he pays you a gross wage of $37,157 per year, he can pay 7.65% of that ($2,843) to the government for Social Security, without exceeding his limit of $50,000:

Wages he pays to you	$ 37,157
His share of Social Security	2,843
His other employment costs	10,000
His total cost of your employment	**$ 50,000**

Since the employer is willing to pay $50,000 for your services, if he didn't have to pay $2,843 to Social Security, that money probably would go to you.

Suppose Social Security were abolished tomorrow morning. Some employers would quickly add the $2,843 to what they pay their employees. However, your employer might decide he could keep for himself what he's been paying to Social Security. But not for long. He'd quickly see his workforce dwindling. Employees who had been considering a job switch would speed up their plans, and look for a company that pays the extra $2,843. And few job seekers would give your employer a second look.

In very little time, the employer would be pressured to pay the $2,843 to you as increased wages. Salaries always rise to the maximum amount available—the amount at which it's still profitable for your employer to hire you.

The tax your employer pays to Social Security today is money that would have gone to you. So, in effect, he pays no tax at all; you pay the full 15%.

SOCIAL SECURITY TAXES GO UP

The Social Security tax has risen from a combined employer-employee rate of 2% in 1935 to today's combined tax of 15.30%.

And there's no reason to believe the tax rate won't continue to rise. As administered by politicians, Social Security is inherently unworkable, because the politicians will always spend the money they take in. This means the money doesn't earn interest, as savings do. So as the retired population grows, it requires higher and higher taxes to pay the benefits the politicians have promised.

The upper graph on page 164 shows how much the tax has risen so far. How high will it go in the future?

We can see where Social Security is headed by looking at the lower graph. It shows Social Security tax rates in countries that have had a Social Security system longer than we have.

In Italy, 56% of a worker's pay goes to the government for Social Security taxes. The worker may not realize the tax is that high, because he sees only a 9.14% deduction on his payroll check stub. But the employer has to pay 46.45%. The worker's net pay could be 61% higher if the employer didn't have to pay Social Security tax.

The rates shown in the graph suggest what we have to look forward to.

Higher Rates or Lower Benefits?

Most people think Congress would never renege on its promises to Social Security recipients—no matter how bad federal finances become.

But when the only alternative is to raise the Social Security tax rate to 35% or 40%—or to cut off food stamps to the poor—there may be no choice but to cut Social Security benefits. The politicians who once were so keen on sharing the wealth will now ask you to share the pain—at a time in your life when you may not have the option to go back to work and make up the difference.

WHAT WE PASS ON TO OUR CHILDREN

Many polls show that most people today believe their children will endure a lower standard of living—unlike generations past, which expected continual improvement. In 1995 a survey by Republican pollster Frank Luntz found that 78% believe it will be more difficult for the next generation to achieve the American dream.

Most people can't explain their pessimism. They just feel the economy is heading into reverse. Simple as the fear may be, it is a correct one. There's a powerful reason for the falling standard of living.

The reason is too much government. The graph on page 3 shows how taxes take more and more of our incomes. Most of this money goes down the drain, providing no benefit to us—even indirectly. That means we're working harder for less. And our children and grandchildren will be working even longer hours to take home even less.

Economists Joel Kotlikoff, Alan Auerbach, and Jagadeesh Gokhale project that Social Security, Medicare, government pensions, and interest on the debt will require future generations to pay the

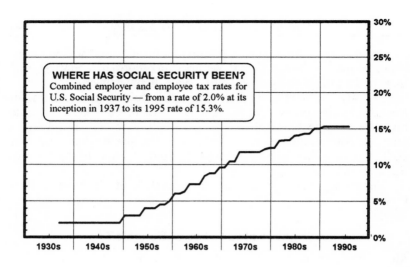

WHERE HAS SOCIAL SECURITY BEEN?
Combined employer and employee tax rates for
U.S. Social Security — from a rate of 2.0% at its
inception in 1937 to its 1995 rate of 15.3%.

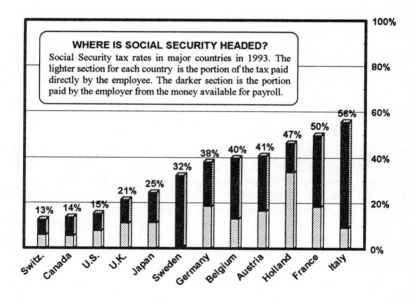

WHERE IS SOCIAL SECURITY HEADED?
Social Security tax rates in major countries in 1993. The
lighter section for each country is the portion of the tax paid
directly by the employee. The darker section is the portion
paid by the employer from the money available for payroll.

government 71% of everything they earn during their lifetimes. The
only alternative is for government to renege on many of the promises it has made.

What kind of lives will our grandchildren have if they can keep
only 29% of what they earn?

It isn't just rhetoric when someone says we're passing the bills for government spending on to our children—although we may think our children will pass the bills on to *their* children.

Each generation may pass the debt on, but it can't pass the interest on. That has to be paid yearly—and it keeps getting larger. Every generation already is suffering from the government spending of earlier generations, and the bills get larger and larger. Our parents paid around 35% of their income in taxes. Now we're paying 47%. What will it be for the next generation? 55%? 60%? 71%?

IGNORING THE PROBLEM

The politicians refuse to acknowledge any of this—and so nothing is done to stop the costs from mounting higher. Politicians still cite Social Security as a crowning achievement of the New Deal—as proof that "government works."

Both Democrats and Republicans use Social Security as a political football—warning the elderly that their opponents will water down their Social Security or Medicare benefits, while denying any intent to do so themselves. And both are afraid the denials won't be believed. Whenever Social Security is mentioned, the politicians rush to say, "If it ain't broke, don't fix it"—as though it didn't break 55 years ago when Congress switched to a pay-as-you-go system.

Public Skepticism

The public, however, knows full well the system *is* broken. Polls routinely show that about two thirds of the American people don't expect to receive a dime from Social Security.

A Wirthlin poll found that 68% of the American people don't believe "Social Security benefits will be available to me when I need them." Here's the breakdown by age group:

Age group	% who expect nothing
18-30 years old	66%
31-49 years old	81%
50 years old & older	40%
All ages	**68%**

Even among people who are only 15 years from retirement, two out of five don't expect Social Security to survive until they start drawing their pensions.

THE PERFECT SYSTEM

The public is right. Social Security is broken, and it soon will collapse.

But until we know what Social Security *should* be, there's no basis for reform. If we were starting from scratch, what kind of system would we create?

Obviously, it should be a fully funded system. The money you put in should be saved and invested on your behalf. And what you receive when you retire would be based on what you put in. With this system, your pension wouldn't depend on contributions from future generations.

Actually, a fully funded system already exists. In fact, there are many of them. They are lifetime annuities offered by private insurance companies. You pay into the annuity over the years, the insurance company invests the money for you, and it pays you a lifetime pension when you retire.

When you own an annuity, you have a firm contract with an insurance company. You know how much you have to pay every year—and, unless you agree otherwise, the amount you pay doesn't change. You know how much you'll receive when you retire—and, unless you agree otherwise, the amount you'll receive never changes.

This is the voluntary, contractual, non-political way of providing for "Social Security." When you have an annuity, you don't have to worry about Congress changing the rules.

Many employers already provide pensions for their employees. If there were no Social Security system, competition for the best employees would inspire a great many more to do the same.

What Should We Do

Private annuities work. They've existed for hundreds of years.

Government doesn't work, although it has existed for thousands of years.

Governmental Social Security is a fraud that can never be fixed. It is headed for bankruptcy. The only question is what to do about it.

In looking for a solution, we must face up to one unchangeable fact:

> *Given the current tax rates and the promised benefits, there is no way everyone can get from Social Security what he's been told he will get.*

Most of the trillions of dollars paid into Social Security over the past 60 years have been spent. The money can't be retrieved. The promised benefits can be paid only if tax rates are raised sharply. On the other hand, tax rates can be kept where they are only by reneging on the promised benefits.

So we really have two choices:

1. Keep patching up Social Security, either by raising taxes until they reach, say, 70%—or by reducing benefits steadily until they're the equivalent of about $100 per month. *Or . . .*
2. Act now to stop the problem from growing. Stop promising increased benefits, and get government out of Social Security entirely, so that no one will ever again be cheated by it.

Social Security will always be a tool for politicians to one-up their opponents by promising bigger benefits now and leaving the necessary taxes for their successors to impose. So it will be a chronic problem until we get it out of the hands of government.

And the longer we wait to get the government out, the more painful it will be when we do.

How to Save Social Security

Because expectations for receiving Social Security benefits are so low, we may be able to solve the problem at a relatively small cost—if we get the government out now.

Millions of people depend on Social Security today. They worked for decades. Their plans assumed that Social Security would provide for them when they retired. I believe these people must be taken care of. But I don't trust the government to do it.

Instead, the government should buy from a private insurance company an annuity for everyone who depends on Social Security. The annuities should provide lifetime incomes similar to what Social Security has promised.[2]

How much will this cost? A mountain of money. The exact size of the mountain is something only the government has the information to calculate. But, based on the amounts now being paid out each year, I estimate the cost to be roughly $5 trillion. This is, in effect, the accumulated deficit of 56 years of "pay as you go."

Because there probably isn't enough money available to the

---

[2]In order to compete I would assume that any private company would participate in a reassurance plan that would guarantee its ability to make good on its annuity.

government to cover all the liabilities, I believe annuities should be provided only for those who truly need them. This means some kind of simple, non-intrusive means test must be applied to each retiree. Those that don't rely on Social Security shouldn't aggravate the problem further. The maximum monthly Social Security benefit is $1,100; there are many retired people to whom that isn't a critical amount.

People over the age of 50 who are nearing retirement and who have made plans based on receiving Social Security should also receive annuities. Those annuities would be smaller and wouldn't begin paying out until age 65.

In the next chapter I'll discuss a way to pay for the annuities.

Of the current retirees and those over 50 who qualify for the annuities, I would hope that a great many would waive the right to an annuity and get along by other means—although we can't count on that.

And what about those under 50? To them we offer the greatest gift possible: *You will never again have to pay the 15% Social Security tax.*

You will be able to fund a real retirement for yourself—putting aside 5%, 10%, 15%, or whatever you want from your pay.

TO THE ELDERLY

If you are one of the elderly who depend on Social Security, you'll get a private annuity you can count on. You'll never again have to worry that Congress will alter your pension.

But if you don't need Social Security to survive, please consider waiving your right to the annuity. I know you paid a great deal into Social Security. But the government squandered all of it. It's gone.

The annuity won't be paid for with your money. It will be taken from your children and your grandchildren. Let them have a clean start. Give them the opportunity to build their own lives without the awful burden of paying taxes for the pensions of others.

You've worked hard and earned a retirement that you can afford without becoming a burden to others, without losing your self-respect, without becoming part of a pressure group.

For your own sake, for the sake of your children, for the sake of your grandchildren, give it up.

WHAT KIND OF AMERICA?

We need to decide what kind of America we want. Do we want a country that sinks ever more deeply into debt—in which generations fight with each other over a constantly shrinking pie?

Or do we make the changes necessary now and get America back on track again—so that people are no longer wards of the state? We can have a country in which our citizens are responsible, self-reliant, and self-respectful.

With regard to Social Security, we have only two choices:

1. Get Social Security completely out of the hands of the government—and do it quickly. Give everyone a fresh start with a guarantee that from now on he'll get what he's promised.
2. Leave it in the government's hands—and put up with periodic crises, higher and higher taxes, and more and more hostility among the generations.

For me the choice is obvious.

Chapter 24

A Freedom Budget

Not long ago Congress passed a program to balance the budget within a few years—a year-by-year blueprint for getting from big deficits to no deficits. After decades of growing debt, the federal government would finally live within its means.

The Congressmen cheered and congratulated themselves, and their friends in the press hailed the historic event.

But the following year, Congress discarded the plan and resumed its old, deficit ways.

I'm referring to the budget plan passed by the Democratic Congress in 1993. Despite the big fanfare, by 1994 the plan was completely forgotten. It was just one more government promise sitting on the trash heap.

In 1980 Ronald Reagan promised to balance the budget by 1984, but in eight years in office he didn't propose a single balanced budget—nor did he use his veto to keep Congress from spending more and more of our money.

The Gramm-Rudman-Hollings plan of 1985 was supposed to bring about a balanced budget in 1991, but it was ignored as soon as it got in the way of Congressional spending.

In 1990 the Republicans and Democrats joined hands to enact a program to balance the budget by 1993; it included an enormous tax increase and stringent spending limits. The plan projected a $156 billion *surplus* in 1995—which turned out to be a $192 billion *deficit*. We still pay the oppressive taxes, but the spending cuts disappeared—and the politicians' projection was off by $348 billion. That's not close enough—not even for government work.

The Republicans had their turn in 1995. They passed a 7-year plan—designed to balance the budget by 2002. But it contained all the usual flaws:

- *No budget cuts:* Despite one side talking about "smaller government" and the other complaining about "mean-spirited cuts," the plan calls for spending increases of $45 billion a year for the next 7 years.
- *More and more debt:* The budget plan projects more than $640 billion dollars in new debt over the next 7 years—money that must be repaid by taxes taken from you, your children, and your grandchildren.
- *Not even balanced:* And the budget won't actually be balanced in 2002. Instead, a projected deficit of $108.4 billion is supposed to be offset by an expected Social Security surplus of $115 billion. (We've already seen how unlikely that is.)
- *No chance:* Even the plan's meek promises are no more likely to be kept than any of its predecessors. It's just a statement of intent—not binding on the future Congresses that are supposed to make the actual spending cuts. Even if Congress tries to stick to the program, the plan will be aborted by the automatic spending increases that kick in during the next recession—surely before 2002.

In other words, the "balanced budget" plan is a sham, pure and simple.

The Mark of Politicians

The budget deficits measure how untrustworthy politicians are.

- Almost every politician claims to oppose deficits. But no one ever proposes the spending cuts needed to balance the budget now. Instead, they talk about some more courageous Congress in some mythical far-off year that will balance the budget without inconvenience to anyone. But the current Congress takes all the bows for its good intentions. They are like drug addicts who promise to enter a rehabilitation program—after one more fix.
- Politicians preach that government is too big and too oppressive, and they call for "smaller government." Then they congratulate themselves for slowing its growth slightly—leaving intact the government they said was too big and too oppressive.
- Politicians say tax rates are outrageous, that high taxes are choking off growth and destroying American families. And then they propose cutting taxes by an insignificant 1% or

2%—to take effect as soon as their impossible budget dream comes true in the year 2002.

- Politicians criticize easy targets like the National Endowment for the Arts or the bee-keeping subsidy, but they don't get rid of them. They cut the programs by only 5% or so—or just slow down their growth—and then act as though they've done us a favor.

We have to understand that *politicians don't want to reduce government.*

And it isn't because they think the spending cuts would hurt too many people. It's because they know it would hurt *them.* No matter what they say, neither Democrats nor Republicans want to give up the power that allows them to bestow favors and exemptions on friends.

Our salvation won't come from politicians. We need people who will go to Washington not to reform government programs or to reduce them, but to get rid of them. We need leaders who don't want to run the country, but who want to restore our right to run our own lives. We need legislators who don't want to be politicians, but simply want to enjoy for themselves the freedom America once knew.

HOW MUCH GOVERNMENT CAN WE STAND?

As we've seen in earlier chapters, all the federal intrusions into education, health care, crime control, welfare, and other areas have done nothing to improve the country. On the contrary, they have degraded education, health care, and crime control, and institutionalized a welfare program that breeds criminals.

The degradation comes from two intrinsic elements of federal programs:

1. The federal government extracts huge taxes from you and your neighbors, takes a healthy cut for itself, and then sends what's left back to your area to perform its intended function. The money would achieve far more if it never left your state.
2. Federal funding means federal rules. It means that 535 politicians in Washington will set rules for your local police department, your board of education, your local hospital, your family doctor, your streets, your town's welfare system. These 535 know-it-alls can't balance the federal checkbook, and they don't have time to read any of the bills they pass, but they claim to know more about running your city than you or any of your neighbors—and they claim to know better than you how to manage your life. No wonder federal programs are such disasters.

The Founding Fathers had good reason to limit the federal government to a few simple functions. They knew that government is coercion—and that coercion is a dangerous weapon. They believed that whatever coercion seemed necessary should be administered very close to home, where citizens could keep it from getting out of control.

We have to get the federal government out of the dozens of areas where it has no business.

Government That's Truly Small

If we shrink the federal government from its current yearly budget of $1.5 trillion down to just its constitutional functions, we could get by with a budget of only $100 billion a year plus the interest that has to be paid on the federal debt (about $285 billion in 1995).

Does $100 billion seem too little?

Consider this: In 1950, the total budget of the federal government, excluding interest, was only $37 billion.[1]

In 1950 there were no Departments of Education, Energy, Housing, or Health & Human Services, no EPA, no War on Drugs, no National Endowment for the Arts, and no Equal Opportunity Commission. There were very few of the thousands of federal programs that today regulate our lives and monitor our every move—and cost so much.

What terrible things happened to America in 1950 in such a government-starved environment?

- New York didn't fall into the Atlantic Ocean.
- Although it was the height of the Cold War, America wasn't overrun by the Soviets.
- The crime rate was a fraction of today's, our children were far better educated, welfare wasn't even a public issue, health care prices weren't going through the roof, federal and state budgets were roughly balanced from year to year, and people weren't shouting at each other the way they do today.

If you value something the federal government has taken on since then, realize that it might be handled more efficiently by state or local governments—or by private agencies.

You may feel you want to hang on to a favorite federal program or two. But government doesn't come with a menu. You can't pick and choose which federal programs you want. When you give the government the power to confiscate money to (for example) take care of your parents, you automatically give it the power to confiscate money to take care of everyone else's parents, everyone's

---

[1]Equivalent to about $241 billion in 1995 dollars.

children, everyone's brother-in-law, people who don't work, people who work but don't make a particular wage, people who prefer a life of drugs or alcohol, people who prefer playing the horses to getting a job, people who are politically connected, people who believe the government owes them a job, and companies who want billion-dollar contracts.

In short, when you give the government the power to confiscate money for whatever you think is important, you give it the power to confiscate money for what everyone else thinks is important.

We can wish for anything we want. But we can choose only from what is possible. Either:

- We shrink the federal government dramatically—to a small fraction of today's size—and "bind it down from mischief with the chains of the Constitution," as Thomas Jefferson said. Or . . .
- We resign ourselves to a government out of control that grows and grows and swamps our children and grandchildren with debt—leaving them with a life that's impoverished compared to what we have enjoyed.

THE DEBT

In its 1995 fiscal year the federal government collected $1.3 trillion in taxes. But that wasn't enough to pay the $1.5 trillion in bills it ran up. So another $200 billion was added to the federal debt.

The federal government has been doing this regularly for decades. In the past 60 years, it has balanced its budget only 8 times. In the past 30 years, it has balanced the budget only once—in 1969.

During this time, the politicians have run up $5 trillion in debt for which you, I, our children, and our grandchildren are obligated.

Obviously, we have to stop the deficits—and stop them *now,* not in seven years.

But we must do more than that. We have to get rid of the federal debt itself—the $5 trillion worth of credit-card bills the politicians have charged to us.

Is the Debt an Investment?

Big government's friends tell us we shouldn't worry about the federal debt. After all, families and corporations go into debt—and some of them carry debt permanently. Why shouldn't government borrow to make investments in our future—investments that will save us money in the long run?

But corporations and families make sound investments in homes, or in business plans and enterprises that build wealth. Government doesn't make investments; it just spends money.

The politicians tell us their spending plans will save us money later—by keeping kids out of jail, or by turning welfare clients into taxpaying workers, or by making the military efficient, or something else that would make sense only if there were evidence that *any* government program works. Never does a politician review the programs enacted ten years ago—to identify a single program that actually did save us money.

But there's an even bigger difference between private and government debt. Families and corporations must repay what they borrow—and repay it out of their own earnings. So most people are cautious about borrowing. And they make regular payments to clear the debt by a specified date.

Politicians don't plan to repay what they borrow in our names. They spend on whatever they want, and the amount exceeding tax receipts is simply put on *our* tab. When they leave office, they have no personal responsibility for the debts they've run up. They just collect enormous pensions and praise themselves for a lifetime of "public service."

In other words, unlike families and corporations, politicians don't feel the burden of debt—only the elation of spending. So *they have no incentive to restrain themselves*. They can spend your money without limit to reward their friends.

This isn't a theory. It's a fact. And the proof is the $5 trillion federal debt—a debt so mind-boggling that few people believe it will ever be paid off.

TWO CHOICES

There's still time to get the debt under control—a little time before tax rates of 50%, 60%, or higher are needed to cover just the interest.

But it will take strong will and determination to get the federal government's hands out of every area not authorized by the Constitution—a determination today's politicians don't possess.

Again, we have to realize we have only two choices.

- Get completely off the politicians' merry-go-round and shrink the federal government to the small, limited enterprise the Founding Fathers envisioned; *or*
- Resign ourselves to government getting larger and larger, taxes getting more and more oppressive, Social Security taxes rising

and rising, and the debt becoming more and more of a burden on our children.

DEBT-FINANCED ASSETS

If we're willing to make the first choice, how can we pull it off?

Over the past 60 years, the federal government collected $19 trillion in taxes—a sum equal to $73,699 for every man, woman, and child living in America today.[2]

During the same 60 years, the government ran up $5 trillion worth of debt. Your share is about $19,045. Your spouse and children each have a similar share. (And this doesn't include the millions of other liabilities to which the government has made you a cosigner—student loans, mortgages, bank deposits, and much more.)

What has the government done with the money it has confiscated or borrowed?

As you would expect when people spend money they did nothing to earn, much of it has been squandered with nothing to show for it. In the past 30 years, for example, over $5 trillion have been spent on poverty programs—leading to more poverty in the 1990s than there was 30 years earlier.

But a good deal of the debt has been used to buy or build things. They may not seem valuable because of the way they're used now. But they might become much more valuable if sold to people who knew how to use them productively.

These assets include such things as:

Buildings, including public housing	Reserves of oil and other commodities
Vacant land	Mineral rights
National parks	Water rights
Vehicles	Unneeded military hardware
Aircraft	Unneeded military bases
Equipment	Dams
Business enterprises	Pipelines
Oil rights	

For example, the federal government owns 29% of all the land in the United States—a total of 649 million acres, or 1 million square miles. It owns 54% of all the land in the 13 western states—365 million acres in Alaska alone. As of 1991 it owned 441,000 buildings.

On the rare occasion when the government closes a facility, such as with the military base closings of the 1990s, it doesn't

---

[2] $19 trillion divided by 262,527,000 people.

usually sell the property; it converts it into a national park or tourist attraction—still owned by the federal government. Although the politicians congratulate themselves for eliminating waste, the facilities continue to cost money.

The assets have been purchased by loading the American people with enormous debt. They may provide the key to getting rid of that debt.

If we shrink the government to what the Constitution permits, it won't need most of these assets. In fact, over 90% of them could be sold—returned to the American people to be used productively.

- Grazing land should be privately owned, so its owners can negotiate with livestock owners for grazing rights—instead of conducting political battles over whether the government should charge ranchers more or less.
- Business enterprises operated by the government—such as public power companies—are the playthings of politicians. They should be sold to private companies to operate as profit-making operations that have to provide their customers with what they want in order to succeed. In addition, the military and other government agencies can save money by selling off their printing facilities, laundry plants, and other auxiliary operations, and then contracting with private owners for the necessary services.
- The government owns thousands of buildings across America that will serve no government purpose—once the federal government stops hampering education, welfare, housing, pension plans, crime control, and health care. These buildings should be sold and put to productive use by private owners.
- National parks should be sold to non-profit trusts and private companies who can continue to operate them for the public, but in ways that keep them clean and valuable—an incentive government employees don't have.

There are those who on principle strongly oppose the sale of the western lands—or some other favorite government properties. And there are those who believe they should be sold even if there were no budget problems.

Whatever you believe, the truth is we have no choice. We must sell these properties in order to reduce the terrifying interest costs awaiting our children. And then we must make sure that politicians can never again put us in the position of having to make such choices.

Realize that selling the properties doesn't make them disappear. Whoever buys them will have to use them for popular purposes, or else lose money on the investment. No one is going to turn Yosemite into a garbage dump; it would be a waste of money to do so.

Realize, too, that there are others who want the same things you do. There already are organizations that buy government properties to keep them off the market. They will make sure that national parks and other properties continue to be used as they are now. But with the government out of the picture, they most likely will make the properties much more attractive and useful.

Benefits from the Sale

How important is it that we sell these assets? Consider this: If the federal government's unneeded assets can be sold for $12 trillion over a 6-year period, we can achieve the following:

1. Everyone who has become dependent on Social Security can receive a private annuity. No retiree will be left in the lurch—and neither you nor your children will ever again have to pay the 15% Social Security tax. You'll be able to establish any retirement plan you want. And you'll undoubtedly be able to achieve a far more comfortable retirement than Social Security offers, while devoting much less than 15% of your working income.

2. We can balance the budget *immediately* in 1998—the first fiscal year of the new presidential term. No more deficits. No more Soviet-style 5-year and 7-year plans to balance the budget. We will stop the bleeding immediately.

3. We can pay off the entire accumulated federal debt by the year 2003. You, your children, and your grandchildren will be freed of the enormous burden the politicians have piled on top of you. Interest costs will be reduced to zero.

4. We can repeal all federal income taxes—the personal income tax, the capital gains tax, taxes on dividends and interest, and the corporate tax—as well as the estate and gift taxes. Everything you earn from 1998 onward will be yours to use as *you* see fit. No more keeping records to please the government, no more living in fear of the IRS.[3]

5. The share of the national income taxed away by government at all levels will drop immediately from 49% to 28%. Your total tax burden will have been cut almost in half within one year. You'll see the difference in larger take-home pay, better working conditions, and lower prices for the things you buy.

The table on the facing page shows how the debt can be eliminated over a 6-year period. The graphs on page 180 show the

---

[3] The remaining taxes would be mostly customs duties and excise taxes.

GETTING RID OF THE INCOME TAX & THE FEDERAL DEBT
The Federal Budget, 1995 - 2004 (billions of dollars)

Fiscal year:	1995	1996	1997	1998	1999	2000	2001	2002	2003	2004
Revenue										
Personal income, estate, & gift taxes	589	617	646	0	0	0	0	0	0	0
Corporate income tax	151	166	183	0	0	0	0	0	0	0
Social Security tax	484	509	534	0	0	0	0	0	0	0
Other taxes	123	131	139	148	157	167	178	189	100	100
Asset sales				2,900	3,200	2,700	1,600	1,100	500	0
Total Revenue	1,347	1,417	1,475	3,048	3,357	2,867	1,778	1,289	600	100
Spending										
Interest	234	250	259	266	266	265	154	80	24	0
Purchase Social Security annuities				2,250	2,800	195	0	0	0	0
Social Security payments	336	357	379	230	15	0	0	0	0	0
Other spending	1,305	1,337	1,368	300	250	200	150	100	100	100
Total Spending	1,539	1,588	1,627	3,046	3,331	660	304	180	124	100
Surplus/(Deficit)	(192)	(170)	(152)	1	26	2,207	1,474	1,109	476	0
Total Debt at End of Fiscal Year	4,962	5,132	5,284	5,283	5,257	3,050	1,577	467	(9)	(9)
Total Budget without Annuities	1,539	1,588	1,627	796	531	465	304	180	124	100
Cumulative asset sales				2,900	6,100	8,800	10,400	11,500	12,000	12,000

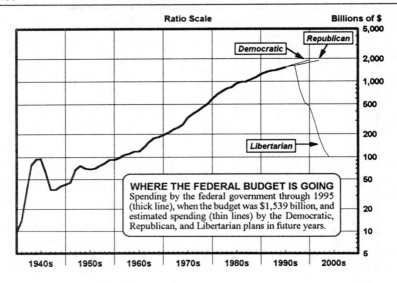

Ratio Scale

Billions of $

WHERE THE FEDERAL BUDGET IS GOING
Spending by the federal government through 1995
(thick line), when the budget was $1,539 billion, and
estimated spending (thin lines) by the Democratic,
Republican, and Libertarian plans in future years.

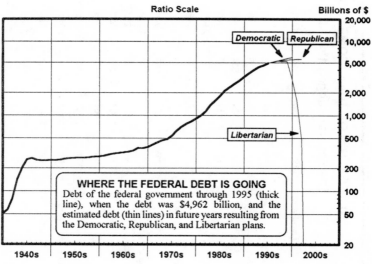

Ratio Scale

Billions of $

WHERE THE FEDERAL DEBT IS GOING
Debt of the federal government through 1995 (thick
line), when the debt was $4,962 billion, and the
estimated debt (thin lines) in future years resulting from
the Democratic, Republican, and Libertarian plans.

difference between this plan and the Republican plan. The latter
merely slows the growth of government—allowing government to
continue taking a larger share of the national income and allowing
the debt to continue growing. My Libertarian plan cuts the government dramatically and reduces the debt to zero.[4]

---

[4]The plans shown in the graphs are those that have been proposed by the
Democratic President, the Republican Congress, and by me. None of them is an

Source of the Purchasing Power

Where will the $12 trillion come from to buy these assets? Over $5 trillion in new capital will come from the cashing in of government bonds—by pension plans, individual investors, and others. Bids will come as well from foreigners, because we should maximize the proceeds by allowing everyone to bid on the properties. We desperately need the money.

And American entrepreneurs, freed of the income tax and crippling regulation, will be eager to acquire these assets and put them to good use—as people with larger take-home pay will demand new products and services.

Not Enough Assets?

We don't know how much the assets are worth, and we won't know until they're put on the auction block and people bid for them.

What if it turns out they aren't worth $12 trillion?

If that's the case, it will mean the government is now insolvent—as is any individual or business with more liabilities than assets. It means government has been surviving only by promising its creditors to force you to pay whatever taxes are necessary to cover its obligations as they come due.

If the government is effectively insolvent, we need to know that as soon as possible.

But whether or not it is insolvent, we need to stop the bleeding immediately—stop letting the debt grow, and stop allowing the government to heap further obligations upon us and our children. The longer we wait, the harder it will be to fix things without imposing enormous hardships on you, me, and other Americans.

ALTERNATIVES

If there aren't sufficient assets to pay off the debt, the job will be more difficult—but it won't be impossible if we act quickly.

The first proceeds from the asset sales should go to liquidate the Social Security system and get the government completely out of it. Additional proceeds beyond that should be used to pay down the debt as far as possible.

If the proceeds can't wipe out the accumulated debt in six years, we will need to budget an amount every year to pay down the

"official" party proposal, but I have identified them by labeling them with their parties' names.

principal. That would mean we couldn't repeal taxes as cleanly and quickly as proposed.

However, under no circumstances can we allow the current tax system to remain in place. The income tax is the biggest single intrusion suffered by the American people. It forces every worker to be a bookkeeper, to open his records to the government, to explain his expenses, to fear conviction for a harmless accounting error. Hundreds of billions of dollars are wasted on attorneys, accountants, tax shelters, and other costs. The tax penalizes savings and drags down the entire economy. Today's income tax is incompatible with a free and prosperous society.[5]

So whatever taxes are needed must be collected without the oppression and terror of the current system.

There are two possibilities. Either would be a great improvement over what we have now.

1. Flat Tax

Some Republicans have proposed a flat tax. But it is big and flat, because they aren't reducing the size of the federal government.

They say you'll be able to file your tax return on a postcard. But there's nothing to stop the IRS from demanding proof that the number you put on the postcard is correct.

A better arrangement—one that honors freedom and privacy—is a flat 10% tax on all income. No deductions, no exemptions. The 10% would be withheld from your paycheck and forwarded to the government by your employer—without your name attached.

You would not have to file a tax return—not even on a postcard—because you've already paid your tax. The same would be true of all dividends and interest you earn; the company paying you would withhold 10% and forward it to the government without your name attached to the payment.

The estate, gift, Social Security, and capital gains taxes would be abolished.

The government wouldn't know how much you make, where you keep it, or what you do with it. You would have no contact with the tax collector at all. It couldn't rummage through your bank account looking for evidence with which to hang you. Your financial life would be private—as it should be in a free country.

Corporations and self-employed persons would pay the same

---

[5]James L. Payne has estimated the cost to America of complying with the federal tax system (aside from the taxes themselves) to be $363 billion, about 7% of the national income.

flat 10% on their profits. This would require filing a tax return with a profit-and-loss statement. But any self-employed person or small corporation could choose to pay 5% of gross sales instead—in order to avoid having to justify one's expenses to the IRS.

Unfortunately, employers would continue to be required to withhold taxes from their employees, as they do now. As reimbursement, they would forward to the government only 95% of whatever they withhold. This doesn't make coercion right, but it does acknowledge the inconvenience being imposed.

In any dispute with self-employed taxpayers, corporations, or employers withholding taxes, the burden of proof would always be on the IRS. No one would be considered guilty until proven so. And if the government lost its case, it would have no right to appeal to a higher court and continue to make the taxpayer's life miserable.

There probably would be little interest in tax evasion—and certainly no tax-shelter industry—because the rate would be too small to warrant the effort and risk. There would be less money wasted trying to hide income or minimize taxes, and no more bad economic decisions made for tax reasons.

A 10% flat tax probably would raise $500 billion or more in today's economy. With a greatly reduced federal budget, it can pay the interest on the debt and pay down the principal.

2. Sales Tax

Another possibility is to eliminate the income tax entirely, and put a 5% retail sales tax in its place. To prevent it from becoming a political football, there should be no exemptions—not for food, medicine, or anything else.

Most likely, the repeal of the personal and corporate income taxes would reduce prices enough that, even with a 5% sales tax, most things would cost less than they do today. But even if prices didn't fall, the 5% tax would be much less oppressive than the current income tax.

As with the flat tax, the estate, gift, Social Security, and capital gains taxes would be abolished, along with the income tax.

You would never again have to file a tax return, never have to fear the IRS, never have the government going through your records, your bank account, or your personal affairs. Your privacy and your life would be your own again.

The federal government should reimburse every retailer for being a tax collector—by taking only 95% of whatever the retailer collects. The rest should be a fee to the retailer to partially compensate for the involuntary servitude he undergoes as a tax collector.

The tax would produce about $250 billion in today's economy—which can amortize the debt and get rid of it.

Maximizing the Return on the Assets

The only virtue of either a 10% flat tax or a 5% sales tax is that it is better than what we have now. Either of them is a poor second choice to abolishing all direct taxes—and once the debt is paid off, the flat tax or the sales tax should be repealed.

But everything possible should be done to avoid having to resort to either tax in the first place. So we need to maximize the proceeds from the asset sales.

It may be suggested that sale prices will be higher if we feed the assets onto the market slowly. However, we can't allow a long period for the sales. Politicians can't be counted on to stick to any plan for very long—at least not a plan that cuts government and reduces the debt. The 6-year plan I've described is the longest I would tolerate—and even *it* is dangerously long.

To maximize the return, we need to set a firm schedule of sales and stick to it. There needs to be a very descriptive inventory of every property—available to anyone in the world who wants a copy. And we must rely on private companies to hold the auctions.

CONSTITUTIONAL AMENDMENT

Even as we liquidate the current debt and cut the federal government to a fraction of its current size, we should look ahead to tomorrow—when future politicians will try to resurrect today's welfare state.

We must bind them down with Constitutional amendments that can't be sidestepped. The first one should:

1. Prohibit any tax on incomes (personal or business), estates, gifts, or capital gains.
2. Specify the taxes that are authorized—such as tariffs and excises—and set absolute limits on their rates.
3. Prohibit the federal government from spending more money than was received in revenue the preceding fiscal year.
4. In case of emergency, Congress could override these restrictions if approved by a 75% majority in both houses. But any such overrride would expire automatically in two years, requiring a 75% majority to reenact.

The third provision, devised by Professor Richard H. Timberlake of the University of Georgia, is the most effective way to prevent future budget deficits.

It is far more realistic than the Republicans' 1995 Balanced Budget Amendment, which limited government spending only to a Congressional estimate of what the next year's revenue would be. But such estimates often are way off. The budget could turn out to be considerably imbalanced, and nothing could be done about it after the fact. In addition, the Balanced Budget Amendment could serve merely as an excuse to raise taxes.

Professor Timberlake's provision avoids tax increases and doesn't depend on revenue estimates. Since a growing economy causes tax revenues to grow automatically, the amount Congress could spend would grow modestly every year—but never faster than the economy.[6]

BENEFITS

The plan I've outlined is a blueprint for restoring freedom, privacy, and prosperity to America.

- It will end the Social Security crisis forever. It will take care of retirees while freeing younger people from the burden of supporting another generation.
- It will end the federal deficits immediately.
- It will get rid of the debt that threatens to impoverish your children and grandchildren.
- It will free all of us from the terror of the IRS. It will give us back our earnings, our freedom, and our lives.
- It should unleash the American economy and produce a greater boost in our standard of living than any of us has seen in his lifetime.
- Government will no longer take almost half the national income in taxes. We will cut the government's share almost in half. And I trust this is only the first step.

Some people may applaud the goals expressed here, but feel this program is too extreme, that it moves too quickly—that it is throwing out the baby with the bath water.

But that is what we have to do. It's Rosemary's baby we're talking about.

Benefits All

Some people may balk because they see that this will benefit the wealthy.

---

[6]In a recession, revenues could decline—causing Congress to spend more than it takes in for a year or two. But such deficits necessarily would be tiny, brief, and infrequent—and would be more than offset by the automatic surpluses a growing economy would produce in other years.

Of course, it will benefit the wealthy—and it will benefit the middle class—and it will benefit the poor, most of whom won't stay that way. The poor no longer will be shut out of jobs by minimum wage laws and federal employment rules. And their labor—even with little experience or training—will be much more valuable in a vigorous economy.

And that growing economy will be able to assimilate all the government employees and welfare clients who today might have trouble finding worthwhile jobs.

How much will it mean to you?

When you get your next paycheck, look at the stub that comes with it. See how much is being taken from you each payday in income tax and Social Security tax.

Then please spend a few minutes with your spouse, discussing what you'd do if that money were available to *you*, instead of the government. What would you do with it?

- Would you put your children in a private school—one that provides the kind of education and values you've always wanted for them?
- Would you set the money aside to save up for the business you've always wanted to start?
- Would you move into a better home, a better neighborhood?
- Would you put the money in the bank to save up for your children's college education?
- Would you make a bigger contribution to your favorite cause or charity?

What would you do? That money is yours, you earned it, so *you* should decide.

It doesn't belong to the politicians—to take from you and then dole back to you as though it were an allowance. The politicians have no moral claim on it. They take it from you in the name of compassion for those supposedly less fortunate. But the only compassion they feel is for their power and their reelections — and their ability to use your money to assure both.

Is there any benefit you're getting from the government now that you couldn't replace several times over with the money you're going to save in income tax?

What would you do with that money? It's time you got it to spend for yourself.

It's time to take back our earnings, our freedom, our lives.

Chapter 25

Do We Really Want Government to Protect Family Values?

Politicians lash out at movies, TV, and popular music. But they say they don't want to censor anyone. They just want entertainers to be more responsible.

But what does a politician mean by "responsibility"? And why must entertainers worry about it? If entertainers aren't breaking the law, and if people want to listen or watch, who cares what the politician-critic thinks?

And what special moral wisdom do politicians possess? Every one of them, at one time or another, has sold his vote for political, personal, or financial gain—pandering as shamelessly as any streetwalker. What moral guidance could they possibly have to offer?

And don't they have more important things to do—such as balancing the budget or repealing laws?

Politicians rail against the entertainment industry because:

- They know that millions of people deplore the social decay of the past 40 years—the epidemic of teenage pregnancies, the incivility of public discourse, the bad moral climate in schools, and the breakdown of families.
- The politicians don't understand what caused this and they don't know what to do to correct it.

So they rail against entertainers—hoping to impress the voters who care about these things.

Or they talk vaguely about getting America "back to basics," even though they never define what those basics are or what government could do to restore them.

Or they propose a Constitutional amendment to permit prayer in government schools—though they must know this won't improve the curriculum or solve any of the social problems infecting schools.

Or they propose tax credits for families with children, even though a connection between that and enhanced family values is hard to discern.

And when their policies produce no positive changes, they may "reluctantly" turn to the only weapon they have—censorship. They started down that road in 1995 with a bill to censor the Internet computer network.

Censorship & Coercion

But censorship isn't the answer. Government doesn't work, and so censorship doesn't work.

It may seem simple to ban just the bad things. But someone else—not you—will decide what is bad and what is good. And his values most likely will differ considerably from yours.

If gratuitous violence is bad, next year's censor may decide the Bible or heroic tales contain too much of it. If sexual promiscuity isn't fit for sensitive eyes, maybe the adulterous story of David and Bathsheba will be excised from Scripture.

You can't control government. So asking it to enforce your values is opening the door to enforce someone else's values on you. Unless you grant to everyone the freedom to read what he wants, you won't have that freedom either.

Coercion isn't the answer. Censorship would be no more effective than efforts to stamp out prostitution, gambling, and drugs have been. Government doesn't work.

A Little Coercion Goes a Long Way

But the politicians recognize public dissatisfaction, and so they feel compelled to do something—right or wrong.

And that something will involve force—even if it isn't outright censorship. Thus politicians propose coercing TV manufacturers to include a computer chip that allows parents to restrict children's access to some programs. But wouldn't manufacturers be doing this voluntarily if the public wanted it enough to pay for it?

There may be many people who think the chip is a good idea in principle, but not enough people who are willing to pay for it in practice. So the politicians will make everyone, including the childless, pay for the chip—no matter who needs or wants it.

The chip's specifications will be dictated by bureaucrats. It may be clumsy, expensive, or easy for children to bypass, and it may even turn your TV picture upside-down—but by golly the politicians can say they've done something to protect children.

WHERE'S THE PROBLEM?

We need to recognize the elements that have encouraged the decay in our culture. Here are a few:

- With government taking 47% of the national income, in too many families both parents have to work outside the home just to keep afloat financially—leaving the children to learn about life on their own.
- Government schools often work against the values you try to teach your child. Many of them teach that all values are morally equal, that your business and the wealth you've earned are somehow tainted, that children should put society's interests (as defined by government) ahead of family and friends, and that your culture should have no special place in your child's affection.
- Social reform programs—such as busing—teach children they aren't responsible individuals, but rather are simple pawns in great social experiments.
- Truancy laws keep trouble-makers in school to disrupt and slow down education—teaching children that the violent, the noisy, and the anti-social elements get their way.
- Child-abuse witch hunts teach children to think of parents as enemies.
- Minimum wage laws and child labor laws keep children from getting jobs—and thus cut them off from the learning that comes with a job.
- Welfare can make low-income parents seem superfluous in the eyes of their children. If the parents can't support the children, what can the children learn from them?
- Welfare makes it profitable for 15-year-old girls to have babies, and it pays Daddy to disappear.

CLEANING UP SOCIETY

Any plan to end America's moral decline should begin by undoing everything on that list. Politicians talk about reversing some of them, but they're not really eager to do so because they don't want to reduce the influence of government.

Taxes

Raising children is a moral challenge. But it's a practical one, too. Your chances of success would be much greater if government left more money in your pocket.

If the income tax were banished from your life:

- You could send your child to a private school that teaches the kind of values you cherish—or at least doesn't oppose those values. You could choose a school with whatever features you want—prayer or no prayer, traditional education or progressive education. No more fighting with the Board of Education over textbooks and curriculum.
- You could afford to have one parent remain home as the children grow up, so that most of their moral education comes from you.
- You could afford more leisure time and longer vacations—during which the family could do things together.

If you can imagine how much repealing the income tax would do for your family, imagine as well what it would do for other families—how much it would help children everywhere to grow up to be decent, peace-loving citizens.

The Schools

The quickest thing we can do to clean up school problems is to get the federal government out of education. When states are no longer following Washington's rules in order to get Washington's money, they will restore some sanity to school systems—and parents will have a better chance to exercise some influence.

And the more parents turn away from government schools to schools that match their values, the easier for them to raise their children in their own beliefs. So we should do nothing to hamper the growth of non-governmental schools.

The Laws

We need to get rid of the minimum wage laws, the child-labor laws, and other regulations that prevent a child from getting the practical job experience that can make him a more responsible person.

Welfare

We need to get the federal government out of welfare—so private charities can help people turn their lives around, rather than encourage them to remain dependent.

TAKING CARE OF OUR OWN

Until society changes, you have to insulate your children from the worst elements of it.

Your church, some teachers, and some friends may help instill the right values in your children. But the final responsibility for your children's moral education rests with you. You have to provide them with the understanding to live ethically, peaceably, and productively in a hostile world.

The local government school won't do this for you. Politicians won't do it. Not even your church can teach all your child needs to know to live a decent life and cope with people who don't hold the same values.

It is not my place to choose how other people should live. But it *is* my place and my job to take care of my own family—to see that those I care for are provided for, and are shielded from the dangers of today's society.

ABORTION

One of the most contentious moral issues of our time is abortion.

Until science can demonstrate otherwise, I must assume that life begins at conception. Thus I believe abortion is wrong—very wrong. But the government that can't win a War on Poverty or a War on Drugs isn't going to win a War on Abortion.

An unfortunate fact of life is that there always will be abortions, just as there always will be people who misuse drugs, no matter what the laws are.

The only practical solution to either problem is a program of education and persuasion—undertaken by people, not government. I applaud the dedication and efforts of those who work so hard to dissuade young women from rushing into abortions, who arrange adoptions for pregnant women, and who spend their own money on advertising that celebrates the lives of children who weren't aborted.

So long as we wait for the government to solve this problem, the abortion clinics will operate at full speed. And, if we have any respect for the Constitution, it surely isn't a matter in which the federal government has any role—either to facilitate or stop abortion, or to prevent state governments from stopping them.

TOO MUCH FREEDOM?

It can seem that the breakdown in moral values has come from too much freedom—from everyone "doing his own thing." So it can seem logical that government must do something more to regulate behavior, to control people, or even to censor what we see and hear.

However, what's happening hasn't been caused by too much freedom, but by too much government.

When government takes responsibility for everyone, no one is responsible for himself—and we shouldn't be surprised when more people act irresponsibly.

As James A. Dorn has said:

> If we learned anything from the failure of communism, it should have been that when freedom disappears, so do security, morality, and civility. We become wards of the state, and our future depends not on our own actions but on the actions of government. Without freedom of choice and without individual responsibility, life loses meaning and there is no real morality or virtue.

The best thing we can do to protect family values is to get government out of the way so that we can take full responsibility for our own families.

Chapter 26

Neither of the Two Old Parties Will Save Us

You may not agree with everything in this book. But, most likely, you agree with me that government is far too large and far too intrusive—and that cutting government substantially would be good for you, good for your neighbors, good for the economy, and good for America.

Most Americans feel the same way. My wife, Pamela, and I have been traveling throughout America during 1995. We've already visited 32 states. I have posed a simple question to hundreds of people I've met:

> If you had your choice, would you want more government than we have now, less government than we have now, or about the same amount as now?

I've asked this question of taxi drivers, store clerks, bellmen, and waiters; I've asked people who are well off and people who aren't; I've asked people who are black and white, men and women, old and young.

Almost invariably, the answer comes right back at me: "Oh, I'd like a lot less government. Taxes are too high, government is too big."

Of the hundreds of people I've asked, very few wanted more government. One who said she did was a young woman of, maybe, 20 years old, working as a clerk in a hotel drugstore in Indianapolis. She thought about the question for several seconds and then said, "I guess I want more government."

When I asked her, "What is it you want government to do that it isn't doing now?" she said, "Get all those people off welfare."

So maybe she should be counted as well among those who want less government.

My informal survey has been confirmed by every formal poll taken in the past few years. More and more Americans say they want government to be smaller. For example, recent polls have found that:

1. 73% believe "the federal government is much too large and has too much power."
2. 67% believe "big government is the biggest threat to the country in the future."
3. 63% think "government regulation of business usually does more harm than good."
4. 60% "favor a smaller government with fewer services."
5. Only 22% "trust the government in Washington to do what is right most of the time."

People everywhere recognize the simple truth that *government doesn't work*. It is failing at everything it tries to do—even as politicians propose new worlds for it to conquer.

Anti-Government Revolution

An anti-government revolution is boiling up in America. It began 30 years ago, expanded slowly during the 1970s, stepped up speed in the 1980s, and has become a tidal wave in the 1990s.

Not everyone wants to see government cut down to size, of course. But I believe an overwhelming majority of Americans do. Not every one of them wants to see government cut as far as I've suggested here—or maybe not even as far as *you* would like.

Each of us differs in his understanding of what freedom means, so each of us may have a different goal in mind when we talk of reducing government. But those differences needn't divide us. What's important now is the direction we want to go, not the precise destination.

And the direction that most of us want is toward less government—a lot less government.

Politicians Look Away

Unfortunately, neither the politicians nor the political journalists want to admit this. They recognize the discontent, but they talk of "reinventing government," in the words of Albert Gore, or making government "user friendly," in the words of Newt Gingrich.

Obviously, reinventing government isn't the answer; we need to *dis*invent it. And you can't make an agency of coercion user friendly; a gun is still a gun—even if the triggerman smiles, calls you "sir" or "ma'am," and lets you fill out a sheet evaluating his performance.

When voters gave control of Congress to the Republicans in 1994, they weren't throwing a "temper tantrum" as TV newscaster Peter Jennings tried to explain it. They were demanding an end to ever-growing government.

Sadly, the Republican Congress has failed to heed the voters. The Republican leadership is merely waging a war of words with the Democrats. They may even be winning it, but words aren't enough. What we want is real change—a dramatic reduction in government—and the Republicans have reduced nothing.

Oh yes, there have been battles over cuts in individual programs. But even these cuts are minor; they often are cuts only in the speed at which a program will grow; and in many cases the cuts aren't scheduled to occur until years from now.

Despite the supposed "cuts," despite the weeping and wailing and gnashing of teeth, one fact stands out: *the government is still growing*.

It's like a bad horror movie of the 1950s:

The Incredible Growing Government
The more you cut it, the bigger it gets!
Coming soon to an IRS office near you

Some Republicans say, in effect, "It took 60 years to build the welfare state, it can't be dismantled overnight." But they aren't even trying. They continue to move in the wrong direction. They continue to make the welfare state bigger.

No Change

And so, after the Republican Congress's first year, what has changed?

Are your taxes lower than they were?

Is government any smaller than it was before?

If you are in business, have the regulators stopped harassing you? Do you have fewer forms to fill out?

Do you expect any improvement—lower taxes, less intrusions, smaller government—to occur in the next year or two?

Of course, Republican politicians say they're hindered by having a Democrat in the White House, and that electing a Republican President will enable them to finally shrink government. That might be believable if the Republicans had passed bills that would have reduced government—even if President Clinton vetoed them. But the Republicans haven't done that, and their differences with President Clinton are trivial.

In effect, the issue between them has been whether government should take 47% of your life or only 46.9%.

Words & Deeds

Meanwhile, the Republican Presidential candidates—recognizing that voters want less government—are touring the country, playing to the crowds. They rant and rave that "government is too big and too oppressive," that "taxes take too much from the American family," that "we must get back to the Constitution."

But these are just words.

Who is your favorite Republican candidate? Imagine for a moment that he held a press conference yesterday—during which he made an announcement:

> I've told you I believe government is too big and too oppressive. I've told you that taxes are way too high. And I've told you we must get back to the Constitution if we're going to save the Republic. I believe those things with all my heart.
>
> But first we must increase government spending every single year for the next seven years. And we must add another $646 billion to the federal debt. If I'm elected and reelected, you have my solemn promise as a career politician that I will try to cut government in the 3rd year of my second term.

Would you still support him if he said that? I doubt it. You'd know his anti-government statements were empty talk.

Well, I have some bad news for you. If your candidate is a U.S. Senator, he already has made the decision to put off cutting government for seven years. In June 1995, he—along with every other Republican Senator—voted for the balanced budget resolution.

The plan calls for the government to grow by an average of 3.0% every year for the next seven years—taking the budget close to $2 trillion. Further, the plan adds $646 billion more in federal debt. That's $646 billion, plus interest, for your children and grandchildren to pay in extra taxes.

Every Republican Senator voted for this plan—including all the

THE REPUBLICAN PLAN FOR BIGGER GOVERNMENT
(billions of $)

Year	Budget Size	Growth	Deficit
1995 *	$ 1,539	+ 5.3%	$ 183.7
1996	1,588	+ 3.2%	170.3
1997	1,627	+ 2.5%	152.2
1998	1,661	+ 2.1%	115.8
1999	1,718	+ 3.4%	100.4
2000	1,778	+ 3.5%	80.8
2001	1,822	+ 2.4%	33.1
2002	1,876	+ 3.0%	** + 6.4

* = Last Democratic year.   ** = Surplus.

presidential candidates. And no Republican candidate who isn't in Congress denounced it. So we must assume that each of them approves of the plan to keep government growing.

None of them will put it this way, but no Republican presidential candidate intends to begin reducing government for at least seven years.

WHY THE GOP IS FAILING

Even if the Republican leadership wanted to cut government, they would fail—because they don't understand that you can't cut government one program at a time.

Put almost any government program to a vote of the American people, and a large majority would choose to eliminate it entirely. But in most cases the cost of a single program to the average American is negligible. So, no matter how silly a program is, no one is inspired to go to Washington to lobby against it—nor even to write or phone his Congressman to demand that the program be eliminated.

Meanwhile, there are a handful of people who profit handsomely from the program, and who will lobby intensely to keep it. The press joins in with horror stories of people whose lives will be shattered if the program is cut.

So all the pressure is on one side—to retain the program, and to increase its funding.

The Package

Is there no hope then?

Yes, there is. But only if the elimination of a program will affect the average American profoundly, so that people everywhere will pressure Congress to get rid of it. How do we do that?

By combining all the cuts in a single package—one bill that will eliminate farm subsidies, foreign aid, the Corporation for Public Broadcasting, all the unconstitutional departments and agencies, all the activities of the federal government that never should have been started in the first place.

And that single package must also reward Americans directly and immediately for all the cuts—by freeing them from the income tax. Only then will everyone have an incentive to see the government reduced to Constitutional levels.

Almost everyone has a favorite federal program he will wish weren't in the package. But whatever the program, most likely it won't mean as much to him as escaping the income tax. For once, the pressure will be reversed—the gain to the taxpayers will be great enough to mobilize them, to make *them* the major influence on the outcome.

This is the only way to overcome the well-known contradiction that most Americans want government to be much smaller, but they don't want their own favorites to be eliminated.

Not only is it impossible to cut government without repealing the income tax, it's impossible to repeal the income tax without cutting government.

The Republican proposals to replace today's progressive income tax with a national sales tax or a flat income tax will never pass. The rate for the new tax will be much too high—20% or more—because government will remain so large, and so the voters won't support the plan.

So you can't repeal the income tax without cutting government dramatically. And you can't cut government without repealing the income tax. The two steps must be part of the same package.

PROFESSIONAL POLITICIANS ARE NO HELP

Since the Republicans haven't combined spending and tax cuts, they're not even able to pass mild spending cuts.

But it's doubtful that they care. The current system suits them just fine. Big government gives them the power of life or death over companies. We can't expect them to lead the fight to change things.

The Democrats are no different—as we saw when they controlled Congress.

We can't rely on politicians to deliver on anything. They profit from government as it is. We will put an end to big government only when we elect citizens who don't want political careers—people who will go to Washington for a few short years, clean up the mess, and then go home to enjoy their newly recovered freedom.

Term Limits

Term limits are necessary to prevent the honest, conscientious citizen from turning into a career politician. Power is seductive. Many a President or Congressman has been transformed from a reformer into a defender of the status quo once it was *his* hand on the wheel.

I strongly support the move to limit Senators to two 6-year terms and Congressmen to three 2-year terms.

Some people say it's anti-democratic to keep people from voting for whomever they want. If so, the First Amendment is anti-democratic, too; it prevents people from voting to outlaw unpopular viewpoints, publications, or religions. The entire Constitution is a limitation on democracy.

The Congressman elected from your district doesn't affect only the people in your district. His votes in Congress affect all Americans. And some Congressmen and Senators have—through years of tenure—amassed such power, such fund-raising connections, and such networks of political back-scratching that they are able to milk all American taxpayers for the benefit of their own constituents. Naturally, the constituents reelect them, but voters elsewhere who pay the bills have no recourse.

Term limits would work against such power-building.

They also would attract better people to Congress—people who don't want a career in politics. Today, they see no point in going to Washington for only a few years, because new Congressmen have no power in a Congress run by political hacks who have been there for decades.

Lastly, no Congressional election is a fair contest. The incumbent has enormous advantages—the ability to get publicity at the drop of a million-dollar federal project, to buy votes with the voters' own money, to mail voters postage-free reelection literature disguised as Washington "reports." These advantages give the incumbent a long headstart in any race. And, as the obvious favorite to win, the incumbent has an easier time raising money—since influence-buyers naturally prefer to bet on a winner.

As we've seen in recent decades, scandals or voter dissatisfaction must be enormous before an incumbent will lose an election.

No campaign reform law will cure these ills. In fact, every "campaign reform" of the last few decades made incumbents harder to beat.

THE THIRD PARTY IS COMING

A decade or so of term limits would make the Republican and Democratic parties more responsive to the American people. The leaders who have done so much to perpetuate big government would be replaced by citizens with much less incentive to perpetuate the system we have now.

But until then, neither party will do anything to take government out of our pocketbooks, our privacy, or our lives. They profit too much from the status quo.

Our only hope is a third party.

The public has expressed a strong desire to see a third alternative in the 1996 presidential race. In 1995 the Gallup Poll found that:

- 60% of Americans want a third party to be in the 1996 race.
- 56% would be inclined to vote for a third alternative if the two old parties nominated Bill Clinton and Robert Dole.
- 54% would vote for the best candidate *even if he seemed to have no chance of winning.*

That doesn't mean all these people will vote for a third-party candidate. It means only that they want the opportunity to do so—they want an alternative to Tweedledum and Tweedledee. With other surveys showing that 73% believe government is too large, it's not hard to figure out what Americans want from a third party.

The press, however, is determined to ignore the obvious. Political pundits say the public wants a third party to avoid the extremes of the Democrats on the left and the Republicans on the right. They say the voters want a "centrist" candidate—a moderate who won't be a big-spender but won't cut government dramatically, someone who will make government more responsible. In other words, someone who can make government work.

But government doesn't work. And the American people know that. They *aren't* looking for someone to slip into the center between the Republicans and Democrats. The gap between them is so small that anyone squeezing in there could get crushed.

The voters want a third party to shrink the government the two old parties have built.

THE THIRD PARTY HAS ARRIVED

Fortunately, there is such a party already.

The Libertarian Party was founded in 1971 by David Nolan. It is the only nationwide party whose platform has consistently opposed big government. It has run a candidate in each presidential election since 1972. It was listed on the ballot of all 50 states in 1992, and will be so again in 1996. It is by far America's largest "third party."

The party's platform is lengthy and discusses alternatives to government in dozens of areas. Its preamble sums up the Libertarian position very well:

> As Libertarians, we seek a world of liberty; a world in which all individuals are sovereign over their own lives, and no one is forced to sacrifice his or her values for the benefit of others.
>
> We believe that respect for individual rights is the essential precondition for a free and prosperous world, that force and fraud must be banished from human relationships, and that only through freedom can peace and prosperity be realized.
>
> Consequently, we defend each person's right to engage in any activity that is peaceful and honest, and welcome the diversity that freedom brings. The world we seek to build is one where individuals are free to follow their own dreams in their own ways, without interference from government or any authoritarian power.[1]

About 160 Libertarians currently hold elective office. There are none in Congress, however.

Libertarians are considerably different from Republicans or Democrats. Their dedication to small government and individual liberty stems from principle, not from opinion polls. So they can be expected to be far more consistent and committed to making changes than the Republican Congress has been:

- Republican politicians want to reform or slow down government programs. Libertarians want to abolish them.
- Republicans want government to "cut" the growth rate of government. Libertarians want to shrink government dramatically.
- Republicans want to use government to promote good causes. Libertarians support the private promotion of good causes—and they don't want government forcing its version of goodness on anyone.
- Republicans say we need a large military to continue our foreign policy successes. Libertarians wonder what those successes are.

---

[1] A copy of the complete party platform can be obtained by calling (800) 314-8611.

- Republicans see that federal, state, and local taxes combined took only 8% of the national income in 1900, and now take 47%; they say that's too much and promise to cut it back to 46%. Libertarians wonder whether 8% was too much.
- Republicans want to increase the budget for seven years, and then balance the bigger budget. Libertarians want to balance a much smaller budget immediately.
- Libertarians won't vote for any bill increasing the size or power of government. Republicans won't vote for any bill their pollsters reject.
- Libertarians aggressively propose and support bills to make huge cuts in the size, scope, and power of government. Republicans support bills their party leaders tell them to vote for.

Over the past 25 to 30 years, libertarian organizations, writers, speakers, and teachers have helped to educate the public that government doesn't work, and that there are far better ways to achieve most goals. During that same time, government has run out of opportunities to hide its failures.

As a result, millions of people are now ready for a candidate and a party that is dedicated not to managing, authorizing, tinkering, ordering, or fixing—but dedicated to reducing government and returning decision-making to the people.

I believe the Libertarian Party is ready to move up from its position as the nation's largest minor party to become America's third major party.

If you're tired of big government, take heart. Help is on the way.

Chapter 27

What the President Can Do

In 1980 the American people elected by a landslide a President who promised to get government off our backs. He said government was the problem, not the solution. He promised to balance the budget within three years, cut government spending drastically, and reduce the awful burden of taxes.

When he left office eight years later, government spending was 69% greater, tax collections were 65% larger, and $1.9 trillion had been added to the federal debt your children are supposed to pay.

It's true he had to deal with a Democratic Congress, so he couldn't get whatever he wanted. But he wasn't helpless. Although Congress votes for the budget and the laws we must live by, the President can veto what Congress does. And Congress can overrule the veto only if two thirds of both houses vote to do so. Thus the President can stop a bad law or a big budget if just one third of one house of Congress will support him.

Since the government grew so much in spite of the President's promises, you'd think Congress must have overridden hundreds of his vetoes—if not thousands of them. But in eight years, he vetoed only 78 of the thousands of bills sent to him. And only four of the 78 vetoes were on major budget bills.

Of the 78 vetoes, Congress overrode only eight. This means *Congress enacted into law only eight bills the President didn't approve of.* And only one of those was a budget bill—the Supplemental Appropriations Act in August 1982.

Only two other overrides significantly affected the power of government—the Clean Water Act of 1987 and the Civil Rights Restoration Act of 1988.[1]

Thus Congress didn't enlarge government over the President's determined opposition. They did only what he allowed.

Pens are cheap. A President can sign thousands of vetoes. Unless his opposition can muster a two-thirds majority in both houses of Congress, nothing can be forced on him.

The determining factor is whether the President has *the will* to reduce government. If he does, no one can stop him. There are many things he can do—whether or not Congress agrees with him.

WHAT I WILL DO

I am running for President of the United States. If elected, I will set to work immediately to make this a freer, safer, more prosperous country—and I won't have to wait for the help of Congress.

By releasing the non-violent federal prisoners we can increase the prison space available for child molesters, rapists, murders, muggers, and other violent criminals. This is something the President can do about crime without raising your taxes or stealing your civil liberties.

So on my first day in office, by Executive Order, I will personally:

- Pardon everyone who has been convicted solely on a federal tax-evasion charge, order the immediate release of those in prison, and restore their civil and voting rights.
- Pardon everyone who has been convicted solely on a federal non-violent drug charge, order the immediate release of those in prison, and restore their civil and voting rights.
- Pardon everyone who has been convicted solely on any federal gun-control charge, order the immediate release of those in prison, and restore their civil and voting rights.
- Instruct the Attorney General to prepare a roster of persons convicted solely of federal victimless crimes, so that I can pardon them, too.

Federal law enforcement agents, prosecutors, and judges will get the message immediately: We are interested only in getting the violent criminals off the streets. Don't waste your time and the taxpayers' money prosecuting people who haven't intruded on

---

[1]Congress overrode the President's veto of one large spending bill, the Highway Reauthorization Act in 1987, but the President had preferred a bill almost as large as the one that passed.

anyone's person or property. We need the prison space to house the people who are terrorizing our citizens.

Since there are no federal violent crimes listed in the Constitution (except for piracy), there will be a great deal of prison space available after the pardons. So we can help the debt-reduction program by selling unneeded federal prisons to state governments that do need them.

There are other steps I can take the first day in office:

- End federal affirmative action. End all federal quotas, set-asides, preferential treatments, and other discriminatory practices of the federal government.
- Establish a policy to penalize, dismiss, or even prosecute any federal officer who violates the Bill of Rights in dealing with citizens.
- Bring an immediate end to all federal asset-forfeiture cases, and initiate steps to make restitution to anyone whose property has been impounded, frozen, or seized by the federal government. Over 80% of such seizures occur when no one has even been charged with a crime.
- As Commander-in-Chief of the Armed Forces, I will quickly and completely remove all American troops from foreign soil. Europe and Japan can pay for their own defense, and they can risk their own sons and daughters in their eternal squabbles. This alone will save billions of dollars a year in taxes, but—more important—it will save American lives.
- As Commander-in-Chief I will remove all American troops from United Nations' operations.
- Everything put into the Federal Register by previous Presidents can be taken out by this President. I will put a hold on regulatory activities while my staff reviews the Constitutionality of all existing regulations.

Budget

I will submit a budget for the fiscal year 1998 (the first budget during the presidential term), as shown in chapter 24 of this book. I will veto any 1998 appropriations that exceed a total of $800 billion—not counting the money appropriated to buy annuities for former Social Security dependents.

Congress may pass a larger budget and expect me to sign it. I won't.

Will Congress override my veto?

I don't know. But we shouldn't assume that it will. If Bill Clinton were to wake up tomorrow morning as a born-again libertarian, and vow to cut the federal government by two thirds, Congress probably would laugh at him and go on its merry way.

But if I were elected on my platform to cut government dramatically, with my intentions set forth clearly in this book, no politician or journalist could hide from what my election meant. No one could claim the American people elected me to make government user-friendly—or to make stirring speeches at the United Nations. It would be obvious that the people had voted for much smaller government. So Congressmen would be taking an enormous political risk by defying such a President.

And if Congress couldn't override my veto, but wouldn't agree to my budget, we would reach an impasse—threatening a closure of most government agencies in October 1997. While this possibility might pressure some other President, it would work in our favor.

Even if Congress did defy me and the electorate, at least the battle finally would be joined. At last there would be two sides arguing in Washington—one to increase government and one to cut it sharply—instead of the current trivial debate between Democrats who want government to grow by 5% a year and Republicans who want it to grow by 3%.

Short Bills

One sign of a government run amok is that many Congressional bills are hundreds and hundreds of pages long—and they often include dozens and dozens of provisions that are irrelevant to the bills' topics.

Congressmen rarely read the bills they vote for, and Presidents almost never read them before signing them. Everyone relies on aides and "experts" to assess the bills—and even the latter can't read a bill that is rushed through to a vote or altered at the last minute.

In too many cases, Congressmen and Presidents don't even care what's in a bill. They approve it not because of its content, but because of its image—"tough on crime," racially correct, welfare reform, "budget-cutting," environmentally pure, or whatever. This is how quotas, asset-forfeiture, draconian regulations, and so many other pernicious practices sneak into the law—as "minor" matters hidden in a skyscraper of words. But the regulators read all these bills thoroughly and enforce every provision. And then some Congressmen are shocked to learn that their constituents are being harassed.

I will not sign any bill I haven't read. I will consult with advisors, but I will always make the final decision myself, based on what a bill actually says. If a bill is too long for me to read during the ten days the Constitution gives the President to make a decision, I will veto it automatically.

If a bill is ambiguous or too complicated to understand, I will veto it—even if I think it might be aimed in the right direction.

If these standards seem too rigid for this modern age, it is not because the standards are wrong, but because government has become too big and complicated. Restore government to a manageable size and bills will be short, government will be less complicated, and Congress can do all its work in a few months each year.

Keep Government in Check

If a bill would increase the size and power of the federal government in any way, I will veto it.

If a bill asks the federal government to do something for which there is no Constitutional authority, I will veto it. If the Constitution is inadequate for today's America, the Constitution should be amended—not violated.

Abiding by the Constitution

I will abide by the Constitution—even parts I might not agree with. I will not carry out any function for which there is no Constitutional authority.

I will take the Bill of Rights seriously. I will refuse to enforce any law that violates it.

Congress or someone else may sue to force me to carry out a policy for which there is no warrant in the Constitution. But that won't deter me. If a President is defending the Constitution, there is no reason to back down.

Over and over I will remind my opponents that the Constitution serves no useful purpose if it can be bent to whatever seems convenient at the moment. If there is no fixed charter that limits the government to specific functions, we will have only so much freedom as the government wishes to allow. It is time to stop paying lip service to the Constitution on national holidays, and instead start taking it seriously 365 days a year.

Over and over I will remind Congress and the American people, "No one is stopping you from voluntarily establishing any program you want, building it with your own wisdom and work and money, and persuading others to join or support you. Charities and churches and service clubs do this every day. But I will not let you use the federal government to force others to support and pay for your project.''

My opponents may take some issue all the way to the Supreme Court. What happens then?

The Supreme Court also can read the election returns. Some of today's justices seem to have a higher regard for the Constitution than their recent predecessors. My election and my actions may encourage them to stand up finally for the absolute supremacy of the Constitution.

And if the Supreme Court rules against me, I will remind them that I am sworn to uphold what the Constitution says—not what they would like it to say. And I will not back down.

The President Can Change Things

Yes, there is a great deal the President can do—with or without the support of Congress.

It requires a President who believes without question in individual liberty and self-responsibility—who will shrink government to only the functions specified in the Constitution—who really knows that government doesn't work and that we must make it as small and inexpensive and as irrelevant to our lives as possible.

It requires a President who has the will and the determination to get government out of our lives no matter what his opponents say, no matter what the press writes, no matter what it takes.

WE NEED A LIBERTARIAN PRESIDENT

Every four years, Republicans dress up as Libertarians to run for President. They talk about cutting taxes and holding government in check. But as soon as one is elected, he puts his Republican business-as-usual suit back on and makes his contribution to bigger government.

In other words, Republicans campaign like Libertarians and govern like Democrats.

Wouldn't it be nice to elect a real Libertarian for a change—one who would run as a Libertarian and govern as one?

Libertarian Candidate

I am that Libertarian.

My philosophy has been unchanged for over 35 years; it isn't going to change now. I have one reason to run for President: to scale the government down to size, so I can go back home and live the last few decades of my life in peace and freedom.

It should be obvious that I hold politicians in very low esteem. I do not want to become one of them.

I have joined the Libertarian Party because it is the only political party in America that consistently and intensely calls for immediate and huge cuts in the size and power of government.

Libertarians don't propose unreliable plans to maybe change things somehow in some way in some uncertain time in the future. We want:

- Huge spending cuts now.
- Huge tax cuts now.
- A balanced budget now.

As a Libertarian, I don't have to compromise to make deals and gain support within the party. I don't have to promise anyone a position in my administration. I don't have to accommodate the contrary views of any wing of the party.

Libertarians are individualists, so they don't agree on everything. There are differences over how far government should be cut, how a campaign should be run, which political stands are philosophically "pure." But, unlike other parties, *all* Libertarians want much less government than we have now. They all want to move in that direction—and no area of government is an exception.

The Libertarian Party's nominating convention will be held July 4–5, 1996, in Washington, D.C. I expect to win the nomination. Although there are other Libertarians running, none is devoting the time, energy, and attention that I am. My campaign is attracting personal and financial support from within and without the Party.

I decided to seek the Presidency on August 14, 1994. The rest of 1994 was devoted to planning and organizing the campaign. During the first nine months of 1995 I concentrated mostly—but not completely—on winning the support of Libertarians within the party.

The groundwork has been laid. And my attention is now focused on the general campaign. Beginning in October 1995, I will be speaking before organizations of all kinds, appearing on radio and TV shows, and campaigning all over America.

So Far

By the time you read this, I will have appeared in a series of nationally televised debates with Democratic and Republican Presidential candidates. These were the CityVote debates, scheduled for October 6, 22, and 29, 1995. Most of the Republican candidates were expected to be there—along with Jesse Jackson and Lyndon LaRouche representing the Democratic Party.

I will wage a full-scale campaign in New Hampshire—in order to draw more votes in the Libertarian Party's primary than many Republican candidates get in their primary.[2] By the spring of 1996, I should be showing up in opinion polls.

Although I don't expect to raise as much money as the older parties will have, I'm determined to raise enough to carry our message to the American people—to let every American know there's a candidate who has the desire and the will to make America a free country again.

Other Candidates

There may be other independent or "third party" candidates in the race—people such as Ross Perot, Colin Powell, Bill Bradley, Jesse Jackson, or maybe someone who wasn't considered a potential candidate in late 1995. The more of these people who decide to run, the better for us.

All of them—along with President Clinton, Senator Dole, Senator Gramm, Steve Forbes, and the other Republican candidates— claim they can make government work. I alone of the major candidates recognize that government doesn't work, and that the only solution is to get rid of as much of it as we can.

If the polls showing overwhelming support for much smaller government are correct, we can make this election a referendum on the question: *Do we reduce government dramatically or do we continue as we are now?* If the issue is framed that way, all the other candidates will be on one side of the fence, while I stand alone on the side of much smaller government.

The differences among the other candidates are trivial. If Bill Clinton, Robert Dole, Phil Gramm, Pat Buchanan, Steve Forbes, Ross Perot, or Colin Powell wins the election, government will be even larger in four years than it is today.

Despite the attempts to pose as a friend of individual liberty, none of those candidates will be able to carry the pretense all the way to Election Day, 1996. Each of them will have to defend too many Senate votes or proposals for more government.

All those candidates will split the vote of those who still have faith that government can work. I will be the candidate of those who want to restore American freedom.

---

[2]The primary for both parties is scheduled for February 17, 1996.

Running to Win

Many people have encouraged my candidacy by saying they hope I will influence the candidates of the two old parties—that I will pressure them to be more libertarian.

That isn't my goal. What politicians say in order to get elected is of no value to us. From "get government off our backs" to "read my lips" to the "New Democrat," a politician's words are meaningless.

We have to understand that politicians—Republicans or Democrats—like government the way it is. They will say whatever they have to in order to win an election. But their purposes are quite different from yours or mine.

So I have no hope of changing them.

I am running this campaign to win the Presidency. I know it is a very long shot, but not nearly as long as it might seem at first glance. The people are on our side. To win we have to show the voters two things:

1. There is a candidate with a realistic, credible plan to reduce government dramatically.
2. Voting for me would not be wasting a vote.

The first task will simply require hard work, money, and help from many people—to get our message to everyone in America.

Spoiler?

The second task will require showing what the stakes are.

Too many people are willing to vote for a bad Republican in order to keep Bill Clinton from being reelected. I can understand their attitude, but electing the "lesser of two evils" guarantees that there will be no substantial improvement.

Every Republican candidate has already made it clear he doesn't plan to cut government significantly. So what difference does it make whether a Democrat or a Republican is elected? Would America be significantly freer if George Bush had been reelected in 1992?

We finally have a chance to reverse the awful trend of bigger government—to turn it around once and for all. Should we throw away that chance by handing the task to a politician who, no matter what he says now, has never demonstrated a commitment to reducing government?

After four years of his administration, should we celebrate that the federal government grew by only $300 billion, instead of $400 billion? Should we feel relieved then that only $600 billion, instead of $700 billion, was added to the federal debt our children must carry?

Shouldn't we be working to elect someone who is determined to reduce government dramatically? Shouldn't we elect the person who wants to get rid of the federal debt entirely? To give our children a fresh start? To relieve them of the obligation to pay for the waste and political mistakes of earlier generations of politicians?

Shouldn't we seize this opportunity to get the federal government out of regulation, out of crime control, out of housing, transportation, welfare, and all its other boondoggles? Or do you believe the opportunity will still be there whenever we happen to get around to acting on it?

Before long, the federal debt—as well as the government's many uncounted liabilities—will be far too large to liquidate without the widespread misery produced by millions of broken promises. Then it won't be possible for a Libertarian to walk into the White House and turn the situation around in four years. We no longer will be able to offer hope to those who have been hurt by federal programs, taxes, and regulation.

Yes, it does make a difference who is elected—an enormous difference.

If a Libertarian is elected, the anti-government revolution will be won.

If Bill Clinton is reelected, at least the revolution will continue, because no one will misread the problem.

But if a Republican is elected, the revolution will go to sleep—and it may not reawaken until it's too late to succeed.

YOUR HELP

I could certainly use your help. There's much you can do to help restore America to the free country it once was.

Obviously, your vote is important. But so is your active support. There are many ways you can provide it.

You can mention my candidacy in letters to the editor, and on call-in radio and TV shows. Whenever the discussion turns to what the Republican Congress is doing, point out that there's a presidential candidate who has a specific program for real cuts in government, not just to slow its growth.

You can display bumper stickers, yard signs, lapel buttons, envelope stickers, and other advertisements. We will have a 30-

minute videocassette available by which you can introduce friends to the message of the campaign.

You can contribute money. What you donate will make it possible for us to reach every American with our message of hope.

If you would like to help, contact:

> The Browne for President Committee
> 4094 Majestic Lane, Suite 240
> Fairfax, Virginia 22033
> Telephone: (800) 314-8611
> World Wide Web site: http://www.harrybrowne96.org

If nothing else, send us your name, so we can inform you of the campaign's progress.

WHY I AM RUNNING

I am 62 years old. I have had a happy, successful life. I have no need to embark upon a new career. And even if I wanted to try something new, politics is the last vocation I would turn to.

Over the past four decades I have watched America become less and less free. I have seen government at all levels take over more and more of our lives. I've seen more and more people drawn into dependency upon government and lose the confidence to stand on their own two feet.

I've also been heartened by a marvelous educational campaign—as libertarian think tanks, magazines, books, speakers, clubs, and other organs, as well as the Libertarian Party, have made more people aware that freedom works and government doesn't. And even more people have been added to the ranks as they've seen firsthand that government doesn't work.

But despite the belief of three out of four Americans that "government is much too large"—and despite the election-year cheering for less government—government continues to get larger. Even if the politicians and journalists are the only Americans left who still believe in government, that's enough to keep government growing.

I have to conclude that, no matter how unpopular government is today, it will continue growing for the rest of my life if we don't change things quickly. It doesn't matter whether Republicans or Democrats control Congress or the White House, government will continue to become more oppressive—even as politicians congratulate themselves on "dismantling the welfare state" or on their "Republican revolution."

The educational battle has been won. The people have chosen

freedom over government. But the political battle continues to be lost.

Only when someone goes to Washington who is determined to clean the stables, who values freedom above political power, who has the will to stand fast against every politician, only then will the trend turn around—and only then will the political battle be won. But it's obvious that there is no such person in two-party politics we can look to.

In 1992 my wife suggested that I run for President. At first I thought the idea was absurd. But we talked about it for two years, and in August 1994 I decided I should run.

I have only one reason for running, a selfish motivation: I want to live in peace and freedom for my remaining 20–40 years.

I don't want to spend those years watching the greatest country in history sink into bankruptcy, into a third-rate socialist state.

And I am determined to do everything in my power to see that it doesn't happen.

I hope you will help me.

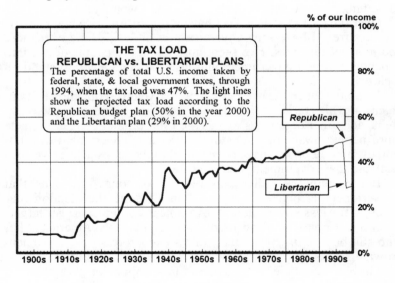

THE TAX LOAD
REPUBLICAN vs. LIBERTARIAN PLANS
The percentage of total U.S. income taken by federal, state, & local government taxes, through 1994, when the tax load was 47%. The light lines show the projected tax load according to the Republican budget plan (50% in the year 2000) and the Libertarian plan (29% in 2000).

EPILOGUE

Chapter 28

A Message of Hope

In the first chapter I asked you to imagine a different kind of America. I'd like you to do it again.

Imagine living in a community where your mother or sister or daughter felt safe walking home at ten in the evening—or even at two in the morning.

Imagine your children going to schools that respect your values; where teachers concentrate on reading, writing, arithmetic, and other fundamentals; and where no one would teach your child alien philosophies.

Imagine keeping half the taxes government takes from you now. You could move into a better home, finance a more comfortable retirement, send your children to the private school of your choice, support your favorite cause or charity in a way that would make a real difference, or save up to go into business for yourself.

With much lower taxes, your family could live well on the income of just one breadwinner—so the other parent could choose to stay home and raise your children with your values, rather than surrendering their moral upbringing to strangers.

This Is Reality

Perhaps now these dreams don't seem as utopian as they did in chapter 1.

We can have that kind of America. We had much of it as recently as the 1950s, and we could have it again. With the progress made in the marketplace since then, we can do even better now. But to get it, we need to break the stranglehold the federal government has over our lives.

I don't envision a nation completely without poverty. But I do see America with much less poverty, and without the bleak, endless, demoralized poverty the government has led millions into during the past three decades.

I don't see a country completely without crime. But I do see an America in which crime is minimized because citizens can defend themselves, the bad guys can't plea-bargain their way out of trouble, and the government doesn't subsidize gang warfare with a War on Drugs.

I don't envision a country completely without meanness, prejudice, or injustice. But I do see America able to soften and minimize such problems and the pain they inflict—an America free of class warfare and organized racial conflict, and free of the resentment and hostility fostered by federal Affirmative Action programs and laws that push people into unwanted relationships.

And I see a country with far less bickering among groups—a nation in which the government doesn't reward those who protest, scream, whine, and vilify. No longer able to use government to coerce others, we will have to learn to communicate, negotiate, and cooperate—to deal with each other civilly—because that's the only way we'll get what we want.

I don't envision a world at peace. But I do see our America at peace—safe from the eternal conflicts and wars of Europe and Asia. Never again should our sons and daughters be crippled and killed in foreign wars.

FORCE OR FREEDOM?

No book can cover every possible issue. I've left out or touched only lightly on the environment, immigration, our money system, Affirmative Action, and housing.

But you know how I stand on these and any other issues: Government doesn't work, and I want the federal government out of them. The answer always is smaller government. Government forces one choice on everyone. Freedom provides a hundred choices.

I haven't covered everything, but I've still asked you to consider many things. We've gone through many issues, principles, and examples. But it all comes down to a simple question:

> Should we rely on force to settle social issues, or would we all live better if we used persuasion to obtain the willing cooperation of those whose help we seek?

We must defend ourselves against those who would hurt us, and that may require force. But it is a mistake to believe we should settle questions among ourselves—including questions regarding defense—by force. Coercion doesn't produce desirable results; persuasion and cooperation do.

For America's first 150 years, force was minimized in social relationships. During the past 60 years, government coercion has become the standard device for settling social questions. Today everything is a political issue—to be decided by the strongest faction at the expense of everyone else. Today political might makes right. The result is an America our grandparents wouldn't recognize.

- Instead of compassion and charity, we have welfare rights.
- Instead of education, we have schools with metal detectors, drug pushers, social indoctrination, and kids who can't read their own diplomas.
- Instead of shining cities, we have war-zone ghettos.
- Instead of safety we have doors with multiple locks.
- Instead of civility we have groups jostling to gain entitlements to the earnings of others.

While private companies have been producing dazzling progress in computers, electronics, pharmaceuticals, and many other areas, everything in the social order has deteriorated. Our public institutions are a wreck.

To correct this, we don't have to turn back the clock. We only have to turn away from government—from the idea that we can cure social problems with a gun, from the fairy-tale belief that government can be made to work for anyone but the politicians. Coercion will never be as effective as freedom and cooperation.

Government doesn't work. It is time to stop trying to fix it, and start finding ways to live with as little of it as possible.

Agreement?

You may have found yourself agreeing with many of the changes I've proposed for the federal government, but still find it hard to accept others. I can understand that. I've asked you to consider a lot all at once.

You may feel you'd like to take the best parts of what I've suggested—get rid of Programs A through J, but perhaps only reform Programs K and L, while keeping Programs M and N as they are. But I'm afraid that can't be done.

If we keep the programs you like, the ones you don't want will be back again in no time. There is no way to avoid that. You can't ask government to do good without giving it the power to do bad. Empowering government "to help those who can't help themselves" empowers the politicians to help themselves.

You have to choose between . . .

- Taking a clear program such as mine, which may include one or two features you don't like, and
- Letting the politicians work out a "compromise"—which means that things will go on as they are, with more trillions in debt to be financed with higher and higher taxes.

There is no middle ground—no slower transition, no moderate compromise. It's huge change or no change, immediate change or no change. Which do you want? . . .

- A country in which the government is bound down from mischief by the chains of the Constitution—a society in which your children can grow up in a safe city, in good schools, in a land of opportunity in which they will be limited only by their own talents and ambition. Or . . .
- A society in which government gets ever larger, ever more intrusive, taxing more and more from you and your children, retarding the economy's growth to a slower and slower pace, running up more and more debt—a society in which civil discourse becomes ever more shrill, crime continues to worsen, education continues to decline, and we become more and more dependent on government.

There is no middle choice, because what you think is middle ground is owned by people who are in the business of making government grow.

Realize that whatever functions you wish the government would keep won't be abandoned just because the federal government lets go of them. If there's any appreciable demand for them, someone else will take them on—state or local governments or, better yet, non-profit groups or companies that can profit only by handling them efficiently.

In the marketplace, you don't have to muster a majority vote to get something done. You need only a few people who want something—and someone will satisfy that desire in order to earn a profit.

Phase Out?

As we get closer to the point of taking the country back from government and returning it to the people, we will hear many warnings—especially from those who want to maintain power over our lives.

They will say we should phase out unneeded programs over several years, to make the change easier. We must say, "No, we're wise to your foot-dragging. We know you're planning to restore the programs as soon as we turn our backs. We must get rid of them now."

They'll say that doing this quickly will cause too many dislocations. We must say, "Nothing can dislocate the economy as badly as the government has. Getting the government out of the economy opens up new business opportunities and jobs. We want it done now."

They'll say, "We must be sure the rich don't profit from these changes." We must say, "The rich are as entitled to profit as we are. They don't live to finance your political schemes. They don't live for us—anymore than we live for them. Leave them alone so they can invest and create new businesses, new products, and new opportunities for all of us."

We must act quickly and decisively if we're going to transform America from the land of welfare back to the land of the free, from the land of dependency back to the land of opportunity, from the land of shrinking incomes back to the land of prosperity. Taking it slowly or starting new government programs "to ease the transition" is a sure route back to where we are now.

MESSAGE OF HOPE

They'll say we're taking something away from people. But we threaten no one, except maybe the politicians.

To everyone else we carry a message of hope.

To the young we say:

> You'll no longer have to pour money down the Social Security rat hole. You'll be free to plan and provide for your own retirement, or make arrangements to have your employer help you. Your future is unlimited because no income tax will keep you from accumulating the fruits of your work. America will once again be the land of opportunity.

To the elderly we say:

> No longer must you fear that Congress will cut your Social Security benefits, because you'll have a firm contract with an honest company that will honor it. And your children and grandchildren will have opportunities far beyond yours. They can live longer, live better, earn more, and keep what they earn.

To minorities in the inner cities we say:

We will end the War on Drugs, so your neighborhood won't be infested with drug deals, gang battles, or pushers preying on your children. We will abolish the income tax—so business and job opportunities will improve, so you can afford a better home and neighborhood, so you can buy a private-school education for your children, so you can finally escape the desperation the government has led you into.

To people of every religion we say:

With the income tax gone, you can afford to put your children in a religious school, and to support your faith to an extent never before possible. You'll be able, if you choose, to survive on one parent's income, so the other parent can be there to raise your children in *your* values. No longer will they be taught alien philosophies by strangers.

To government employees we say:

The new economy will be big enough to accommodate everyone. A private company may need exactly what you're doing now. If not, there will be new opportunities everywhere. And you, too, will keep what you earn. The price of your current job has been an enormous tax. But in your new job, everything you make will be yours to spend as you see fit—or to save or give as you choose. Your retirement will be more secure. And going to work may be more exciting than you ever imagined.

To reformers we say:

No one will stop you from trying to create a better world. You just won't be able to force your way on others. You must prevail by persuasion, rather than coercion. But what you achieve will be far more satisfying, and it will provoke gratitude rather than resentment.

To people on welfare we say:

Take heart, help is on the way. We will tear down the Berlin Wall of government programs, regulations, and taxes that have imprisoned you in hopelessness. A prosperity is coming that will let everyone work who wants to—that will set you free from dependence on government—free to assert your dignity, self-respect, and responsibility for your own life—free to give your children a better life than you've had.

And to everyone we say:

With the federal government out of your everyday life, your city can be safe, your school can reflect your values, your earnings are yours to use as *you* think best. You can buy what you want, sell what you want, deal with your employer without the government to interfere, and live your own life by your own values.

The blessings of liberty touch everyone. And liberty is America's destiny.

Let's make America a free country again.

Nashville, Tennessee
September 25, 1995

Appendix A

Acknowledgments

Every book I've written since 1975 has relied heavily on the talents of Terry Coxon. His understanding of government, economics, and good writing has contributed something to every page. This book is no exception; it would have been quite different, and much less readable, without his help. His advice, support, and willingness to accommodate my unusual schedule are deeply appreciated.

I'm also grateful to Michael Emerling Cloud of my campaign staff, who made a number of important suggestions—and who has made invaluable contributions to the development of specific proposals.

St. Martin's Press—in particular, editor George Witte—has been extremely patient, as I tried to finish this book while campaigning. The ideas have been in development for about 40 years, but it has required almost a year to put them in readable form while pursuing the Presidency. George Witte has been tolerant beyond what any writer could hope for. And I especially appreciate St. Martin's effort in delivering the book to the stores just eight weeks after I finished the final manuscript.

The book couldn't have been ready in time with accurate facts and figures without the excellent research done by Brian Doherty, with the help of Phil Blumel and Margaret Griffis. I have never come across a faster, more effective, more conscientious researcher than Mr. Doherty.

In addition, I'm indebted to Stephen Moore and Jeanne Hill at the Cato Institute, Fred Smith at the Competitive Enterprise Institute, and Joe Cobb at the Heritage Foundation for important background help.

Further, I'm grateful for specific suggestions made by A.J. Davies, Richard Timberlake, Robert Prechter, Jr., and others.

I've been able to write this book while campaigning full-time only because Terry Bronson has taken over the running of my office. Without her, many things would not have been possible, and I'm very fortunate to have her services.

In addition, I appreciate the encouragement given by Sharon Ayres, Perry Willis, Jack Dean, Phyllis Westberg, Oscar Collier, John Chandler, Charles Smith, and many other friends, associates, and campaign supporters who were determined to see this book published.

Most of all, none of this would have been possible without the suggestions, encouragement, support, respect, and love of my wife, Pamela.

Appendix B

Notes & Background Information

This appendix provides background information and sources for some of the statements made in the book. See Appendix C for details of some of the publications mentioned here.

Graphs

All the graphs in the book were created by the author.

Most of the graphs are plotted on a ratio scale (also called a *logarithmic*, *log*, or *semi-log* scale), which is different from a normal linear scale.

On a *linear* scale a vertical inch (or any other distance) represents the same *number of units* (such as dollars) wherever it appears on the graph. For example, a change from 100 to 120 would appear to be 20 times as large as the change from 5 to 6—even though each is, proportionately, a 20% increase.

A ratio scale provides a more realistic view of growth. A vertical inch (or any other distance) represents the same *degree of growth* wherever it appears on the graph. Thus the vertical distance between, say, 100 and 120 on a ratio scale would be the same as between 5 and 6—because each represents a 20% increase.

All the graphs showing the growth of government would have looked more terrifying had they been plotted on a linear scale. But they would have been misleading.

1. THE BREAKDOWN OF GOVERNMENT

The crime comparison between 1950 and 1994 is calculated from data in the FBI report *Urban Crime Reports: Crime in the United States 1991* (1992), reported in *The Universal Almanac 1994* (page 239), and *Historical Statistics of the United States, Colonial Times to 1970*, table H952–961 (page 413).

In the graph on page 3, tax data is from the U.S. Bureau of the Census series "All Governments—Summary of Finances," which is published in *Historical Statistics of the United States, Colonial Times to 1970*, Series Y-533, pages 1120–1121, and in various issues of *The Statistical Abstract*. This series eliminates all duplication among levels of government. The national income data are taken from *Economic Indicators 1980 Historical Supplement* (Joint Economic Committee of Congress), and from *Historical Statistics of the United States, Colonial Times to 1970*, page 224.

2. WHAT IS GOVERNMENT?

The General Motors revenues are from *The World Almanac and Book of Facts, 1994*, page 112. The Pacific Bell announcement appeared in the *San Francisco Examiner*, November 11, 1993, page A-1.

3. OOPS! WHY GOVERNMENT PROGRAMS ALWAYS GO ASTRAY

Regarding the increased costs to the elderly brought on by Medicare: In 1961 the average elderly family spent $1,589 per year on health care (in 1991 dollars). In 1991 this had risen to $3,305 per year. This was reported in "The Health Care Squeeze on Older Americans," a study by the Families USA Foundation, using data from the Consumer Expenditure Survey of the U.S. Bureau of the Census.

5. IF YOU WERE KING (THE DICTATOR SYNDROME)

The Denny's suit was announced in the *San Francisco Examiner*, May 24, 1993. The settlement was reported in *The New York Times*, May 29, 1994, Section 4, page 4, column 1.

The woman with the microchip in her tooth, the employee who brought a gun to work, and the National Guard case were all described in *Reason* magazine, May 1995, page 15.

The case of the couple ejected from the airliner was reported in the *San Francisco Examiner*, October 22, 1993.

The case of the woman requiring a segregated workplace was brought against Fuqua Industries, Inc. in Florida, and was reported in *The Wall Street Journal*, December 23, 1992.

7. GOVERNMENT DOESN'T WORK

The U.S. war casualty figures are from the *1995 World Almanac*, page 163, which compiled data from the U.S. Department of Defense. According to figures I compiled from *Historical Statistics of the United States, Colonial Times to 1970*, tables Y458–473, pages 1114–1115; *Economic Indicators* (Joint Economic Committee of Congress); and various issues of the *Statistical Abstract of the U.S.*, the U.S. government since its inception has spent $7,108,424,000,000 ($7.1 trillion) on the military, equivalent to $19.2 trillion when adjusted for inflation to 1995 dollars.

8. ONCE THE LAND OF THE FREE

The James Madison quote is taken from the summarized House floor debate in *The History of Congress*, page 170.

The George Washington quote regarding the nature of government has been cited in many places, but I've never found an original source for it.

9. HOW FREEDOM WAS LOST

When the income tax began in 1913, the lowest rate was 1%, and was levied only on incomes greater than $20,000 (equivalent to $300,000 in 1995 dollars). The maximum rate of 7% applied to incomes greater than $500,000 (equivalent to $7,500,000 in 1995). Since World War I, the lowest maximum rate was 24%—which became effective in 1929 but lasted only one year.

The statistics on consumer prices are from *Historical Statistics of the United States, Colonial Times to 1970*, page 211, table E-135, and from various issues of *Economic Indicators* (Joint Economic Committee of Congress).

The data on government spending and tax rates are taken from *Historical Statistics of the United States, Colonial Times to 1970*. Government spending figures are from table R188, page 1105. Tax figures are from table VIII, page 1095. Data on price levels are from table E135, page 211.

The unemployment rate was 15.9% in 1931 and 17.2% in 1939 (*Historical Statistics of the United States, Colonial Times to 1970*, table D-86, page 135).

The data on teenage pregnancies are from *Historical Statistics of the United States, Colonial Times to 1970*, table B30, page 52; and the *Statistical Abstract of the United States, 1994–1995*, table 100, page 80. The tables cover girls 15–19.

10. HOW MUCH FREEDOM IS LEFT?

The debate over the crime bill in which the 4th amendment was voted down is recorded in *The Congressional Record*, February 7, 1995, pages H1340–1341.

The President's decision to try to circumvent the Constitution on the gun-control law was described in *The Detroit News*, April 30, 1995, page 5A.

A study by Thomas D. Hopkins of the Rochester Institute of Technology estimated the cost of regulation at $600 billion annually, which is 11% of the $5,599 billion national income at the end of 1994. A 1992 study for the Heritage Foundation by William G. Laffer III and Nancy A. Bord estimated the net cost of regulation (after allowing for the benefits it might produce) to be between 16% and 32% of the national income.

11. YOUR INNOCENCE IS NO PROTECTION

The story of the Reverend Acelynne Williams is described in detail in *Reason* magazine, May 1995, page 48. The story of Donald Scott is described in *The Wall Street Journal*, August 25, 1993, page A11. The stories of the other victims who were shot, vandalized, or imprisoned are recounted in *Lost Rights* by James Bovard (listed in Appendix C on page 238), pages 233–237.

Henry Hyde points out in *Forfeiting Our Property Rights* (page 24, listed in Appendix C on page 237) that the first modern law containing asset forfeiture procedures was the Comprehensive Drug Abuse Prevention and Control Act of 1970. It provided only for the forfeiture of property used to make or exchange drugs. The 1978 Psychotropic Substances Act allowed money and other valuable things to be forfeited if they were connected to a crime in any way. The 1984 Comprehensive Crime Control Act expanded the concept further to encompass any real estate connected to a drug crime. The 1986 Anti-Drug Abuse Act added all proceeds of money-laundering. Amendments passed in 1990 brought counterfeiting and financial crimes into the circle. And in 1992 Congress added just about every other offense imaginable, including car theft, and allowed virtually any property to be seized. Another demonstration that a government program will always expand to encompass far more than originally intended.

The enumeration of the many federal agencies using asset forfeiture laws is given in *Forfeiting Our Property Rights*, page 24.

The details of the process involved in recovering your property were given in *National Review*, February 20, 1995, page 36. In 1993 the Supreme Court put some limits on asset forfeiture procedures. But you still have to undergo an enormous effort to retrieve your property.

The quote from Congressman Conyers appeared in "S.C. Woman: Criminal Asset Forfeiture Program Needs Reforms" by Paul Kirby, States News Service, June 22, 1993, and was reprinted in *Lost Rights* by James Bovard (listed in Appendix C on page 238).

Billy Munnerlyn's story was recounted in "Jet Seized, Trashed, Offered Back for $66,000" by Andrew Schneider and Mary Pat Flaherty, *The Pittsburgh Press*, August 16, 1991, and was confirmed by Mr. Munnerlyn. Willie Jones' story was told in "Drug Agents More Likely to Stop Minorities" by Andrew Schneider and Mary Pat Flaherty, *The Pittsburgh Press*, August 16, 1991. Tracy Thomas' story was recounted in "Government Seizures Victimize Innocent" by Andrew Schneider and Mary Pat Flaherty, *The Pittsburgh Press*, August 16, 1991.

The statement that only 20% of the people who lost their property to seizures were charged with a crime was given in "Government Seizures Victimize Innocent" by Andrew Schneider and Mary Pat Flaherty, *The Pittsburgh Press*, August 16, 1991.

John Thorpe's run-in with the salt marsh harvest mouse was described in "Mice and Men: Whose interest shall we serve?" by Ike Sugg, *The Detroit News*, July 17, 1992. It was also cited in *Red Tape in America*, Heritage Foundation, page 64 (listed in Appendix C on page 238).

The *Money* magazine article was "Tax Penalty Ambush" by Greg Anrig, Jr., and Elizabeth M. MacDonald, *Money*, June 1992, page 156. The U.S. General Accounting Office report is "Tax Administration Extent and Causes of Erroneous Levies," December 21, 1990.

James Payne's estimate of the average cost of fighting a tax case is explained in *Costly Returns: The Burdens of the U.S. Tax System* by James L. Payne (listed in Appendix C on page 237), pages 58, 62.

12. ON THE ROAD TO A BETTER WORLD

The number of people killed by the Soviet Union and the 119 million people killed by their own governments in the 20th century are taken from "War Isn't This Century's Biggest Killer" by R. J. Rummel, *The Wall Street Journal*, July 7, 1986, editorial page.

15. HOW YOUR LIFE IS REGULATED

The information on the Clean Air Act and Intel's consideration of moving offshore were compiled by Ben Lieberman of the Competitive Enterprise Institute, and were summarized in a *National Review* editorial, August 28, 1995, page 14.

16. HEALTH CARE—THE PROBLEM

Suits against doctors for turning down patients are discussed in "Dr. Dean's Health-Care Reform Plan" by Ward Dean, M.D., *Forefront Health Investigations*, August 1994, page 6.

Regarding the cost to get a new drug to market, Joseph DiMasi and Louis Lasagna of Tufts University, Ronald Hansen of the University of Rochester, and Henry Grabowski of Duke University calculated in 1990 the average cost of a new drug during the period 1970–1982 to be $315 million in 1995 dollars ($231 million in 1987 dollars in the original). The U.S. Office of Technology Assessment, using the same data, increased the cost to $400 million by adding in time and opportunity costs and the costs of failed projects. Dr. Mary J. Ruwart (in "Death by Regulation," ISIL Educational Pamphlet Series) and Jarret Wollstein (in "We *Can* Have Affordable Health Care," ISIL Educational Pamphlet Series) both use a figure of $359 million.

The legal problems involved in ordering medicines from overseas are discussed in "Dr. Dean's Health-Care Reform Plan" by Ward Dean, M.D., *Forefront Health Investigations*, August 1994, pages 5–6.

The Arthur D. Little study of the lives lost due to the FDA's withholding of propanolol from treatment of angina and hypertension is reported in "Cost Effectiveness of Pharmaceuticals #7: Beta-Blocker Reduction of Mortality and Reinfarction Rate in Survivors of Myocardial Infarction: A Cost-Benefit Study" (Pharmaceutical Manufacturers Association, Washington, D.C., 1984), pages 1–5. Also, William M. Wardell said "The proper use of the [the B-blocker] practolol . . . could now be saving 10,000 lives each year in the U.S. at a cost, in terms of side effects, that can now be made trivial by comparison." (Quoted in "Deadly Overcaution: FDA's Drug Approval Process" by Sam Kazman, *Journal of Regulation and Social Costs*, Vol. 1, No. 1, page 104). This was in reference to the FDA's 10-year delay, from 1967 to 1976, in approving a variety of beta blockers to reduce heart attacks.

Dr. Mary J. Ruwart's statement comparing the deaths due to withholding propanolol and the deaths due to the taking of unsafe drugs was made in "Death by Regulation," ISIL Educational Pamphlet Series. Robert Goldberg's statement appeared in *The Wall Street Journal*, August 15, 1995, page A16.

The FDA's policy against vitamin makers is discussed in "FDA Anti-Information Policy Assailed," *Human Events*, August 25, 1995, page 6.

The effect of litigation costs on DuPont's decision to stop selling polyester for medical devices is discussed in "Material Risk" by Thomas G. Donlon, *Barron's*, June 13, 1994, page 58.

Hospitals that receive Medicare payments have to admit all patients because of the Consolidated Omnibus Budget Reconciliation Act (COBRA) of 1985 (P.L. 99–272). The ramifications of this are discussed in *Emergency Departments: Unevenly Affected by Growth and Change in Patient Use*, U.S. General Accounting Office report, 1990.

States that force insurance companies to include unwanted and costly benefits in all policies are discussed in "Health Insurance for All" by Elizabeth McCaughey, *The Wall Street Journal*, April 28, 1994, page A14.

The estimate of Medicare's 1990 cost is recounted in "The Great Patriotic War" by Grover G. Norquist, *The American Spectator*, December 1993, page 70. It is mentioned also in "American Health Care Today" by Edward R. Annis, M.D., *National Review*, health care supplement, date unknown, page 8. The actual cost of $98 billion is given in *Economic Indicators* (Joint Economic Committee of Congress), July 1995.

The history of Medicare taxes and the actuarial projections are described in "Get Ready for the Pain" by Suzanne Oliver, *Forbes*, March 28, 1994, page 45, and in "Physicians Heal Themselves" by Lawrence Kudlow and Stephen Moore, *National Review*, September 26, 1994, page 54.

The Medicare "cuts" in the 1990 deficit-reduction package are discussed in "The President's Costly Budget" by Daniel J. Mitchell, *The Wall Street Journal*, December 23, 1993, page A8. The actual increase in spending is taken from *Economic Indicators* (Joint Economic Committee of Congress), July 1995. The mid-1980s series of cost-control provisions are discussed in "American Health Care Today" by Edward R. Annis, M.D., *National Review*, health care supplement, date unknown, page 8.

Medicaid's costs are discussed in "The Great Patriotic War" by Grover G. Norquist, *The American Spectator*, December 1993, page 71, and in "Physicians Heal Themselves" by Lawrence Kudlow and Stephen Moore, *National Review*, September 26, 1994, page 52.

The passing of Medicare shortfalls onto other hospital patients is discussed in "American Health Care Today" by Edward R. Annis, M.D., *National Review*, health care supplement, date unknown, page 8, and in a statement by Steven L. Gosik, Vice President, Bethesda General Hospital, St. Louis, *The Wall Street Journal*, March 23, 1992, Op-Ed page.

The data on who spends the health-care dollars are from *The New York Times*, June 13, 1993, Business section, page 4.

17. HEALTH CARE—THE SOLUTION

The words used in the various health-care proposals were tabulated in "Removing Our Freedom," a table from the National Taxpayers Union

Foundation, appearing in *The Wall Street Journal*, June 27, 1994, page A12. The principal Republican plan was the Chafee-Thomas proposal; the plan publicized as being the most "free market" was the Gramm-Santorum proposal.

The example of a five-year prison sentence for a person withholding information about his medical history was given in "Clinton Health Plan Coerces Cooperation" by Jane M. Orient, *Human Events*, December 25, 1993, page 10. The example of Medicare fining a doctor for filing the wrong form was given in "Please Do No Harm" by Lois J. Copeland, M.D., *Policy Review*, Summer 1993, page 8.

The New York experience with "guaranteed-issue" health insurance was described in "New York Finds Fewer People Have Health Insurance a Year after Reform" by Leslie Scism, *The Wall Street Journal*, May 27, 1994, page A2. The effects of Washington State's program were described in the *San Francisco Examiner*, June 30, 1994, page A-10, and in *The Wall Street Journal*, July 27, 1994, page A16. The American Society of Actuaries study was reported in "Cooper Plan, Clinton Lite" by Mike Tanner, *The Wall Street Journal*, February 14, 1994, page A14.

The sad state of medical care in Veterans Administration hospitals is described in "I've Seen the Future of Health Reform" by Robert L. Rold, *Medical Economics*, May 9, 1994, Vol. 71, No. 9, page 27. The comparison between emergency-room care in the U.S. and normal care in the governmental systems of Europe was given in "The Good Health Guide" by Norman Macrae, deputy editor of *The Economist*, in *National Review*, December 16, 1991, page 28.

18. IMPROVING EDUCATION

The 6% figure for federal involvement in education was taken from "The Incredible Shrinking Government" by Spencer Abraham, *National Review*, June 26, 1995, page 40.

In the graph "More Federal Aid, Less Education," data for federal spending are from *Historical Statistics of the United States, Colonial Times to 1970*, page 1116, table Y-479, and from the *Budget of the United States Government, 1995*, Historical Tables. The SAT scores are taken from "The Condition of Education 1994," National Center for Education Statistics, U.S. Department of Education; and various publications of the College Entrance Examination Board.

The graph "Not Enough Money for Schools?" was plotted from data in *Historical Statistics of the United States, Colonial Times to 1970*, table H-493, pages 374–375; and various issues of the *Statistical Abstract of the United States*, in the table "Public Elementary and Secondary Schools—Summary." The figures used are current expenditures per pupil enrolled, based on average daily attendance.

19. WELFARE

The statements from John F. Kennedy, *The New York Times*, and Lyndon B. Johnson are reported in *Losing Ground* by Charles Murray (Basic Books, 1984), pages 15 and 23.

Data on federal welfare spending in 1962 are from *Historical Statistics of the United States, Colonial Times to 1970*, series H32, H33, H40, and H41, page 341.

The 1991 figures on social welfare spending were the latest the U.S. government had published as of August 1995.

The quotation by Merritt Ierley is from *With Charity for All* (Praeger Special Studies, 1984), page 191.

The results from the AFDC reform of 1988 are taken from "Welfare Reform: There They Go Again" by Robert B. Carleson, *The Wall Street Journal*, July 13, 1995, page A10.

The data on social welfare spending between 1962 and 1991 are taken from the table "Social Welfare Expenditures Under Public Programs," which appears in *Historical Statistics of the United States, Colonial Times to 1970*, page 341, table 32; and in various issues of the *Statistical Abstract of the United States*, table 572 in the 1994–1995 edition.

Data for the graph "More for Welfare, More in Poverty," on page 114, are taken from the following sources: "Social welfare spending" in the series "Social Welfare Expenditures Under Public Programs, by Source of Funds: 1890 to 1970," from *Historical Statistics of the United States, Colonial Times to 1970*, table H32, page 341. Data for years after 1970 are from various issues of the *Statistical Abstract of the U.S.*, the same series. The original source of the data is the U.S. Social Security Administration. 1991 is the latest year for which data were given in the *Statistical Abstract of the U.S., 1994–95*.

Poverty level information after 1980 is from the table "Persons Below Poverty Level and Below 125 Percent of Poverty Level" in various issues of the *Statistical Abstract of the U.S.* Earlier years are from the same series published in *Losing Ground* by Charles Murray, appendix C on page 238. The original source of the data is the U.S. Census Bureau. Apparently, 1959 is the first year for which the government tracked the poverty level. 1992 is the latest year for which data were given in the *Statistical Abstract of the U.S., 1994–95*.

I am indebted to Charles Murray's book *Losing Ground* for much of the historical background of welfare, and the details of the shift in emphasis that took place in the 1960s. This is an excellent book, well researched and documented, and yet very engrossing.

20. FIGHTING CRIME OR PLAYING GAMES?

The "Rising U.S. Crime Rate" graph is taken from data in *Historical Statistics of the United States, Colonial Times to 1970*, tables H-952, 953, and 958, page 413; and from various issues of the *Statistical Abstract of the United States*, "Crime & Crime Rates, By Type" table, which is table 301, page 198, in the 1994–95 edition. The FBI is the original source of the data.

The data on the 1993 prison population is from "Prisoners in 1994," a U.S. Department of Justice report, page 10.

The "Prohibition" graph is taken from data in *Historical Statistics of the United States, Colonial Times to 1970*, table H-971, page 414; and from various issues of the *Statistical Abstract of the United States*, "Homicide Victims, by Race and Sex" table, which is table 307, page 201, in the 1994–95 edition. The FBI is the original source of the data.

The comparison between cocaine and crack, and mind-altering stimulants, sedatives, tranquilizers, and analgesics is taken from the *Statistical Abstract of the U.S., 1994–95,* table 211, page 142. The comparison between deaths from illegal drugs and accidental poisonings is from the same source, table 134, page 100.

The Donald Scott case is discussed in "Never Mind, Only Property Rights Were Violated" by Gideon Kanner, *The Wall Street Journal*, August 25, 1993, page A11. The FBI projection on property seizures was reported in the U.S. Department of Justice *Annual Report*, page 27, and is cited in *Lost Rights* by James Bovard, page 17.

The statement by New York City police commissioner Patrick Murphy was quoted in "What Can Government Take From you?," *Investors Business Daily*, December 9, 1993, page 1, and repeated in *Forfeiting Our Property Rights* by Henry Hyde, page 9.

21. A WEAK NATIONAL DEFENSE

Figures for casualties in U.S. wars are reported in the table "Casualties in Principal Wars of the U.S." in *The World Almanac, 1995*, page 163, and in the *Statistical Abstract of the U.S., 1994–1995*, page 362.

Total spending on the military and foreign affairs since 1790 has been $7.1 trillion (equivalent to $19.2 trillion in 1995 dollars). Since 1946, total spending has been $6.8 trillion (equivalent to $15.9 trillion in 1995 dollars). Source: *Historical Statistics of the United States, Colonial Times to 1970,* pages 1114–1116, tables Y-458–460, 467–469, 473, 474, 476; various issues of the *Statistical Abstract of the United States,* tables "National Defense Outlays and Veterans Benefits" (table 537 in the 1994–95 edition); and from various issues of *Economic Indicators* (Joint Economic Committee of Congress).

U.S. foreign economic and military aid are reported in *U.S. Overseas Loans and Grants,* July 1, 1945–September 30, 1993, Cong-R-0105, U.S. Agency for International Development.

The Charles Beard epigram is cited in *Perpetual War for Perpetual Peace,* edited by Harry Elmer Barnes, page viii of the 1953 Caxton Printers edition.

22. AN EFFECTIVE NATIONAL DEFENSE

Arms sales are reported in "World Military Expenditures and Arms Transfers" for various years, a report of the U.S. Arms Control and Disarmament Agency. I don't have every year's report, so there probably are more than 102 countries. The list includes such staunch American allies as Iraq, Iran, Syria, Jordan, China, and Yugoslavia.

The total of foreign aid was taken from *Historical Statistics of the*

United States, Colonial Times to 1970, pages 1115–1116, tables Y-468 & Y-474; various issues of the *Statistical Abstract of the United States;* and *Economic Indicators* (Joint Economic Committee of Congress), July 1995.

The references to foreign aid for tennis courts and empty hospitals are from "A New Aid Policy for a New World" by Doug Bandow, Cato Institute Policy Analysis #226, May 15, 1995, page 22.

Thomas Jefferson's quotation is from his first inaugural address, March 4, 1801.

The Winston Churchill quotes are from the book *Free Trade,* originally published in 1906, and now out of print. They were cited by Michael McMenamin in *Reason* magazine, January 1991, pages 37–39.

The statement about Japanese trade "aggression" was made by Patrick Buchanan on John McLaughlin's *One on One* television show, May 12, 1995.

The data on trade with Japan were downloaded from the National Trade Data Bank of the U.S. Department of Commerce on April 27, 1995.

The deaths in the Libyan air raid are reported in *The Peoples Chronology*, Microsoft Bookshelf 1994, a CD-ROM.

The Robert Higgs quote is from *Liberty* magazine, February 1991, page 19.

I'm indebted to Robert Prechter, Jr., for the idea of posting a reward for the assassination of a foreign leader who threatens us.

The list of 14 governments with nuclear missile capability is up to date as of February 1995, and was compiled by the Carnegie Endowment for International Peace, and reprinted in *Nuclear Proliferation: The Post-Cold-War Challenge* by Ronald J. Bee, Headline Series, Foreign Policy Association.

23. HOW TO FIX SOCIAL SECURITY ONCE AND FOR ALL

A claim that Social Security taxes are put into trust funds is made in "Your Social Security Taxes . . . What They're Paying For and Where the Money Goes," Social Security Administration, U.S. Department of Health and Human Services, SSA Publication #05–10010, January 1994.

The changeover from a fully funded to a pay-as-you-go system is discussed in "Social Security: Averting the Crisis" by Peter J. Ferrara, Cato Institute, 1982, page 6.

The Luntz poll showing expectations of a declining standard of living was reported in *Financial World*, August 29, 1995, page 53.

The study on lifetime tax rates for future generations is in "Generational Accounting: A Meaningful Way to Evaluate Fiscal Policy" by Joel Kotlikoff of Boston University, Alan Auerbach of the University of California, and Jagadeesh Gokhale of the Cleveland Federal Reserve Bank, *Journal of Economic Perspectives*, Volume 8, Number 1, Winter 1994, pages 73–94.

The poll results on Social Security expectations are from *The Wirthlin Report*, January 1995, Research Supplement, page 4.

24. A FREEDOM BUDGET

The Reagan promises for a balanced budget are discussed in *The Triumph of Politics: How the Reagan Revolution Failed* by David Stockman (Harper & Row, 1986), page 123. The Gramm-Rudman-Hollings plans are reviewed in *Financial World*, August 29, 1995, page 68. Details of the 1995 Republican plan were given in an analysis by Brian Nutting in *Congressional Quarterly*, July 16, 1995, and by Llewellyn Rockwell, Jr., in "Budget Tricks," *The Free Market*, July 1995, page 2.

The federal holdings of land and buildings are summarized in the *Statistical Abstract of the United States, 1994–1995*, table 354, page 225.

James L. Payne's estimate of the cost of complying with the tax system is in *Costly Returns: The Burdens of the U.S. Tax System* (Institute for Contemporary Studies, San Francisco, 1993), page 150.

Table of the Federal Budget

Figures for 1995 are government estimates as of June 1995. The 1996 and 1997 figures are estimated from news reports of the Republican budget plan.

1998 is the first year affected by the next Presidential term.

The cost of the annuities to replace Social Security is estimated as $13.02 for each $1 currently spent yearly by the Social Security Administration. At current spending rates, 1998's Social Security cost is estimated to be $403 billion—which, multiplied by $13.02, equals $5,245 billion as the total cost of the annuities. This is based on rates prevailing in 1995 for annuities for 65-year-olds of either sex from State Farm Insurance Company. To arrive at a precise total cost would require an audit of the Social Security books. The cost would be less if the annuities are means tested and some retirees forgo the annuities voluntarily.

Interest expense is assumed to be 5% of the total debt—the average rate in 1995.

25. FAMILY VALUES

The quote from James A. Dorn is taken from "The Moral State of the Union," in *The Cato Handbook for Congress*, page 11.

26. NEITHER OF THE TWO OLD PARTIES WILL SAVE US

The five surveys regarding the public's attitude toward government were taken by, respectively:

1. Luntz Research Companies, November 9, 1994.
2. The Roper Center for *Reader's Digest in* 1994.
3. The Times Mirror Center for the People & the Press, July 12–27, 1994.

4. The Times Mirror Center for the People & the Press, June 12–24, 1993.
5. CBS News and *The New York Times,* October 29–November 1, 1994.

Item #3 was published in *The Los Angeles Times*, September 21, 1994. The other four were reported in *The American Enterprise*, March/April 1995, page 101.

The Gallup Poll regarding third-party and independent candidates was taken April 17–19, 1995, and was reported by AP-Dataport-NY, July 6, 1995.

Peter Jennings' commentary on the November 1994 elections said, "The voters had a temper tantrum last week." He blamed the election on "a nation full of uncontrolled two-year-old rage." The commentary was reported in *Media Watch*, February 1995.

27. WHAT THE PRESIDENT CAN DO

All data on Ronald Reagan's vetoes came from the *Congressional Quarterly Almanac* for 1985 and for 1988.

The statement that 80% of the people who lost their property to seizures weren't charged with crimes was given in "Government Seizures Victimize Innocent" by Andrew Schneider and Mary Pat Flaherty, *The Pittsburgh Press*, August 16, 1991.

Appendix C

Further Exploration

This appendix provides sources of ideas and information concerning many of the topics we've covered.

Fortunately, there now are hundreds and hundreds of books, publications, and organizations explaining the problems inherent in government, showing how the marketplace provides what we need without the government's help, and assisting people to insulate themselves from the worst abuses of government.

This list is just a taste of what's available. I put it together quickly as this book was going to press, so it's far from complete. But it will give you a start.

BOOKS

Here are a few good introductory books. You won't agree with all their ideas; I don't either. But they offer new ways of looking at old questions.

They'll help stretch your thinking with new ways to deal with old social issues.

Many of the books can be bought or ordered at any bookstore. For those not sold in stores, I've included the publishers' addresses.

Laissez Faire Books carries almost all of them. To buy a book, or to receive a catalog describing hundreds of libertarian books, contact:

Laissez Faire Books
942 Howard Street
San Francisco, California 94103
(800) 326-0996, (415) 541-9780; fax (415) 541-0597

The Case for Free Trade and Open Immigration, edited by Richard M. Ebeling and Jacob G. Hornberger. There wasn't room for me to cover much on this subject. But this anthology provides a number of perceptive articles on the twin subjects of international trade and immigration. (The Future of Freedom Foundation, address below; 142 pages, hardcover $17.95; cardcover, $9.95.)

The Cato Handbook for Congress. A series of position papers covering most of the political and social issues of the day, including specific proposals for reducing government, written by a variety of libertarian thinkers. (Cato Institute, address below; cardcover, 358 pages, $25.00.)

Costly Returns: The Burdens of the U.S. Tax System by James L. Payne. Facts and figures demonstrating the tyranny of the income tax and the IRS, as well as the awful waste of resources required to comply with the current tax system. (ICS Press, 1205 O'Neill Highway, Dunmore, Pennsylvania 18512; (800) 326-0263; 256 pages, hardcover, $34.95; cardcover, $14.95.)

Economics in One Lesson by Henry Hazlitt. A 50-year-old classic work by a master of clear and persuasive writing, it explains many of the errors in thinking that lead people to believe the government must do something to improve the economy. (Crown Books, New York; cardcover, 218 pages, $9.95.)

The Economics of Liberty, edited by Llewellyn H. Rockwell, Jr. An anthology of articles by distinguished libertarian and conservative writers, providing an introduction to alternative views on many social and political subjects. (Ludwig von Mises Institute, address below; cardcover, 373 pages, $12.00.)

Environmental Gore, edited by John A. Baden. An anthology of articles written in response to various aspects of Albert Gore's hysterical book on the environment. It explains the fallacies in much of what we hear about the environment—covering issues such as the ozone hole, global warming, the disappearing rain forests, and more. The book also explains what could be done to reduce pollution and save resources without resorting to coercion. (Pacific Research Institute for Public Policy, 755 Sansome Street, San Francisco, California 94111, (415) 989-0833; hardcover, 262 pages, $21.95.)

Forfeiting Our Property Rights by Henry Hyde. A useful presentation of the background of the asset-forfeiture laws, and of the problems they cause. (Cato Institute, address below; 100 pages, hardcover, $16.95; card-cover, $8.95.)

Government: America's #1 Growth Industry by Stephen Moore. An excellent quick introduction to an out-of-control government in Washington. (Institute for Policy Innovation, 250 South Stemmons, Suite 306, Lewisville, Texas 75067, (214) 219-0811; cardcover, 97 pages, $9.95.)

Healing Our World by Mary J. Ruwart. A thoughtful presentation of why programs based on coercion always lead to unanticipated and undesired results. It is full of timely examples of the problems coercion has created, as well as ways by which voluntary solutions could produce much better results. (SunStar Press, P.O. Box 342, Kalamazoo, Michigan 49005; hardcover, 304 pages, $14.95.)

The Law by Frederick Bastiat. A masterpiece of writing, this brief book explains why it's just as wrong for government to rob your neighbor on your behalf as it is for you to do it yourself. (Foundation for Economic Education, address below; paperback, 75 pages, $3.00.)

Libertarianism in One Lesson by David Bergland. An articulate introduction to libertarian thought, it also includes a lengthy list of good books and libertarian organizations that are a source of more good literature. (Orpheus Publications, 1773 Bahama Place, Costa Mesa, California 92626; cardcover, 126 pages, $8.95.)

Losing Ground by Charles Murray. One of the best books written on America's welfare system and how the federal government turned it into today's mess. (Basic Books; cardcover, 323 pages, $15.95.)

Lost Rights by James Bovard. An encyclopedia of examples of the way government has usurped your Constitutional rights—through asset forfeiture, gun laws, the War on Drugs, IRS abuses, suppression of free speech, and so on. (St. Martin's Press, New York; hardcover, 392 pages, $24.95.)

Persuasion Versus Force by Mark Skousen. This short pamphlet is a powerful explanation of the alternatives of using peaceful cooperation vs. using force to achieve social goals. (Phillips Publishing, Inc., 7811 Montrose Road, Potomac, Maryland 20854; (800) 777-5005; cardcover, 16 pages, no charge.)

Red Tape in America, edited by Craig E. Richardson and Geoff C. Ziebart. A survey of the many ways government regulation has tied America in red tape—reducing your income and causing you to pay more than necessary for products and services. (The Heritage Foundation, address below; large paperback, 111 pages, $14.95.)

Separating School & State by Sheldon Richman. One of the best discussions of school problems I've seen. The author shows why those problems stem from government ownership and control. (The Future of Freedom Foundation, address below; 121 pages, hardcover, $19.95; card-cover, $12.95.)

What Has Government Done to Our Money? by Murray N. Rothbard. A subject I wish I'd had the space to cover here, our money system has been subverted by government tinkering that has led to inflation, recessions, and other problems that are often attributed to the free market. Professor

Rothbard provides an excellent, easy-to-follow explanation of how our monetary system works and how government has distorted it. (Ludwig von Mises Institute, address below; cardcover, 119 pages, $6.00.)

Whatever Happened to Justice? by Richard J. Maybury. A wonderful, easy-to-understand presentation of the difference between the common law, which supported a stable social order, and political law, which has brought chaos and uncertainty. It is must reading for anyone who wants to understand what law is and what it ought to be. (Bluestocking Press, P.O. Box 1014, Placerville, California 95667, (916) 621-1123; cardcover, 249 pages, $14.95.)

STATISTICAL SOURCES

Historical Statistics of the United States, Colonial Times to 1970. This 2-volume, 1200-page set was published by the U.S. Bureau of the Census. It provides thousands of statistical series describing American life back to the founding of the Republic. Much of the data in my book came from these series. Unfortunately, it is now out of print, but a used book store may be able to get a copy for you.

Statistical Abstract of the U.S.,1994–95. Using material prepared by the U.S. Census Bureau, this is the follow-up to *Historical Statistics*—a yearly updating of most of the same statistical series. (The Reference Press, 6448 Highway 290E, Suite E-104, Austin, Texas 78723, (800) 486-8666; cardcover, 958 pages, $17.95.)

PERIODICALS

Here are three magazines that provide libertarian viewpoints, news, and insights—as well as book and movie reviews, humor, and discussions of cultural topics.

Liberty
P.O. Box 1181
Port Townsend, Washington 98368
(800) 854-6991; $19.50 for six bi-monthly issues

Includes articles that are profound, lighthearted, or informative. Always good reading.

National Review
P.O. Box 668
Mount Morris, Illinois 61054
(815) 734-1232; $57 per 25 bi-weekly issues.

Although a conservative publication, it intersperses libertarian ideas with the standard conservative proposals for government to solve problems. Entertaining as well as informative.

Reason
P.O. Box 526

Mount Morris, Illinois 61054
(815) 734-1102; $26 for 11 monthly issues

The oldest continuous libertarian magazine, it includes thought-provoking articles on a variety of topics.

ORGANIZATIONS

These organizations all promote libertarian ideas—through the publication of papers and books, through policy proposals, or through programs to bring libertarian ideas to people unfamiliar with them. Rather than my describing each one, I suggest you call them to have information sent to you. (A more complete list appears in *Libertarianism in One Lesson*, described on page 238.)

Advocates for Self-Government
3955 Pleasantdale Road, Suite 106A
Atlanta, Georgia 30340
(800) 932-1776; (770) 417-1304

Browne for President Committee
4094 Majestic Lane, Suite 240
Fairfax, Virginia 22033
Telephone: (800) 314-8611

Cato Institute
1000 Massachusetts Avenue, N.W.
Washington, D.C. 20001
(202) 842-0200

Competitive Enterprise Institute
1001 Connecticut Avenue, N.W.,
   Suite 1250
Washington, D.C. 20036
(202) 331-1010

Foundation for Economic
   Education
30 S. Broadway
Irvington-on-Hudson, New York
   10533
(914) 591-7230

Fully Informed Jury Association
P.O. Box 59
Helmville, Montana 59843
(406) 793-5550

The Future of Freedom Foundation
11350 Random Hills Road, Suite 800
Fairfax, Virginia 22030
(703) 934-6101; fax (703) 803-1480

The Heritage Foundation
214 Massachusetts Avenue, N.E.
Washington, D.C. 20002
(202) 546-4400

The Independent Institute
134 98th Avenue
Oakland, California 94603
(510) 632-1366

Libertarian Party Headquarters
2600 Virginia Avenue, NW, Suite
   B100
Washington, D.C. 20037
(800) 682-1776, (202) 333-0008

Ludwig von Mises Institute
Auburn, Alabama 38649-5301
(334) 844-2500

Separation of School & State
   Alliance
4578 North First
P.O. Box 310
Fresno, California 93726
(209) 292-1776

HELP YOURSELF

I wrote this book to help bring about much smaller government in America. But even if we succeed, it will take time. Meanwhile, you will have only as much freedom as you can secure for yourself.

A large part of my life has been spent helping people arrange their finances for greater personal independence. That involves more than just seeking profitable investments. It also means finding realistic ways to insulate yourself from the problems government creates—such as chronic inflation, high taxes, loss of privacy, and confiscation of your savings through lawsuits and seizures.

Individual protection from such problems is beyond the scope of this book. But at least I can point you to a few sources of help.

These are all companies with which I'm associated in some way, because creating or encouraging such mechanisms has been my principal work for the past 30 years. So please understand that I'm not an unbiased appraiser of these sources. You'll need to decide for yourself whether any of them can help you.

Book & Newsletter

Rather than try to explain here the strategy I suggest for financial protection against whatever the economy and government have in store, I'll refer you to my last investment book, *The Economic Time Bomb*, published in 1989 (St. Martin's Press, 294 pages; hardcover, $19.95; paperback, $5.95). It explains government intervention into the economy in much more detail than the current book does.

Since my financial strategy doesn't depend on current trends or predictions, the investment suggestions made in the book still hold. It also lists numerous sources for help in insulating yourself from inflation, setting up a Swiss bank account, or using other devices to ward off the government until the cavalry arrives.

Updated information is available in my newsletter, *Harry Browne's Special Reports*, published irregularly (whenever I have something to say). The newsletter covers the economy, investments, privacy, asset protection, politics, and social issues. A sample issue is available for $10. Call (800) 531-5142 or (512) 453-7313, or write Harry Browne's Special Reports, Box 5586, Austin, Texas 78763.

Tax Efficient Investing

Much of the tax bill on your investments may be coming from the *way* you invest. Without changing your investment strategy, you can cut the tax bill by changing *how* you place money in the kinds of assets you've selected.

For most people, mutual funds are the most convenient way to invest. You can use them to invest in almost anything—stocks, bonds, even bank CDs. But very few mutual funds seem to recognize that their shareholders don't like paying taxes.

One exception is the Permanent Portfolio Family of Funds. These funds—which cover stocks, bonds, money markets, and diversified investing—provide their shareholders with valuable tax-saving advantages. I'm a consultant to the funds and to their investment advisor.

For a free prospectus, contact

Permanent Portfolio Family of Funds
207 Jefferson Square
1601 West 38th Street
Austin, Texas 78731
(800) 531-5142; (512) 453-7558

Privacy & Safety

There's no place I'd rather live than here, in America. Apart from the government and its mischief, there is very little to criticize, and much to celebrate.

And it's home. Almost no American wants to leave. But you might enjoy living here even more if you didn't keep all your savings here—in plain sight, tempting potential litigants and your government to lay their hands on it.

Until recently, offshore trusts were used only by the very wealthy, to protect against lawsuits and taxes. But as those problems have grown, so has interest in finding legal ways of insulating one's wealth from attack. Now a program is available that makes an offshore trust practical for anyone with enough wealth to attract a predatory lawsuit.

The program allows you to continue to live in America, and invest in America or anywhere else, while your financial affairs are as private as you would like them to be. I am an editorial consultant to the company that sponsors the program.

For information, contact

Passport Financial, Inc.
P.O. Box 5586
Austin, Texas 78763
(800) 531-5142

GOOD WISHES

I wish you well in your search for more knowledge and understanding of all these topics.

Appendix D

The Author

Harry Browne is a financial advisor and the author of nine books prior to this one.

He was born in New York City in 1933 and grew up in Los Angeles. He graduated from high school, but attended college for only two weeks. Thereafter, he educated himself in economics, finance, music, and political science. He has lived in Canada, Switzerland, and Northern California. He now resides in Tennessee.

He was unknown to the investment world when his first book, *How You Can Profit from the Coming Devaluation*, was published in 1970. The book warned that the U.S. dollar would be devalued; inflation would become severe; and gold, silver, and foreign currencies would skyrocket in value. The book's message clashed with the prevailing wisdom, but it was in tune with the concerns of hundreds of thousands of Americans, and the book made the *New York Times* best-seller list. His warnings proved to be well-founded when the dollar was devalued twice and the recommended investments rose many times over.

His 1974 book, *You Can Profit from a Monetary Crisis*, was a greater success yet, reaching #1 on the *Times* best-seller list. Its message amplified the themes in his 1970 book, and allowed thousands of investors to profit from the turmoil of the late 1970s.

Meanwhile, in 1973, he had published *How I Found Freedom in an Unfree World*. The book describes an individualist way of life, and continues to be in demand today.

In all, his previous nine books sold over two million copies.

Since 1974, he has been writing *Harry Browne's Special Reports*, a newsletter providing opinions on the economy, politics, and investments. He is widely respected for his honest, down-to-earth investment advice.

Over the years he has become one of America's better-known financial advisors. He has been constantly in demand as a public speaker and for radio and TV interviews, making appearances on the *Today* show, *Wall Street Week*, the Cable News Network (CNN), the Larry King show, and national and local radio and TV shows.

Since 1985 he has been married to the former Pamela Lanier Wolfe. He has a grown daughter, Autumn Browne Wilson. His main non-professional interests are classical music, opera, good food and wine, sports, drama, old movies, and fiction.

On August 14, 1994, he announced his intention to run for President as a Libertarian candidate.

A Message from Pamela Browne

Dear Reader:

When I first read the above biographical note, my immediate reaction was that the statistics concerning my husband's birth, business and books were all accurate, but they conveyed little about the man—his character, personality, or mindset. So I asked if I could write a letter to you describing Harry Browne.

I was asked to make the letter brief because the length of Harry's book had already reached the publisher's limit. So I began my original short letter with adjectives that I believe describe my husband—such as truthful. But I quickly discovered that the words didn't accurately paint a portrait of Harry. For how would you know that by "truthful" I mean he never lies—even a white lie—to anyone for any reason. And that on occasion when I've been tempted to fib, and have looked to him for his blessing, he's often said, "All I can tell you is that the truth has always served me well."

I felt it crucial that you get to know Harry, so I was granted more space to tell you about him. So let me begin by telling you that although we've been married for only ten years, I've known Harry for nearly 25 years—since December of 1970.

He was a gentleman then, in the old-fashioned sense of the word, and he is a gentleman today. Profanity is not a part of his vocabulary in front of ladies, nor even in the company of men. He listens carefully and thoughtfully without interruption when someone speaks. He goes to great lengths to be on time for his appointments, for he believes everyone's time is as valuable as his. He's even-tempered, patient, and understanding. In fact, I can count on both hands the number of times he's raised his voice in anger. When he has, it's been with good reason.

Harry is a kind, gentle, and benevolent man. Yet he's very passionate about many things—from music to politics. When he speaks he's charismatic, and you can hear the quiet passion and enthusiasm in his voice. Yet he's not overbearing or threatening in his eagerness to convey his thoughts.

He's a devoted husband—a romantic and a sentimentalist who remembers, without reminders, those days throughout the year that have special meaning to us. His moral character is beyond reproach, and he's never once betrayed my trust in him.

Harry treats people with respect. And he's a natural diplomat. I've often listened and watched as he smoothed over a disagreement among people with a simple statement or two. He craves privacy, peace, and tranquillity. And he's the essence of civility.

He loves life, all forms, and respects it. It's not unusual to see him catch a bug he's discovered crawling indoors—only to carry it outdoors to its natural habitat.

He loves animals and has had numerous pets prior to and during our marriage. He's especially fond of cats. And often I find him reading in his favorite chair or working at his computer with our old stray, Sable, perched in his lap.

He's a brilliant man, an original thinker, and he's knowledgeable about nearly every subject imaginable. Because he's an avid reader he continues his education daily. He's also a very wise man who has an abundance of common sense.

I believe his greatest gift is the ability to comprehend very complex issues and explain them in terms anyone, even a child, could understand.

One of his greatest attributes is his quick wit. He has the ability to make people laugh, yet he can laugh at himself. In addition, he's great fun to be around because he loves and enjoys life so much.

Thus far I've painted a rather glowing portrait of Harry Browne. But no one is perfect, including my husband. However, his imperfections are very few, and in my estimation, though sometimes annoying, they tend to make him a better person.

For example, Harry has difficulty meeting deadlines for two reasons. First, he's a perfectionist. It's said his first drafts are better than most writers' fifth or tenth drafts, but he insists on polishing and polishing his material until it meets his high standards.

Second, he procrastinates. Sometimes it's because he dreads a certain task. But more often it's because his mind has not yet assimilated the facts and figures he's accumulated. And he refuses to release any material until it's original, precise, and carefully calculated.

If I'd been given space enough to give only one example of Harry's character, I would have told you that long before Harry and I married I knew he was uninterested in having another child. And I'd accepted that fact even though I'd never had children. But six years into our marriage I discovered I longed to have a child. So I timidly approached him with the idea of adoption.

Harry was amazed at my announcement. But, as always, he considered my proposal carefully. And after months of soul-searching and thoughtful discussions, we made application for a foster/adopt child. Harry endured an extensive investigation and what I considered an invasion of our privacy. Nevertheless, he complied with all the agency's rules, and eventually a special needs adolescent was placed in our home.

The young child lived with us for about six months—until it became clear that we were unable to fulfill her special needs. The ultimate decision to return her to the agency was mine, and it was one of the most heart-wrenching decisions I'd ever made. But I believe I made the correct decision for the child and for us, and Harry supported me.

Although the experience broke my heart I'm still searching for the words to thank Harry for enabling me to experience motherhood. He was not only a wonderful father, but he was a loving, patient, and understanding husband. And for that I will be eternally grateful to him.

I suppose it's only natural that you'd be skeptical about the content of this letter, for after all we've never met. And I did admit previously that on occasion I've been tempted to fib! But I tell you honestly that Harry Browne is the most wise, kind, civil, and benevolent man I've known in my life. And I consider it an honor to stand beside him at all times—especially now while he seeks the Presidency of the United States of America.

Most sincerely,

Pamela Wolfe Browne